Hinduism:
Tradition and Philosophy

Hinduism: Tradition and Philosophy

Edited by

RATAN SINGH

GLOBAL PUBLICATIONS

NEW DELHI-110 002 (INDIA)

GLOBAL PUBLICATIONS
4378/4B, G-4 JMD House
Murari Lal Street, Ansari Road
Daryaganj, New Delhi - 110 002
Phone : 23278062 (Off.)
e-mail : omega_publications@yahoo.com

Head Office :
79/23, Laxmi Garden
Near Satya Jyoti School,
Gurgaon (Haryana)
Mob : 9213562438

Hinduism : Tradition and Philosophy

First Published : 2011

ISBN : 978-93-80833-23-1

PRINTED IN INDIA

Published by Ishwari Prasad Garg for Global Publications, New Delhi-110 002 and Printed at Suman Printers, Delhi

Preface

Hinduism comprises numerous sects or denominations. The denominations are roughly comparable to different religions. The main divisions in current Hinduism are Shaivism, Shaktism, Vaishnavism, and Smartism. These four denominations share rituals, beliefs, and traditions, but each denomination has a different philosophy on how to achieve life's ultimate goal (moksa, liberation).

An established philosophical school within a denomination is called a *sampradaya* and a traditional lineage of teachers from any sampradaya is a *parampara.*

The presence of different denominations and schools within Hinduism should not be viewed as a schism, as there was no original unity. On the contrary, there is at present no great animosity between the different "religions" which constitute Hinduism, and among Hindu followers as a whole, there is a strong belief that there are many paths leading to the One God or the Source, whatever one chooses to call that ultimate Truth. Whether Shiva is same as Vishnu or different from Vishnu, is a matter of dispute among adherents but now most keep their disputes private.

Instead, there is a healthy cross-pollination of ideas and logical debate that serves to refine each school's philosophy. It is not uncommon, or disallowed, for an individual to follow one school but take the point of view of another school for a certain issue.

The major topics dealt in this book are : *Introduction to Hindu Philosophy; Hindu and Hindu Deities; Hindu Denominations; Hinduism in India; Marriage in Hinduism; Hindu Wedding Rituals; Ayyavazhi's Teachings and Impact; Hinduism and Islam; Indian Religions and Philosophy; Hindu Cuisine and Costumes; etc.*

We are thankful to all those who rendered ready help and cooperation while working on this project. We express our gratitude to various scholars, teachers and friends for their assistance and guidance. Finally, we thank our publishers for bringing out this book in very limited time.

—Editor

Contents

1

Introducation to Hindu Philosophy

Hindu philosophy is divided into six Sanskrit *âstika* ("orthodox") schools of thought, or *darshanas* (literally, "views"), which accept the Vedas as supreme revealed scriptures, and three *nâstika* ("heterodox") schools, which do not accept the Vedas as supreme. The âstika schools are:

1. Sankhya, a strongly dualist theoretical exposition of mind and matter.
2. Yoga, a school emphasizing meditation closely based on Sankhya
3. Nyaya or logics
4. Vaisheshika, an empiricist school of atomism
5. Mimamsa, an anti-ascetic and anti-mysticist school of orthopraxy
6. Vedanta, opposing Vedic ritualism in favour of mysticism. Vedanta came to be the dominant current of Hinduism in the post-medieval period.

The nâstika schools are:

1. Buddhism
2. Jainism
3. Cârvâka, a skeptical materialist school, which died out in the 15th century and whose primary texts have been lost.

These nine philosophies form the nine gems of the Sanâtana Dharma.

In Hindu history, the distinction of these six schools was current in the Gupta period "golden age" of Hinduism. With the disappearance of Vaishshika and Mimamsa, it was obsolete by the later Middle Ages, when the various sub-schools of Vedanta (Dvaita "dualism", Advaita "non-dualism" and others) began to rise to prominence as the main divisions of religious philosophy. Nyaya survived into the 17th century as *Navya Nyaya* "Neo-Nyaya", while Sankhya gradually lost its status as an independent school, its tenets absorbed into Yoga and Vedanta.

Samkhya

Samkhya or Sankhya is the oldest of the orthodox philosophical systems in Hinduism. Samkhya postulates that everything in reality stems from **purusha** and **prakriti** (matter, creative agency or energy). There are many living souls (*Jeevatmas*) and they possess consciousness. *Prakriti* consists of three dispositions known as qualities (gunas): activity (rajas), inactivity (tamas) and steadiness (sattva) which arises when the two other gunas are held in equilibrium. Because of the intertwined relationship between the soul and these dispositions, an imbalance in disposition causes the world to evolve. Liberation of the soul happens when it realizes that it is above and beyond these three dispositions. Samkhya is a dualistic philosophy, but there are differences between Samkhya and other forms of dualism. In the West, dualism is between the mind and the body, whereas in Samkhya it is between the soul and matter. The concept of the atma (soul) is different from the concept of the mind. Soul is absolute reality that is all-pervasive, eternal, indivisible, attributeless, pure consiousness. It is non-matter and is beyond intellect. Originally, Samkhya was not theistic, but in confluence with Yoga it developed a theistic variant.

Yoga

In Indian philosophy, Yoga is the name of one of the six orthodox philosophical schools. The Yoga philosophical system is closely allied with the Samkhya school. The Yoga school as expounded by Patanjali accepts the Samkhya psychology and metaphysics, but is more theistic than the Samkhya, as evidenced by the addition of a divine entity to the Samkhya's twenty-five elements of reality. The parallels between Yoga and Samkhya were so close that Max Müller says that "the two philosophies were in popular parlance distinguished from each other as Samkhya with and Samkhya without a Lord...." The intimate relationship between Samkhya and Yoga is explained by Heinrich Zimmer:

"These two are regarded in India as twins, the two aspects of a single discipline. SâEkhya provides a basic theoretical exposition of human nature, enumerating and defining its elements, analyzing their manner of co-operation in a state of bondage (*bandha*), and describing their state of disentanglement or separation in release (*mokca*), while Yoga treats specifically of the dynamics of the process for the disentanglement, and outlines practical techniques for the gaining of release, or 'isolation-integration' (*kaivalya*)."

The foundational text of the Yoga school is the Yoga Sutras of Patanjali, who is regarded as the founder of the formal Yoga philosophy. The Sutras of the Yoga philosophy are ascribed to Patanjali, who may have been, as Max Müller explains, "the author or representative of the Yoga-philosophy without being necessarily the author of the Sutras."

Nyaya

The Nyaya school is based on the Nyaya Sutras. They were written by Aksapada Gautama, probably in the second century B.C.E. The most important contribution made by this school is its methodology. This methodology is based on a system of logic that has subsequently been adopted by the majority of the Indian schools. This is comparable to the relationship between Western science and philosophy, which was derived largely from Aristotelian logic.

Nevertheless, Nyaya was seen by its followers as more than logical in its own right. They believed that obtaining valid knowledge was the only way to gain release from suffering, and they took great pains to identify valid sources of knowledge and distinguish these from mere false opinions. According to Nyaya, there are exactly four sources of knowledge: perception, inference, comparison, and testimony. Knowledge obtained through each of these is either valid or invalid. Nyaya developed several criteria of validity. In this sense, Nyaya is probably the closest Indian equivalent to analytic philosophy. The later Naiyanikas gave logical proofs for the existence and uniqueness of Ishvara in response to Buddhism, which, at that time, was fundamentally non-theistic. An important later development in Nyaya was the system of *Navya*.

Vaisheshika

The Vaisheshika school was founded by Kanada and postulates an atomic pluralism. All objects in the physical universe are reducible to certain types of atoms, and Brahman is regarded as the fundamental force that causes consciousness in these atoms.

Although the Vaisheshika school developed independently from the Nyaya, the two eventually merged because of their closely related metaphysical theories. In its classical form, however, the Vaisheshika school differed from the Nyaya in one crucial respect: where Nyaya accepted four sources of valid knowledge, the Vaisheshika accepted only two—–perception and inference.

Purva Mimamsa

The main objective of the Purva Mimamsa school was to establish the authority of the Vedas. Consequently, this school's most valuable contribution to Hinduism was its formulation of the rules of Vedic interpretation. Its adherents believe that one must have unquestionable faith in the Vedas and perform the *yajñas*, or fire-sacrifices, regularly. They believe in the power of the mantras and yajñas to sustain all the activity of the universe. In keeping with this belief, they place great emphasis on *dharma*, which consists of the performance of Vedic rituals.

The Mimamsa accepted the logical and philosophical teachings of the other schools, but felt they did not sufficiently emphasize attention to right action. They believed that the other schools of thought that aimed for release (*moksha*) are not allowed for complete freedom from desire and selfishness, because the very striving for liberation stemmed from a simple desire to be free. According to Mimamsa thought, only by acting in accordance with the prescriptions of the Vedas may one attain salvation.

The Mimamsa school later shifted its views and began to teach the doctrines of Brahman and freedom. Its adherents then advocated the release or escape of the soul from its constraints through enlightened activity. Although Mimamsa does not receive much scholarly attention, its influence can be felt in the life of the practising Hindu, because all Hindu ritual, ceremony, and law is influenced by this school.

Vedanta

The Vedanta, or *later* Mimamsa school, concentrates on the philosophical teachings of the Upanishads rather than the ritualistic injunctions of the Brahmanas.

While the traditional Vedic rituals continued to be practised as meditative and propitiatory rites, a more knowledge-centered understanding began to emerge. These were mystical aspects of Vedic religion that focused on meditation, self-discipline, and spiritual connectivity, more than traditional ritualism.

The more abstruse Vedanta is the essence of the Vedas, as encapsulated in the Upanishads. Vedantic thought drew on Vedic cosmology, hymns and philosophy. The Brihadaranyaka Upanishad is believed to have appeared as far back as 3,000 years ago. While thirteen or so Upanishads are accepted as principal, over a hundred exist. The most significant contribution of Vedantic thought is the idea that self-consciousness is continuous with and indistinguishable from consciousness of Brahman.

The aphorisms of the Vedanta sutras are presented in a cryptic, poetic style, which allows for a variety of interpretations. Consequently, the Vedanta separated into six sub-schools, each interpreting the texts in its own way and producing its own series of sub-commentaries. Four of them are given here.

Advaita

Advaita literally means "non duality." Its first great consolidator was Adi Shankaracharya (788-820), who continued the line of thought of some of the Upanishadic teachers, and that of his teacher's teacher Gaudapada. By analysing the three states of experience—–waking, dreaming, and deep sleep—–he established the singular reality of Brahman, in which the soul and Brahman are one and the same. He saw this form as that of Vishnu. He wrote a thesis on the Vishnu Sahasranama (1008 names of Vishnu), and also composed poems like the Bhaja Govindham instructing people to think about Govinda (Vishnu) all the time. Ishvara is the manifestation of Brahman to human minds under the influence of an illusionary power called *Avidya*.

Visishtadvaita

Ramanujacharya (1040-1137) was the foremost proponent of the concept of the Supreme Being having a definite form, name, and attributes. He saw this form as that of Vishnu, and taught that reality has three aspects: Vishnu, soul (jiva), and matter (prakrti). Vishnu is the only independent reality, while souls and matter are dependent on Vishnu for their existence. Thus, Ramanuja's system is known as *qualified* non-dualism.

Dvaita

Madhvacharya (1238-1317) identified Brahman with Vishnu, but his view of reality was pluralistic. According to Dvaita, there are three ultimate realities: Vishnu, soul, and matter. Five distinctions are made: (1) Vishnu is distinct from souls; (2) Vishnu is distinct from matter; (3) Souls are distinct from matter; (4) A soul is distinct from another soul, and (5) Matter is distinct from other matter. Souls are eternal and are dependent upon the will of Vishnu. This theology attempts to address the problem of evil with the idea that souls are not created.

Dvaitadvaita (Bhedabheda)

Dvaitadvaita was proposed by Nimbarka, a 13th century Vaishnava Philosopher from the Andhra region. According to this philosophy there are three categories of existence: Brahman, soul, and matter. Soul and matter are different from Brahman in that they have attributes and capacities different from Brahman. Brahman exists independently, while soul and matter are dependent. Thus soul and matter have an existence that is separate yet dependent. Further, Brahman is a controller, the soul is the enjoyer, and matter the thing enjoyed. Also, the highest object of worship is Krishna and his consort Radha, attended by thousands of *gopis*, or cowherdesses; of the celestial Vrindavana; and devotion consists in self-surrender.

Shuddhadvaita

Shuddhadvaita was proposed by Vallabhacharya (1479 - 1531), who came from the Andhra region but eventually settled in Gujarat.

Acintya Bheda Abheda

Chaitanya Mahaprabhu (1486-1534), was stating that the soul or energy of God is both distinct and non-distinct from God, whom he identified as Krishna, Govinda, and that this, although unthinkable, may be experienced through a process of loving devotion (*bhakti*).He followed the Dvaita concept of Sri Madhva. This philosophy of "inconceivable oneness and difference" is followed by a number of modern Gaudiya Vaishnava movements, including ISKCON. ISKCON has recently participated in bringing the academic study of Krishna-related philosophies into Western academia through the theological discourse on Krishnology.

HINDU IDEALISM

There are currents of idealism in classical Hindu philosophy. Idealism and materialism are the principal monist ontologies. A related branch is the Buddhist concept of consciousness-only.

Idealist notions have been supported by the Vedanta and Yoga schools opposed by dualist Samkhya, the atomist Vaisheshika, the materialist Nyaya and Mimamsa as well as the atheist Cârvâka schools.

Like Platonic idealism, Hindu idealism is essentially monotheist, espousing the view that consciousness, which at its root emanates from God (Brahman,Purusha or Svayam bhagavan), is the essence or meaning of the phenomenal reality.

The presence of idealist concepts in Indian thought has been emphasized by Rupert Sheldrake and Fritjof Capra. These ideas have also been developed by P.R. Sarkar and advanced by his disciple Sohail Inayatullah, notably in the theory of Microvitum.

Liberation

The essence of Hindu Idealism is captured by such modern spiritual teachers as Sri Nisargadatta Maharaj, Sri Aurobindo and Sri Anandamurti, also known as P.R. Sarkar. Sri Nisargadatta advocated discovery of the *real self*. By establishing oneself in the earnestness of spiritual pursuits, it is possible to transcend the temporal self, limited by desires, fears, memories and mental constructs, and gain blissful immersion in the *pure* consciousness of God. Sarkar went further by emphasising that liberation was best achieved through service to self and society, exemplified by his socio-spiritual movement Ananda Marga, or the "Path of Bliss".

Âstika and Nâstika

Astika and Nastika are technical terms in Hinduism used to classify philosophical schools and persons, according to whether they accept the authority of the Vedas as supreme revealed scriptures, or not. By this definition, Nyaya, Vaisheshika, Samkhya, Yoga, Purva Mimamsa and Vedanta are classified as *astika* schools; while Charvaka, Jainism and Buddhism are considered *nastika* schools. The distinction is similar to the orthodox/heterodox distinction in the West.

In non-technical usage, the term *astika* is sometimes loosely translated as "theist" while *nastika* is translated as "atheist". However this interpretation is distinct from the use of the term in Hindu philosophy. Notably even among the *astika* schools, *samkhya*and the early *mimamsa* school do not accept a God (see Atheism in Hinduism) while accepting the authority of the Vedas; they thus are "atheistic *astika* schools".

The different usages of these terms are explained by Chatterjee and Datta as follows:

> In modern Indian languages, 'âstika' and 'nâstika' generally mean 'theist' and 'atheist', respectively. But in Sanskrit philosophical literature, 'âstika' means 'one who believes in the authority of the Vedas' or 'one who believes in life after death'. ('nâstika' means the opposite of these). The word is used here in the first sense. In the second sense, even the Jaina and Buddha schools are

'âstika', as they believe in life after death. The six orthodox schools are 'âstika', and the Cârvâka is 'nâstika' in both the senses.

Etymology

Astika is a Sanskrit adjective (and noun) that is derived from *asti* ("it is or exists") meaning "believing" or "pious"; or "one who believes in the existence (of God, of another world, etc.)." *Nastika* (*na* (not) + *âstika*) is its negative, literally meaning "not believing" or "not pious". As used in Hindu philosophy the differentiation between *astika* and *nastika* refers to belief in Vedic authority, not belief or lack of belief in theism. As N. N. Bhattacharyya writes:

> The followers of Tantra are often branded as Nâstika by the upholders of the Vedic tradition. The term Nâstika does not denote an atheist. It is applied only to those who do not believe in the Vedas. The SâEkhyas and MîmâCsakas do not believe in God, but they believe in the Vedas and hence they are not Nâstikas. The Buddhists, Jains, and Cârvâkas do not believe in the Vedas; hence they are Nâstikas.

Classification of Schools

Many Indian intellectual traditions were codified during the medieval period into a standard list of six orthodox systems, the shaddarshanas, all of which cite Vedic authority as their source:

- Nyaya, the school of logic
- Vaisheshika, the atomist school
- Samkhya, the enumeration school
- Yoga, the school of Patanjali (which assumes the metaphysics of Samkhya)
- Purva Mimamsa (or simply Mimamsa), the tradition of Vedic exegesis, and
- Vedanta (also called Uttara Mimamsa), the Upanishadic tradition.

These are often coupled into three groups for both historical and conceptual reasons: Nyaya-Vaishesika, Samkhya-Yoga, and Mimamsa-Vedanta.

The three main schools of Indian philosophy that do not base their beliefs on the Vedas were regarded as heterodox by Brahmans:

- Buddhism
- Jainism
- Cârvâka

The use of the term *nastika* to describe Buddhism and Jainism in India is explained by Gavin Flood as follows:

> At an early period, during the formation of the Upaniºads and the rise of Buddhism and Jainism, we must envisage a common heritage of meditation and mental discipline practiced by renouncers with varying affiliations to non-orthodox (Veda-rejecting) and orthodox (Veda-accepting) traditions.... These schools [such as Buddhism and Jainism] are understandably regarded as heterodox (*nâstika*) by orthodox (*âstika*) Brahmanism.

BUDDHISM AND HINDUISM

Buddhism and Hinduism are two closely related religions that are in some ways parallel and in other ways divergent in theory and practice.

The Vedic, Buddhist, and Jain religions share a common regional culture situated near and around north eastern India – modern day eastern Uttar Pradesh, Bihar and Nepal. Both the Buddha and Mahavira (the historical founder of Jainism), hailed from this region. Also the Brihadaranyaka Upanishad, considered to be among the very earliest Upanishads, was compiled in this region, under King Janaka of Mithila.

Ancient India had two philosophical streams of thought, the Shramana religions and the Vedic religion, parallel traditions that have existed side by side for thousands of years. Both Buddhism and Jainism are continuations of Shramana traditions, while modern Hinduism is a continuation of the Vedic tradition. These co-existing traditions have been mutually influential.

The Buddha rejected relying on Vedas for salvation, which included the earliest Upanishads. He redefined Indian cosmology, incorporating many existing terms in his doctrine, but redefining them for his purposes in explaining the Middle Path, also teaching that to achieve salvation one did not have to accept the authority of the scriptures or the existence of God. As regards Vedanta, though at the time of the early Buddhists there was no independent Vedanta school with a developed and organized philosophical system, the various philosophical theories of the Upanishads were quite widely disseminated. These intellectual trends are mentioned in the Buddhist texts, and rejected as "pernicious views".

Later Indian religious thought was in turn influenced by the new interpretations and novel ideas of the Buddhist tradition. Buddhism attained prominence on the Indian subcontinent, but was ultimately eclipsed (in the 11th century C.E.) at its point of origin by Hinduism and Islam. After this, Buddhism continued to flourish outside of India. Tibetan Buddhism predominates in the Himalayan region, as does Theravada Buddhism in Sri Lanka and Southeast Asia, and Mahayana Buddhism in East Asia.

Early History

Evidence from both Buddhist and Hindu scriptures show that the two traditions were in dialogue with one another from a very early date. The Buddha is mentioned in several of the Puranas that are believed to have been composed after his birth. Certain Buddhist teachings appear to have been formulated in response to ideas presented in the early Upanishads – in some cases concurring with them, and in other cases criticizing or re-interpreting them.

The Bhagavad Gita is a post-Buddhist text, and some scholars believe it was composed as part of the Hindu reaction to Buddhism. Prominent Indian scholars see the Bhagavad Gita as rather the product of intellectual currents then prevalent in India that pre-dated the emergence of Buddhism.

In later years, there is significant evidence that both Buddhism and Hinduism were supported by Indian rulers, regardless of the rulers own religious identity. Buddhist kings continued to revere Hindu deities and teachers, and many Buddhist temples were built under the patronage of Hindu rulers.

SIMILARITIES BETWEEN HINDUISM AND BUDDHISM

Technical Language

The Buddha adopted many of the terms already used in philosophical discussions of his era; however, many of these terms were then re-interpreted or redefined in the Buddhist tradition. For example, in the Samanna-phala Sutta, the Buddha is depicted presenting a notion of the 'three knowledges' (*tevijja*) – a term also used in the Vedic tradition to describe knowledge of the Vedas – as being not texts, but things that he had experienced. The true 'three knowledges' are said to be constituted by the process of achieving enlightenment, which is what the Buddha is said to have achieved in the three watches of the night of his enlightenment.

Ahimsa

Ahimsa is a religious concept which advocates non-violence and a respect for all life. *Ahimsa* is Sanskrit for avoidance of sacrificial *himsa*, or injury. The Buddha's dialogue in the *Culakammavibhanga Sutta* with the Brahmin Subha on killing is interesting considering the Vedic emphasis on sacrificial *himsa*. The focus on *ahimsa*, non-harm to all beings, in Buddhist ethics was a definitive move away from the killing inherent in the sacrifices of the Vedic ritual tradition. This move away from sacrificial *himsa* was also being made in other Sramana traditions. The Upanishadic literature, for example, is often critical of Vedic ritual and emphasises the internalization of the meaning and symbolism of sacrifice, rather than its literal enactment. Long life-span was much sought after by the composers of the Vedas. The Buddha's explanation of karma in the *Culakammavibhanga Sutta* challenges the Vedic idea that a life of sacrifice accrues benefits and excellence for oneself and one's family. The Buddha expounds his view that intentionally killing living beings leads not to the good, but to something that was problematic for the brahmins of his day, that is, shortness of life.

Karma

Karma is a word meaning *action* or *activity* and, often implies its subsequent results (also called karma-phala, "the fruits of action"). It is commonly understood as a term to denote the entire cycle of cause and effect as described in the philosophies of a number of cosmologies, including those of Buddhism and Hinduism.

Karma is a central part of Buddhist teachings. Buddhist teachings re-interpret certain aspects of the pre-Buddhist conception of karma, removing the idea of a perfect moral equilibrium present in some versions of those teachings.

Meanwhile, certain aspects of Buddhist teachings on karma, such as the 'transfer of merit' (Sanskrit: PariGâmanâ) or transfer of karma, seem to have been borrowed directly from earlier Hindu teachings, despite presenting apparent inconsistencies with the Buddhist doctrine of karma.

Dharma

Dharma means Natural Law or Reality, and with respect to its significance for spirituality and religion might be considered the Way of the Higher Truths. A Hindu appellation for Hinduism itself is *Sanatana Dharma* which translates to "the eternal dharma." Similarly, Buddhadharma in an appellation for Buddhism. The general concept of dharma forms a basis for philosophies, beliefs and practices originating in India. The four main ones are Hinduism, Buddhism, Jainism (Jaina Dharma), and Sikhism (Sikha Dharma), all of whom retain the centrality of dharma in their teachings. In these traditions, beings that live in harmony with dharma proceed more quickly toward, according to the tradition, Dharma Yukam, Moksha, or Nirvana (personal liberation). Dharma can refer generally to religious duty, and also mean social order, right conduct, or simply virtue.

Mantra

A mantra is a religious syllable or poem, typically from the Sanskrit language. Their use varies according to the school and philosophy associated with the mantra. They are primarily used as spiritual conduits, words or vibrations that instill one-pointed concentration in the devotee. Other purposes have included religious ceremonies to accumulate wealth, avoid danger, or eliminate enemies. Mantras existed in the Vedic religion and were later adopted by Buddhists, Sikhs and Jains, now popular in various modern forms of spiritual practice which are loosely based on practices of these Eastern religions.

Meditation

Meditation was an aspect of the practice of the yogis in the centuries preceding the Buddha. The Buddha built upon the yogis' concern with introspection and developed their meditative techniques, but rejected their theories of liberation.

In Buddhism, sati and sampajanna (both translated into English as mindfulness) are to be developed at all times, in pre-Buddhist yogic practices there is no such injunction. A yogi in the Brahmanical tradition is not to practice while defecating, for example, while a Buddhist monastic should do so. This difference is due the different goals of the practice. The former practitioner is aiming for gnosis of an object outside of the world, while for the latter there is no such object; experience in the world is the object, which must be purified. Another new teaching of the Buddha was that meditative absorption should be combined with the practice of mindfulness.

Religious knowledge or 'vision' was indicated as a result of practice both within and outside of the Buddhist fold. According to the *Samaññaphala Sutta* this sort of vision arose for the Buddhist adept as a result of the perfection of 'meditation' (Sanskrit: dhyâna) coupled with the perfection of 'ethics' (Sanskrit: úîla). Some of the Buddha's meditative techniques were shared with other traditions of his day, but the idea that ethics are causally related to the attainment of 'religious insight' (Sanskrit: prajñâ) was original.

The Buddhist texts are probably the earliest describing meditation techniques. They describe meditative practices and states which had existed before the Buddha as well as those which were first developed within Buddhism. Two Upanishads written after the rise of Buddhism do contain full-fledged descriptions of yoga as a means to liberation.

While there is no convincing evidence for meditation pre-Buddhist early Brahminic texts, Wynne argues that formless meditation originated in the Brahminic tradition, based on strong parallels between Upanishadic cosmological statements and the meditative goals of the two teachers of the Buddha as recorded in the early Buddhist texts. He mentions less likely possibilities as well. Having argued that the cosmological statements in the Upanishads also reflect a contemplative tradition, he argues that the Nasadiya Sukta contains evidence for a contemplative tradition, even as early as the late Rg Vedic period.

Reincarnation

In the Rig Veda, man is thought to be born and die only once. The Rig Veda mentions life after death in heaven in the company of ancestors. The ritual system of the Vedas was central to Vedic life and thought and depended 'on the notion of constant sacrifice, the reintegration of multiple elements into a moment of unity before a new dispersal into being'.

It is highly probable that in India the concept of reincarnation (along with karma, samsara, and moksha) was developed by non-Aryan people outside of the caste system whose spiritual ideas greatly influenced later Indian religious thought. Buddhism and Jainism are continuations of this tradition, and the early Upanishadic movement was influenced by it. Reincarnation was likely adopted from this religious culture by Brahmin orthodoxy, and Brahmins composed the earliest known scriptures containing these ideas in the early Upanishads. According to the Oxford Handbook of Eschatology, the Upanishadic treatments of samsara, karma, and reincarnation are "fundamental contributions of the Upanishads to Hindu—indeed, South Asian—eschatology."

According to Hinduism, the soul (*atman*) is immortal, while the body is subject to birth, decay, old age and death. The meme of reincarnation is intricately linked with the notion of karma, another concept first recorded in the Upanishads. Karma (literally: action) is the sum of one's actions, and the force that determines one's next reincarnation. The cycle of death and rebirth, governed by karma, is referred to as samsara.

The Shakyamuni Buddha rejected all theories according to which beings have an eternal, immutable self that transmigrated – the 'dweller within the body' or *atman* – he also criticized the statement "I have no self" (See below). Buddhism developed an understanding of a 'continuum or stream of skanda' through such disciplines as vipassanâ and shamata, which has become reified in later Buddhist discourse as the Mindstream doctrine, a reification that Shakyamuni Buddha would have challenged. Hence, it is to be understood as an upaya doctrine, as are all doctrines of the Buddhadharma. The mindstream was further developed by the Cittamatra and Yogacara schools and it impacted on the development of the 'store consciousness' (âlâyavijñâna) and the buddha nature conceptions and tathagatagarbha literature. In English Buddhist discourse the nomenclature 'reincarnation' is unfavoured due the insidious bias of an 'entity' that 'incarnates'. Buddhism challenges all such 'entities'. Instead of an 'entity', what is reborn is an 'evolving consciousness' (M.1.256) or 'stream of consciousness' (D.3.105), whose quality has been conditioned by karma.

Buddhist scriptures regularly discuss what is generally understood by the lay person as future and past lives, though these are more appropriately understood following Buddhavacana as the continuity of the mindstream of sentient beings. The phenomenon and institution of tulku within the Vajrayana tradition is an interesting qualification and analogue to the reification of the entity and the transmigration and reincarnation meme within many of the plethora of schools and sects of the Sanatana Dharma.

Yoga

The practice of Yoga is intimately connected to the religious beliefs and practices of both Buddhism and Hinduism. However there are distinct variations in the usage of yoga terminology in the two religions. In Hinduism, the term "Yoga" commonly refers to the eight limbs of yoga as defined in the Yoga Sutras of Patanjali, written some time after 100

BCE. Whereas in the Vajrayana Buddhism of Tibet, the term "Yoga" is used to refer to any type of spiritual practice; from the various types of tantra (like Kriyayoga or Charyayoga) to 'Deity yoga' and 'guru yoga'. In the early translation phase of the Sutrayana and Tantrayana from India, China and other regions to Tibet, along with the practice lineages of sadhana, codified in the Nyingmapa canon, the most subtle 'conveyance' (Sanskrit: yana) is Adi Yoga (Sanskrit). A contemporary scholar with a focus on Tibetan Buddhism, Robert Thurman writes that Patanjali was influenced by the success of the Buddhist monastic system to formulate his own matrix for the version of thought he considered orthodox.

There is a range of common terminology and common descriptions of the meditative states that are seen as the foundation of meditation practice in both Hindu Yoga and Buddhism. Many scholars have noted that the concepts of dhyana and samâdhi - technical terms describing stages of meditative absorption - are common to meditative practices in both Hinduism and Buddhism. Most notable in this context is the relationship between the system of four Buddhist *dhyana* states (Pali: *jhana*) and the *samprajnata samadhi* states of Classical Yoga. Also, many (Tibetan) Vajrayana practices of the generation stage and completion stage work with the chakras, inner energy channels (nadis) and kundalini, called tummo in Tibetan.

Zen Buddhism

Zen is a form of Mahayana Buddhism. The Mahayana school of Buddhism is noted for its proximity with Yoga. In the west, Zen is often set alongside Yoga, the two schools of meditation display obvious family resemblances. Zen Buddhism traces some of its roots to yogic practices. Certain essential elements of Yoga are important both for Buddhism in general and for Zen in particular.

Tibetan Buddhism

Tibetan Buddhism is not a monolithic entity. What is known as Tibetan Buddhism, a particular tradition of Vajrayana, is a collection of practice lineages or traditions of sadhana transmission. These practice lineages are entwined and historically come from throughout the Asian region and include tantric elements from non-Buddhist schools. The modern nomenclature of western discourse that reifies a 'Buddhism' and a 'Hinduism' obscured the varigated and manifold entwined lineages of Tantra. It is important to remember that though Buddhism values scholarship, it is not a textual tradition (in the sense of the written word), but primarily one based on the practitioner's investigation and direct experience as demonstrated by the example of Shakyamuni, culminating in enlightenment under the Bodhi Tree. Aspects of vipashyana and shamatha are entwined within tantric techniques. It is commonly held that Buddhism was introduced to Tibet from India, and though this is true, Buddhism from other areas such as China, Kashmir, Japan entered the Himalaya and is integrated with the practice lineages of the Nyingma, Kagyupa, Sakyapa and Gelukpa schools of Tibetan Buddhism, which in turn dialogued with the indigenous Bonpo traditions of the Himalaya.

Yoga is central to Tibetan Buddhism. In the Nyingma tradition, certain practitioners progress to increasingly profound levels of yoga, starting with Mahâ yoga, continuing to Anu yoga and ultimately undertaking the most subtle, Ati yoga. In qualification, the Nyingmapa do not equate a value judgment with the yana, one is not better than another, the yana most appropriate for a practitioner is determined by their karma, propensity and proclivity. The majority of practitioners stay within one yana for the duration of their lifetime. The Nyingmapa view all traditions, not just their own through the modal of the nine yana. The Bonpo have a comparable modal of nine. Elements of Adi Yoga for both the Bonpo and Nyingmapa are perceived in other traditions. Indeed, Nyingmapa and Bonpo are not the only source of Ati Yoga teachings as both traditions testify, as Adi Yoga is propagated in other worlds and dimensions. In the Sarma traditions, the Anuttara yoga class is equivalent to the three most subtle yana of the Nyingmapa. Other tantra yoga practices include a system of 108 bodily postures practiced with breath and heart rhythm timing in movement exercises is known as Trul khor or union of moon and sun (channel) prajna energies, and the body postures of Tibetan ancient yogis are depicted on the walls of the Dalai Lama's summer temple of Lukhang.

Tibetan Buddhist doctrines unite a seemingly diverse group of practices to offer a variety of ways to 'truth' (Sanskrit: satya; refer Two Truths) and 'enlightenment' (Sanskrit: bodhi) in accordance with the different qualities and capacities of sentient beings. These practices involve the use of tantra and yoga. Yoga used as a way to enhance concentration.

Nagarjuna's Madhyamika view and Yogacara's Mind-only view are used in Tibetan Buddhism as bases for Yoga practices. Focused meditation clears the mind of unenlightened concepts.

In the 13th and the 14th centuries, the Sarma traditions developed a fourfold classification system for Tantric texts based on the types of practices each contained, especially their relative emphasis on external ritual or internal yoga. The first two classes, the so-called lower tantras, are called the Kriya and the Chatya tantras; the two classes of higher tantras are the Yoga and the Anuttara Yoga (Highest Yoga).

Symbolism

- **Mudra**: This is a symbolic hand-gesture expressing an emotion. Depictions of the Buddha are almost always depicted performing a mudra.

- **Dharma Chakra**: The Dharma Chakra, which appears on the national flag of India and the flag of the Thai royal family, is a Buddhist symbol that is used by members of both religions.
- **Rudraraksh**: These are beads which devotees, usually monks use for praying.
- **Tilak**: Many Hindu devotees mark their heads with a tilak, which is interpreted as a third eye. A similar mark is one of the characteristic physical characteristics of the Buddha.
- **Swastika** and **Sauvastika**: both are sacred symbols. It can be either clockwise or counter-clockwise and both are seen in Hinduism and Buddhism. The Buddha is sometimes depicted with a swastika on his chest or the palms of his hands.

Cosmology and Worldview

Both Hinduism and Buddhism have the concept of Naraka and Svarga lokas, the mountain Sumeru, Jambudvipa, entities such as devas, asuras, nâga, preta, yaksha, gandharvas, kinnars, brahma, etc. Cosmological time is measured in kalpas.

Fire Ritual

In Japan, the Shingon Fire Ritual is derived from Hindu traditions. Similar rituals are common in Tibetan Buddhism.

DIFFERENCES BETWEEN THE TWO RELIGIONS

Despite the similarities there exist differences between the two religions. The major differences are mentioned below.

God

Gautama Buddha (as portrayed in the Pali scriptures, the agamas) set an important trend in nontheism in Buddhism in the sense of denying the notion of an omnipotent god. Nevertheless, in many passages in the Tripitaka gods (devas in Sanskrit) are mentioned and specific examples are given of individuals who were reborn as a god, or gods who were reborn as humans. Buddhist cosmology recognizes various levels and types of gods, but none of these gods is considered the creator of the world or of the human race.

Buddhist canonical views about God and the priests are mentioned below:

> 13. 'Well then, Vasettha, those ancient sages versed in ancient scriptures, the authors of the verses, the utterers of the verses, whose, ancient form of words so chanted, uttered, or composed, the priests of to-day chant over again or repeat; intoning or reciting exactly as has been intoned or recited-to wit, Atthaka, Vamaka, Vamadeva, Vessamitta, Yamataggi, Angirasa, Bharadvaja, Vasettha, Kassapa, and Bhagu — did even they speak thus, saying: " We know it, we have seen it", where the creator is whence the creator is, whither the creator is?

From the Buddhist perspective, man has created God out of the psychologically deep-rooted idea of self-protection. Walpola Rahula writes that man depends on this creation "for his own protection, safety, and security, just as a child depends on his parent." He describes this as a product of "ignorance, weakness, fear, and desire," and writes that this "deeply and fanatically held belief" for man's consolation is "false and empty" from the perspective of Buddhism. He writes that man does not wish to hear or understand teachings against this belief, and that the Buddha described his teachings as "against the current" for this reason.

The Vedas

The Buddha is recorded in the Canki Sutta (Majjhima Nikaya 95) as saying to a group of Brahmins:

> O Vasettha, those priests who know the scriptures are just like a line of blind men tied together where the first sees nothing, the middle man nothing, and the last sees nothing.

In the same discourse, he says:

> It is not proper for a wise man who maintains truth to come to the conclusion: This alone is Truth, and everything else is false.

He is also recorded as saying:

> To be attached to one thing (to a certain view) and to look down upon other things (views) as inferior - this the wise men call a fetter.

Walpola Rahula writes, "It is always a question of knowing and seeing, and not that of believing. The teaching of the Buddha is qualified as *ehi-passika,* inviting you to 'come and see,' but not to come and believe... It is always seeing through knowledge or wisdom, and not believing through faith."

In the Samanna-phala Sutta, the Buddha is depicted presenting a notion of the 'three knowledges' (*tevijja*)- a term also used in the Vedic tradition to describe knowledge of the Vedas- as being not of texts, but things that he had experienced. The true 'three knowledges' are said to be constituted by the process of achieving enlightenment, which is what the Buddha is said to have achieved in the three watches of the night of his enlightenment. These three are: memory of previous lives, seeing the rebirth of others according to their karma, and the four noble truths and the destruction of spiritual faults which fester in the mind and keep it unenlightened - the third is a composite. The third knowledge, according to the early Buddhist texts, was completed at dawn, and brought the perfect enlightenment he had been seeking. Gombrich notes that this definition of the true "three knowledges" occurs in multiple places in the Canon, and was likely intended to parallel and trump the "three knowledges" of the brahmins.

In Hinduism, philosophies are classified either as Astika or Nastika, that is, philosophies which either affirm or reject the authorities of the Vedas. According to this tradition, Buddhism is a Nastika school since it rejects the authority of the Vedas. Buddhists on the whole called those who did not believe in Buddhism the "outer path-farers" (*tiirthika*).

Conversion

Since the Hindu scriptures are essentially silent on the issue of religious conversion, the issue of whether Hindus evangelize is open to interpretations. Those who view Hinduism as an ethnicity more than as a religion tend to believe that to be a Hindu, one must be born a Hindu. However, those who see Hinduism primarily as a philosophy, a set of beliefs, or a way of life generally believe that one can convert to Hinduism by incorporating Hindu beliefs into one's life and by considering oneself a Hindu. The Supreme Court of India has taken the latter view, holding that the question of whether a person is a Hindu should be determined by the person's belief system, not by their ethnic or racial heritage.

Buddhism spread throughout Asia via evangelism and conversion. Buddhist scriptures depict such conversions in the form of lay followers declaring their support for the Buddha and his teachings, or via ordination as a Buddhist monk. Buddhist identity has been broadly defined as one who "takes refuge" in the Buddha, Dharma, and Sangha, echoing a formula seen in Buddhist texts. In some communities, formal conversion rituals are observed. No specific ethnicity has typically been associated with Buddhism, and as it spread beyond its origin in India immigrant monastics were replaced with newly ordained members of the local ethnic or tribal group.

Early Buddhism and Early Vedanta

Early Buddhist scriptures do not mention schools of learning directly connected with the Upanishads. Though the earliest Upanishads had been completed by the Buddha's time, they are not cited in the early Buddhist texts as Upanishads or Vedanta. For the early Buddhists they were likely not thought of as having any outstanding significance in and of themselves, and as simply one section of the Vedas.

The Buddhist texts do describe wandering, mendicant Brahmins who appear to have valued the early Upanishads' promotion of this lifestyle as opposed to living the life of the householder and accruing wealth from nobles in exchange for performing Vedic sacrifices. Furthermore, the early Buddhist texts mention ideas similar to those expounded in the early Upanishads, before controverting them.

Brahman

The old Upanishads largely consider Brahman (masculine gender, Brahmâ in the nominative case, henceforth "Brahmâ") to be a personal god, and Brahman (neuter gender, Brahma in the nominative case, henceforth "Brahman") to be the impersonal world principle. They do not strictly distinguish between the two, however. The old Upanishads ascribe these characteristics to Brahmâ: first, he has light and luster as his marks; second, he is invisible; third, he is unknowable, and it is impossible to know his nature; fourth, he is omniscient. The old Upanishads ascribe these characteristics to Brahman as well.

In the Buddhist texts, there are many Brahmâs. There they form a class of superhuman beings, and rebirth into the realm of Brahmâs is possible by pursuing Buddhist practices.

In the early texts, the Buddha gives arguments to refute the existence of a creator.

In the Pâli scriptures, the neuter Brahman does not appear (though the word *brahma* is standardly used in compound words to mean "best", or "supreme"), however ideas are mentioned as held by various Brahmins in connection with Brahmâ that match exactly with the concept of Brahman in the Upanishads. Brahmins who appear in the Tevijja-suttanta of the Digha Nikaya regard "union with Brahmâ" as liberation, and earnestly seek it. In that text, Brahmins of the time are reported to assert: "Truly every Brahmin versed in the three Vedas has said thus: 'We shall expound the path for the sake of union with that which we do not know and do not see. This is the correct path. This path is the truth, and leads to liberation. If one practices it, he shall be able to enter into association with Brahmâ." The early Upanishads frequently expound "association with Brahmâ", and "that which we do not know and do not see" matches exactly with the early Upanishadic Brahman.

In the earliest Upanishad, the Brihadaranyaka Upanishad, the Absolute, which came to be referred to as Brahman, is referred to as "the imperishable". The Pâli scriptures present a "pernicious view" that is set up as an absolute principle corresponding to Brahman: "O Bhikkhus! At that time Baka, the Brahmâ, produced the following pernicious view: 'It is permanent. It is eternal. It is always existent. It is independent existence. It has the dharma of non-perishing. Truly it is not born, does not become old, does not die, does not disappear, and is not born again. Furthermore, no liberation superior to it exists elsewhere." The principle expounded here corresponds to the concept of Brahman laid out in the Upanishads. According to this text the Buddha criticized this notion: "Truly the Baka Brahmâ is covered with unwisdom."

The Buddha confined himself to what is empirically given. This empiricism is based broadly on both ordinary sense experience and extrasensory perception enabled by high degrees of mental concentration.

Atman

In Hinduism, the atman is considered the essential 'self' of a person.

The pre-Buddhist Upanishads link the Self to the feeling "I am." The Chandogya Upanishad for example does, and it sees Self as underlying the whole world, being "below," "above," and in the four directions. In contrast, the Buddhist Arahant says: "Above, below, everywhere set free, not considering 'this I am.'"

While the pre-Buddhist Upanishads link the Self to the attitude "I am," others like the post-Buddhist Maitri Upanishad hold that only the defiled individual self, rather than the universal self, thinks "this is I" or "this is mine". According to Peter Harvey,

This is very reminiscent of Buddhism, and may well have been influenced by it to divorce the universal Self from such egocentric associations.

The Upanishadic "Self" shares certain characteristics with nibbana; both are permanent, beyond suffering, and unconditioned. However, the Buddha shunned any attempt to see the spiritual goal in terms of "Self" because in his framework, the craving for a permanent self is the very thing which keeps a person in the round of uncontrollable rebirth, preventing him or her from attaining nibbana. Harvey continues:

Both in the Upanishads and in common usage, self/Self is linked to the sense of "I am" ... If the later Upanishads came to see ultimate reality as beyond the sense of "I am", Buddhism would then say: why call it 'Self', then?

Buddhist mysticism is also of a different sort from that found in systems revolving around the concept of a "God" or "Self":

> If one would characterize the forms of mysticism found in the Pali discourses, it is none of the nature-, God-, or soul-mysticism of F.C. Happold. Though nearest to the latter, it goes beyond any ideas of 'soul' in the sense of immortal 'self' and is better styled 'consciousness-mysticism.'

Possibly the main philosophical difference between Hinduism and Buddhism is that the concept of atman was rejected by the Buddha. Terms like anatman (not-self) and shunyata (voidness) are at the core of all Buddhist traditions. The permanent transcendence of the belief in the separate existence of the self is integral to the enlightenment of an Arhat.

The Buddha criticized conceiving theories even of a unitary soul or identity immanent in all things as unskillful. In fact, according to the Buddha's statement in Khandha Samyutta 47, all thoughts about self are necessarily, whether the thinker is aware of it or not, thoughts about the five aggregates or one of them.

At the time of the Buddha some philosophers and meditators posited a "root": an abstract principle out of which all things emanated and which was immanent in all things. When asked about this, instead of following this pattern of thinking, the Buddha attacks it at its very root: the notion of a principle in the abstract, superimposed on experience. In contrast, a person in training should look for a different kind of "root" — the root of dukkha experienced in the present. According to one Buddhist scholar, theories of this sort have most often originated among meditators who label a particular meditative experience as the ultimate goal, and identify with it in a subtle way.

B. Alan Wallace writes that the transcendental notion of the self is an "idol" that cannot "withstand empirical investigation or rational analysis."

Rahula writes,

> Two ideas are psychologically deep-rooted in man: self-protection and self-preservation. For self-protection man has created God, on whom he depends for his own protection, safety, and security, just as a child depends on its parent. For self-preservation man has conceived the idea of an immortal Soul or Atman, which will live eternally. In his ignorance, fear, weakness, and desire, man needs these two things to console himself. Hence he clings to them deeply and fanatically. The Buddha's teaching does not support this ignorance, fear, weakness, and desire, but aims at making man enlightened by removing them and destroying them, striking at their very root. According to Buddhism, our ideas of God and Soul are false and empty. Though highly developed as theories, they are all the same extremely subtle mental projections, garbed in an intricate metaphysical and philosophical phraseology. These ideas are so deep-rooted in man, and so near and dear to him, that he does not wish to hear, nor does he want to understand, any teaching against them. The Buddha knew this quite well. In fact, he said that his teaching was 'against the current,' against man's selfish desires.

Upanishadic Self Declared Non-Existent

The Buddha denies the existence of Self in the Alagaddupama Sutta (M I 135-136). Possibly the most famous Upanishadic dictum is *tat tvam asi,* "thou art that." Transposed into first person, the Pali version is *eso 'ham asmi,* "I am this." This is said in several suttas to be false. The full statement declared to be incorrect is "This is mine, I am this, this is my self/essence." This is often rejected as a wrong view. The

Alagaduppama Sutta rejects this and other obvious echoes of surviving Upanishadic statements as well (these are not mentioned as such in the commentaries, and seem not to have been noticed until modern times). Moreover, the passage denies that one's self is the same as the world and that one will become the world self at death. The Buddha tells the monks that people worry about something that is non-existent externally (*bahiddhaa asati*) and non-existent internally (*ajjhattam asati*); he is referring respectively to the soul/essence of the world and of the individual. A similar rejection of "internal" Self and "external" Self occurs at AN II 212. Both are referring to the Upanishads. The most basic presupposition of early Brahminic cosmology is the identification of man and the cosmos (instances of this occur at TU II.1 and Mbh XII.195), and liberation for the yogin was thought to only occur at death, with the adept's union with brahman (as at Mbh XII.192.22). The Buddha's rejection of these theories is therefore one instance of the Buddha's attack on the whole enterprise of Upanishadic ontology.

Caste

The Buddha repudiated the caste distinctions of the Brahmanical religion, and was as a result described as a corrupter and opposed to true dharma in some of the Puranas.

Buddhism implicitly denied the validity of caste distinctions by offering ordination to all regardless of caste. The Buddhist writer Ashvaghosa directly opposed the caste system of Hinduism by drawing upon anomalous episodes in Hindu scriptures. While the caste system constitutes an assumed background to the stories told in Buddhist scriptures, the sutras do not attempt to justify or explain the system, and the caste system was not generally propagated along with the Buddhist teachings. The early texts state that caste is not determined by karma.

The notion of ritual purity also provided a conceptual foundation for the caste system, by identifying occupations and duties associated with impure or taboo objects as being themselves impure. Regulations imposing such a system of purity and taboos are absent from the Buddhist monastic code, and not generally regarded as being part of Buddhist teachings.

Soteriology

Upanishadic soteriology is focused on the static Self, while the Buddha's is focused on dynamic agency. In the former paradigm, change and movement are an illusion; to realize the Self as the only reality is to realize something that has always been the case. In the Buddha's system by contrast, one has to make things happen.

The fire metaphor used in the Aggi-Vacchagotta Sutta (which is also used elsewhere) is a radical way of making the point that the liberated sage is beyond phenomenal experience. It also makes the additional point that this indefinable, transcendent state is the sage's state even during life. This idea goes against the early Brahminic notion of liberation at death.

Liberation for the Brahminic yogin was thought to be the permanent realization at death of a nondual meditative state anticipated in life. In fact, old Brahminic metaphors for the liberation at death of the yogic adept ("becoming cool", "going out") were given a new meaning by the Buddha; their point of reference became the sage who is liberated in life. The Buddha taught that these meditative states alone do not offer a decisive and permanent end to suffering either during life or after death.

He stated that achieving a formless attainment with no further practice would only lead to temporary rebirth in a formless realm after death. Moreover, he gave a pragmatic refutation of early Brahminical theories according to which the meditator, the meditative state, and the proposed uncaused, unborn, unanalyzable Self, are identical. These theories are undergirded by the Upanishadic correspondence between macrocosm and microcosm, from which perspective it is not surprising that meditative states of consciousness were thought to be identical to the subtle strata of the cosmos. The Buddha, in contrast, argued that states of consciousness come about caused and conditioned by the yogi's training and techniques, and therefore no state of consciousness could be this eternal Self.

Nonduality

Both the Buddha's conception of the liberated person and the goal of early Brahminic yoga can be characterized as nondual, but in different ways. The nondual goal in early Brahminism was conceived in ontological terms; the goal was that into which one merges after death. According to Wynne, liberation for the Buddha "... is nondual in another, more radical, sense. This is made clear in the dialogue with Upasiva, where the liberated sage is defined as someone who has passed beyond conceptual dualities. Concepts that might have some meaning in ordinary discourse, such as consciousness or the lack of it, existence and non-existence, etc., do not apply to the sage. For the Buddha, propositions are not applicable to the liberated person, because language and concepts (Sn 1076: *vaadapathaa, dhammaa*), as well as any sort of intellectual reckoning (*sankhaa*) do not apply to the liberated sage."

The Term "Nirvana"

The word nirvana (Pali: Nibbana) was first used in its technical sense in Buddhism, and cannot be found in any of the pre-Buddhist Upanishads. The use of the term in the Bhagavad Gita may be a sign of the strong Buddhist influence upon Hindu thought. Although the word nirvana is absent from the Upanishads, the word itself existed prior to the Buddha. It must be kept in mind that nirvana is one of many terms for salvation that occur in the orthodox Buddhist scriptures. Other terms that appear are 'Vimokha', or 'Vimutti', implying 'salvation' and 'deliverance' respectively. Some more words synonymously used for nirvana in Buddhist scriptures are 'mokkha/moksha', meaning 'liberation' and 'kevala/ kaivalya', meaning 'wholeness'; these words were given a new Buddhist meaning.

The Buddha in Hindu Scriptures

In many Puranas, the Buddha is described as an incarnation of Vishnu who incarnated in order to delude either demons or mankind away from the Vedic dharma. The Bhavishya Purana posits:

> At this time, reminded of the Kali Age, the god Vishnu became born as Gautama, the Shakyamuni, and taught the Buddhist dharma for ten years. Then Shuddodana ruled for twenty years, and Shakyasimha for twenty. At the first stage of the Kali Age, the path of the Vedas was destroyed and all men became Buddhists. Those who sought refuge with Vishnu were deluded.

It is believed by some scholars that the Buddha avatar, which occurs in different versions in various Puranas, may represent an attempt by Brahmin orthodoxy to slander the Buddhists by identifying them with the demons. Helmuth von Glasenapp attributed these developments to a Hindu desire to absorb Buddhism in a peaceful manner, both to win Buddhists to Vishnuism and also to account for the fact that such a significant heresy could exist in India.

Notable Views

Sarvepalli Radhakrishnan has claimed that the Buddha did not look upon himself as an innovator, but only a restorer of the way of the Upanishads, despite the fact that the Buddha did not accept the Upanishads, viewing them as comprising a pretentious tradition, foreign to his paradigm.

The Hindu philosopher, Vivekananda, wrote in glowing terms about Buddha, and visited Bodh Gaya several times.

Ananda Coomaraswamy, a proponent of the Perennial Philosophy, claimed:

> Hinduism is a religion both of Eternity and Time, while Gautama looks upon Eternity alone. it is not really fair to Gautama or to the Brahmans to contrast their Dharma; for they do not seek to cover the same ground. We must compare the Buddhist ethical ideal with the identical standard of Brahmanhood expected of the Brahman born; we must contrast the Buddhist monastic system with the Brahmanical orders; the doctrine of Anatta with the doctrine of Atman, and here we shall find identity. Buddhism stands for a restricted ideal, which contrasts with Brahmanism as a part contrasts with the whole.

He also maintained:

> The more superficially one studies Buddhism, the more it seems to differ from Brahmanism in which it originated; the more profound our study, the more difficult it becomes to distinguish Buddhism from Brahmanism, or to say in what respects, if any, Buddhism is really unorthodox.

Some Hindu scholars have also accepted Buddhism as a fulfillment of Sanatana Dharma philosophy:

> The relation between Hinduism (by Hinduism, I mean the religion of the Vedas) and what is called Buddhism at the present day, is nearly the same as between Judaism and Christianity. Jesus Christ was a Jew, and Shakya

> Muni was a Hindu. The Jews rejected Jesus Christ, nay, crucified him, and the Hindus have accepted Shakya Muni as God and worship him. But the real difference that we Hindus want to show between modern Buddhism and what we should understand as the teachings of Lord Buddha, lies principally in this: Shakya Muni came to preach nothing new. He also, like Jesus, came to fulfill and not to destroy.

Steven Collins sees such Hindu claims regarding Buddhism as part of an effort - itself a reaction to Christian proselytizing efforts in India - to show that "all religions are one", and that Hinduism is uniquely valuable because it alone recognizes this fact.

Some scholars have written that Buddhism should be regarded as "reformed Brahmanism", and many Hindus consider Buddhism a sect of Hinduism.

Alan Watts wrote the following:

> Being a Hindu really involves living in India. Because of the differences of climate, or arts, crafts, and technology, you cannot be a Hindu in the full sense in Japan or in the United States. Buddhism is Hinduism stripped for export. The Buddha was a reformer in the highest sense: someone who wants to go to the original form, or to re-form it for the needs of a certain time... Buddha is the man who woke up, who discovered who he really was. The crucial issue wherein Buddhism differs from Hinduism is that it doesn't say who you are; it has no idea, no concept. I emphasize the words *idea* and *concept.* It has no idea and no concept of God because Buddhism is not interested in concepts, it is interested in direct experience only.

Buddhist scholar Rahula Walpole has written that the Buddha fundamentally denied all speculative views, such as the doctrinal Upanishadic belief in Atman.

B. R. Ambedkar, the founder of the Dalit Buddhist movement, believed that Buddhism offered an opportunity for low-caste and untouchable Hindus to achieve greater respect and dignity because of its non-caste doctrines. Among the 22 vows he prescribed to his followers is an injunction against having faith in Brahma, Vishnu and Mahesh. He also regarded the belief that the Buddha was an incarnation of Vishnu as "false propaganda".

●●

2
Hindu and Hindu Deities

A Hindu is an adherent of Hinduism, a set of religious, philosophical and cultural systems that originated in the Indian subcontinent. The vast body of Hindu scriptures, divided into Œruti ("revealed") and Smriti ("remembered"), lay the foundation of Hindu beliefs which primarily include dhárma, kárma, ahimsa and saCsâra. Vedânta and yoga are one of the several core schools of Hindu philosophy.

Hinduism is regarded as the oldest of world's major religions and Hindu mythology and philosophy has had a profound impact in many parts of the world, especially southern Asia. With more than a billion adherents, Hinduism is the world's third largest religion. Vast majority of Hindus, approximately 900 million, live in India. Other countries with large Hindu populations can be found in various parts of the world.

Etymology

The word *Hindu* first appeared in the Old Persian language which was derived from the Sanskrit word *Sindhu*, the historic local appellation for the Indus River in the northwestern part of the Indian subcontinent. The usage of the word *Hindu* was further popularized by the Arabic term *al-Hind* referring to the land of the people who live across river Indus. By 13th century, *Hindustân* emerged as a popular alternative name of India, meaning the "land of *Hindus*". 'Hindus' came to be used for people regardless of their religious affiliation and mainly as a geographical term. It was only towards the end of the

18th century, the European merchants and colonists referred collectively to the followers of Dharmic religions in *Hindustan* — which geographically referred to most parts of the northern Indian subcontinent — as *Hindus*. Eventually, it came to define a precisely religious identity that includes any person of Indian origin who did not practice Abrahamic religions or religions such as Jainism, Zoroastrianism, Sikhism or Buddhism and came to be known as a Hindu, thereby encompassing a wide range of religious beliefs and practices..

One of the accepted views is that *ism* was added to *Hindu* around 1830 to denote the culture and religion of the high-caste Brahmans in contrast to other religions. The term *Hinduism* was soon appropriated by the Hindus in India themselves as they tried to establish a national, social and cultural identity opposed to European colonialism in India.

Definition

The roots of the diverse set of religious beliefs, traditions and philosophy of Hindus were laid during the Vedic age which originated in India between 2000 and 1500 BC. The ancient Vedic religion is considered by most scholars as the predecessor of the modern religion of Hindus and it has had a profound impact on India's history, culture and philosophy. The *Vedas* is oldest sacred book of Hinduism and lays the foundation of several schools of Hindu thought. The *Upanishads* refers to those scriptures which form the core teachings of the *Vedânta* philosophy. Adi Shankara's commentaries on the Upanishads led to the rise of *Advaita Vedanta*, the most influential sub-school of *Vedanta*.

Hinduism consists of several sects and denominations, of which *Vaishnavism* and *Shaivism* are by far the most popular. Other aspects include folk and conservative Vedic Hinduism. Since 18th century, Hinduism has accommodated a host of new religious and reform movements, with *Arya Samaj* being one of the most notable Hindu revivalist organizations. Due to the wide diversity in the beliefs, practices and traditions encompassed by Hinduism, there is no universally accepted definition on who a Hindu is, or even agreement on whether term Hinduism represents a religious, cultural or socio-political entity. In 1995, Chief Justice P. B. Gajendragadkar was quoted in an Indian Supreme Court ruling:

> When we think of the Hindu religion, unlike other religions in the world, the Hindu religion does not claim any one prophet; it does not worship any one god; it does not subscribe to any one dogma; it does not believe in any one philosophic concept; it does not follow any one set of religious rites or performances; in fact, it does not appear to satisfy the narrow traditional features of any religion or creed. It may broadly be described as a way of life and nothing more.

Thus some scholars argue that the Hinduism is not a religion *per se* but rather a reification of a diverse set of traditions and practices by scholars who constituted a unified system and arbitrarily labeled it Hinduism. The usage may also have been necessitated by the desire to distinguish between "Hindus" and followers of other religions during the periodic census undertaken by the colonial British government in India. Other scholars, while seeing Hinduism as a 19th century construct, view Hinduism as a response to British colonialism by Indian nationalists who forged a unified tradition centered on oral and written Sanskrit texts adopted as scriptures.

A commonly held view, though, is that while Hinduism contains both "uniting and dispersing tendencies", it has a common central thread of philosophical concepts (including dharma, moksha and samsara), practices (puja, bhakti etc) and cultural traditions. These common elements originating (or being codified within) the Vedic, Upanishad and Puranic scriptures and epics. Thus a Hindu could:

- follow any of the Hindu schools of philosophy, such as Advaita (non-dualism), Vishishtadvaita (non-dualism of the qualified whole), Dvaita (dualism), Dvaitadvaita (dualism with non-dualism), etc.
- follow a tradition centered on any particular form of the Divine, such as Shaivism, Vaishnavism, Shaktism, etc.
- practice any one of the various forms of yoga systems; including bhakti (devotion) in order to achieve *moksha*.

In 1995, while considering the question "who are Hindus and what are the broad features of Hindu religion", the Supreme Court of India highlighted Bal Gangadhar Tilak's formulation of Hinduism's defining features:

> Acceptance of the Vedas with reverence; recognition of the fact that the means or ways to salvation are diverse; and the realization of the truth that the number of gods to be worshipped is large, that indeed is the distinguishing feature of Hindu religion.

Some thinkers have attempted to distinguish between the concept of Hinduism as a religion, and a Hindu as a member of a nationalist or socio-political class. Veer Savarkar in his influential pamphlet "Hindutva: Who is a Hindu?" considered geographical unity, common culture and common race to be the defining qualities of Hindus; thus a Hindu was a person who saw India "as his Fatherland as well as his Holy land, that is, the cradle land of his religion". This conceptualization of Hinduism, has led to establishment of Hindutva as the dominant force in Hindu nationalism over the last century.

Customs and Traditions

Ethnic and Cultural Fabric

Hinduism, its religious doctrines, traditions and observances are very typical and inextricably linked to the culture and demographics of India. Hinduism has one of the most ethnically diverse bodies of adherents in the world.It is hard to classify Hinduism as a religion because the framework, symbols, leaders and books of reference that make up a typical religion are not uniquely identified in the case of Hinduism. Most commonly it can be seen as a "way of life" which gives rise to many other civilized forms of religions.

Large tribes and communities indigenous to India are closely linked to the synthesis and formation of Hindu civilization. Peoples of East Asian roots living in the states of north eastern India and Nepal were also a part of the earliest Hindu civilization. Immigration and settlement of peoples from Central Asia and peoples of Indo-Greek heritage have brought their own influence on Hindu society.

The roots of Hinduism in southern India, and amongst tribal and indigenous communities is just as ancient and fundamentally contributive to the foundations of the religious and philosophical system.

Ancient Hindu kingdoms arose and spread the religion and traditions across South East Asia, particularly Thailand, Nepal, Burma, Malaysia, Indonesia, Cambodia and what is now central Vietnam. A form of Hinduism particularly different from Indian roots and traditions is practiced in Bali, Indonesia, where Hindus form 90% of the population. Indian migrants have taken Hinduism and Hindu culture to South Africa, Fiji, Mauritius and other countries in and around the Indian Ocean, and in the nations of the West Indies and the Caribbean.

Hindu Ceremonies, Observances and Pilgrimages

Hinduism is also very diverse in the religious ceremonies performed by its adherents for different periods and events in life, and for death. Principal Festivity of the Hindus also vary from region to region which include Diwali, Shivratri, Ram

Navami, Janmashtmi, Ganapati, Durgapuja, Holi, Navaratri, etc.

Many Hindus make pilgrimages to the holy shrines (known as *tirthas*). Hindu holy shrines include Mount Kailash, Amarnath, Vaishno Devi, Rameshwaram, and Kedarnath. Prominent Hindu holy cities include Varanasi (Benaras), Tirupati, Haridwar, Nashik,Ujjain, Dwarka, Puri, Prayaga, Mathura, Mayapur and Ayodhya.

Goddess Durga's holy shrine in Vaishno Devi attracts thousands of devotees every year. Hundreds of millions of Hindus annually visit holy rivers such as the Ganges ("Ganga" in Sanskrit) and temples near them, wash and bathe themselves to purify their sins. The Kumbha Mela (*the Great Fair*) is a gathering of between 10 to 20 million Hindus upon the banks of the holy rivers at Allahabad (Prayag), Ujjain, Nashik, as periodically ordained in different parts of India by Hinduism's priestly leadership. The most famous is at the confluence of the Ganga and Yamuna in Uttar Pradesh which is known as "Sangam".

Sixteen Sanskars (Rituals)

These are various rituals necessary within a life of Hindu. These *samskaram* are applied during different phases of life. Some of those are:

1. *Garbhadharana* (conception)
2. *Jatakarma* (birth ceremony)
3. *Namakarana* (naming ceremony)
4. *Annaprasana* (first feeding solid food)
5. *Choodakarana* (first tonsure)
6. *Vidhyarambha* (starting of education)
7. *Upanayanam* (thread ceremony- initiation)
8. *Vivaha* (marriage)
9. *Anthyesthi* (funeral rites)

Some Hindus, may perform initiation ceremonies like Upanayana or *Janoy* or 'Bratabandha'. These ceremonies have variants depending on the caste, the culture and the region.

In a ceremony administered by a priest, a coir string, known as Janoy, Poonool (lit. "flower thread,"Tamil), janivara (Kannada, Marathi), is hung from around a young boy's left shoulder to his right waist line for Brahmins and from right shoulders to left waistline by Kshatriyas. The ceremony varies from region to community, and includes reading from the Vedas and special *Mantras* and *Slokas*.

Religion for the Common Hindu

To many Hindus, the Vedas, a large corpus of texts that originated in Ancient India, are the main source of religious social and religious practices in Hindu society. By tradition, the distinction between "believer" and "unbeliever" (Nastika) was simply whether the person, in principle, accepted the authority of the Vedas. Such acceptance was in many cases a matter of common terminology and wildly different belief systems coexist (including atheistic, polytheistic, monotheistic, among others) within the community of "believers." Consequently, for the common Hindu, the connection to the Vedas is mostly through certain chants that are performed at various ceremonies, and not through an emotional/spiritual connection to the content of the Vedas.

The Puranas are a wide collection of religious treatises, biographies and stories on the historical, mythological and religious characters in Hindu folklore, classic literature and sacred scriptures. They are often the source of popular Hindu folk tales and religious lessons and thus play a much bigger role in the emotional/spiritual dimension of the common Hindu's life.

Yoga is an important connection for a Hindu to his religious and historical heritage. The art of spiritual and physical exercises are a distinguished native tradition pursued by millions of Hindus worldwide.

Indian Vedic astrology is important to the conduct of any of life's important events such as marriage, applying for a post or admission, buying a house or starting a new business. To millions of Hindus the kundali is an invaluable possession that charts the course of life for a man or a woman from the time of his birth, all ascertained by Vedic mathematics and astrology.

Perhaps the most popular Hindu scripture is the Mahabharata, depicting a civil war within a family that takes on dimensions of the struggle between *dharma* and *adharma*. Krishna's discourse to the warrior prince Arjuna, known as the Bhagavad Gita and contained in the Mahabharata, is the guide book on life for the common Hindu. For many Hindus the Bhagavad Gita is considered a source of divine guidance and inspiration. Devotional readers apply Krishna's teachings to the personal and worldly contexts of their life. It is often considered as the main source of religious teaching for Hindu practitioners.

Similarly, the Ramayana, depicting the life of the prince and king Rama, also plays a big role through its many different versions. To hundreds of millions of Hindus, Rama is more than just an incarnation of the Supreme, or simply a just king of Ayodhya. He is the still living, thriving soul and identity of real Hinduism. Rama is the image of Hinduism, the Perfect Man, its conscience and undying hope of deliverance.

The doctrines of moksha by the diligent discharge of personal, social and religious duty is the cornerstone of Hindu society. By following one's duty (Swa-Dharma) one gains merit and, when the process is completed, union with the Godhead and cessation of the cycle of birth and death. Dereliction of duty will result in all sorts of misfortunes, including birth into a lower level in the social hierarchy. This is a strong motivation to stick to the right path of human nature. Commonly this swa-dharma or varna is misunderstood as caste, the class identity in Hindu society. Varna is determined by a soul's karma, while Jat or caste is determined by birth and not necessarily in a person's nature. So it is important for a person to follow their true nature and seek to do their duty in life.

HINDU DEITIES

Within Hinduism a large number of personalities, or 'forms', are worshipped as murtis. These beings are either aspects of the supreme Brahman, avatars of the supreme being, or significantly powerful entities known as devas. The exact nature of belief in regards to each deity varies between differing Hindu denominations and philosophies. Often these beings are depicted in humanoid, or partially-humanoid forms, complete with a set of unique and complex iconography in each case. In total, there are 330,000,000 (33 crores or 330 million) of these supernatural beings in various Hindu traditions.

Bhagavan and Ishvara

Hinduism is a religion unlike any other, this is because it has no founder and no specific religious text, though the Bhagavad-Gita could be considered as one. According to Hindu traditions as expounded in Bhagavad-Gita, the religion is timeless and was first given to the Sun god by Lord Krishna over 2.2 million years ago in the last Treta Yuga and transmitted to the worldly beings in various steps. Many religions' (such as Sikhism, Jainism and Buddhism) founders arose out of the same milieu as modern Hinduism and therefore many beliefs and customs are the same. Contrary to popular belief, Hindus believe in many gods, but one supreme God as well . All in all Hinduism is more than a religion (though some try to argue this). Besides a wide diverse set of beliefs, it has a set of customs and traditions that were synonymous with the people of India. As invaders came and left India, the term "hinduism" loosely defined the people who believed in Indian customs and tradition (to separate the people who originally lived in India, from the invading people), for example in the past a Christian or Muslim could have been a Hindu as well, because the term only defined Indian customs and beliefs. More recently (last five hundred years), only people who believe in the traditional Hindu gods are called Hindus, hence it is now defined as a religion. Often Hindus celebrate Christmas, despite Christian origins and many people of other religions also celebrate Deepavali (Diwali), the festival of light, and Holi, the festival of colour despite their Hindu origins.

"Bhagavân" is a word used to refer to the personal aspect of God in general; it is not specific to a particular deity. Bhagavân transcends gender, yet can be looked upon as both father and mother, child, or sweetheart. Most Hindus, in their daily devotional practices, worship some form of this personal aspect of God, although they believe in the more abstract concept of Brahman as well. This may mean worshiping God through an image or a picture, or simply thinking of God as a personal being.

"Ishvara" is a name or title used to emphasize God's role and function as controller of the universe. When Hindus refer to God as Ishvara, they are emphasizing a monistic idea of God as a principle of the universe, rather than a person.

"Ishwar" is the ultimate supreme being Hindus believe in - there is only one God and similar to the way society functions, Ishwar had taken many forms to function the universe; Lord Brahma the creator, Lord Vishnu the preserver and Lord Shiva the destroyer.

Different names and, frequently, different images of God will be used, depending on which aspect of Bhagavâ is being discussed. For instance, when God is talked about in the aspect as the creator, God is called Brahmâ. If one is emphasizing God's capacity as preserver of the world, the name Vishnu is used. When referred to in the capacity as destroyer of the world, God is called Shiva. Many of these individual aspects of God also have other names and images. For example, Krishna and Rama are considered forms of Vishnu. All the various deities and images one finds in Hinduism are considered manifestations of the same God, called Bhagavân in the personal aspect and Brahman when referred to as an abstract concept.

Avatars as Incarnations of God

Many denominations of Hinduism, such as Vaishnavism and Saivism, teach that occasionally, God comes to Earth as a human being to help humans in their struggle toward enlightenment and salvation (moksha.) Such an incarnation of God is called an avatar (or avatâra.) In some respects, the Hindu concept of avatar is similar to the belief found in Christianity that God came to the earth incarnated in the form of Jesus. However, whereas most Christians believe that God has assumed a human body only once, Hinduism teaches that there have been multiple avatars throughout history and that there will be more. Thus Lord Krishna, who is not only viewed as an incarnation but also source of all incarnations, says:

> Whenever righteousness declines (Yada yada hi dharmasya, glanir bhavati bharata)
>
> And unrighteousness increases, (Abhyuth-thanam adharmasya)
>
> I incarnate myself as a human; (Tadat-manam srijamyaham)
>
> To deliver the holy, (Paritranaya sadhunam)
>
> To destroy the sin of the sinner, (Vinasha-yacha dush-kritam)

To establish righteousness. (Dharma sansthapan-arthaya)

I come into being from age to age (Sambhawami yugay yugay)

Ten Avatars

The most famous of the divine incarnations are Rama, whose life is depicted in the Ramayana, and Krishna, whose life is depicted in the Mahâbhârata and the Srimad Bhagavatam. The Bhagavad Gita, which contains the spiritual teachings of Krishna, is one of the most widely-read scriptures in Hinduism.

1. Matsya, the fish, appeared in the Satya Yuga. Represents beginning of life.

2. Kurma, the tortoise, appeared in the Satya Yuga. Represents a human embryo just growing tiny legs, with a huge belly.

3. Varaha, the boar,appeared in the Satya Yuga. Represents a human embryo which is almost ready. Its features are visible.

4. Narasimha, the Man-Lion (Nara = man, simha = lion), appeared in the Satya Yuga. Represents a newborn baby, hairy and cranky, bawling and full of blood.

5. Vamana, the Dwarf, appeared in the Treta Yuga. Represents a young child.

6. Parashurama, Rama with the axe, appeared in the Treta Yuga. Represents both an angry young man and a grumpy old man simultaneously.

7. Rama, Sri Ramachandra, the prince and king of Ayodhya, appeared in the Treta Yuga. Represents a married man with children in a very ideological society

8. Krishna (meaning dark or black; see also other meanings in the article about him.), appeared in the

Dwapara Yuga. Represents a person in more practical society, where there is one good or bad. Good or bad depends on society you live in.

9. Gautama Buddha is considered an avatar that returned pure dharma to the world.

10. Kalki ("Eternity", or "time", or "The Destroyer of foulness"), who is expected to appear at the end of Kali Yuga, the time period in which we currently exist.

There is also a "hidden avatar" mentioned in 11th canto of the Bhagavata Purana.

Some consider Balarama, brother of Krishna to be the eighth avatar of Vishnu, and delete Buddha. The Buddha avatar, which occurs in different versions in various Puranas, may represent an attempt by orthodox Brahminism to slander the Buddhists by identifying them with the demons. Helmuth von Glasenapp attributed these developments to a Hindu desire to absorb Buddhism in a peaceful manner, both to win Buddhists to Vaishnavism and also to account for the fact that such a significant heresy could exist in India.

Devas and Devis

The pantheon in Œrauta consists of many deities. Gods are called devas (or devatâs) and goddesses are called devis. The various devas and devis are personifications of different aspects of one and the same God. For instance, when a Hindu thinks of Ishvara as the giver of knowledge and learning, that aspect of Ishvara is personified as the deity Saraswati. In the same manner, the deity Lakshmi personifies Ishvara as the giver of wealth and prosperity. This does not imply that Ishvara is a kind of supreme god or lord of all the other deities; Ishvara is just the name used to refer to God in general, when no particular deity is being referred to. Devas represent certain forces. For instance, Agni has one aspect as the flame, but this flame symbolises the psychological power associated with Agni—namely, the power of will. Agni can be called God-will. Similarly Indra is the God-mind; Sarasvati is the power of inspiration, not merely of learning.

The devas constitute an integral part of the colorful Hindu culture. These various forms of God are depicted in innumerable paintings, statues, murals, and scriptural stories that can be found in temples, homes, businesses, and other places. In Hinduism, the scriptures recommend that for the satisfaction of a particular material desire a person may worship a particular deity. For example, shopkeepers frequently keep a statue or picture of the devi Lakshmi in their shops for financial prosperity. The elephant-headed deva known as Ganesha is worshiped before commencing any important undertaking, as he represents God's aspect as the remover of obstacles. Students and scholars may propitiate Saraswati, the devi of learning, before taking an exam or giving a lecture.

The most ancient Vedic devas included Indra, Agni, Soma, Varuna, Mitra, Savitri, Rudra, Prajapati, Vishnu, Aryaman, and the ashvins. Important devis were Sarasvati, Ushas, and Prithvi. Later scriptures called the *Puranas* recount traditional stories about each individual deity, such as Ganesha and Hanuman, and avatars such as Rama and Krishna.

Trimurti

Shiva and Vishnu are not regarded as ordinary devas but as Mahâdevas ("great gods") because of their central positions in worship and scriptures. These two along with Brahma are considered the Trimurti—the most supreme individual deities. These three symbolize the entire circle of samsara in Hinduism: Brahma as creator, Vishnu as preserver or protector, and Shiva as destroyer or judge.

Devas in the Vedas

The main devas are (vide 6th anuvaka of Chamakam):

- Aditya
- Agni
- Antariksha
- Ashwinis
- Brahma
- Brihaspati
- Dishas
- Dyaus
- Indra
- Ganesha
- Marutas
- Moordha
- Prajapati
- Prithvi
- Pusha
- Rudra
- Savitr
- Shiva
- Soma
- Varuna
- Vayu
- Vishnu
- Vishvedavas

The main devis are:

- Durga or Parvati
- Lakshmi or Shri
- Sarasvati or Vaak

Popular Deities

In their personal religious practices, Hindus may worship primarily one or another of these deities, known as their "Ishta Devata," or chosen deity. The particular form of God worshiped as one's chosen ideal is a matter of individual preference, although regional and family traditions can play a large part in influencing this choice. Hindus may also take guidance about this choice from scriptures.

Although Hindus do worship deities other than their chosen deity from time to time, depending on the occasion and their personal inclinations, it is not expected that they will worship, or even know about, every form of God. Hindus generally choose one concept of God (popular choices include Krishna, Rama, Shiva, or Kali), and cultivate devotion to that chosen form, while at the same time respecting the chosen ideals of other people.

Some popular Hindu deities include Durga, Krishna, Vishnu, Shiva, Ganesha, Hanuman, Kali, Murugan, Venkateshwara, Nataraja, Rama, and Lakshmi.

Denominations of Hinduism

Contemporary Hinduism has four major divisions: Saivism, Shaktism, Smartism, and Vaishnavism.

Hinduism is a very rich and complex religion. Each of its four denominations shares rituals, beliefs, traditions and personal gods with one another, but each sect has a unique philosophy on how to achieve life's ultimate goal (moksa, liberation). For example a person can be a devotee to Shiva and a Vishnu devotee but one can practice the Advaita Vedanta philosophy which believes there is no difference between Brahman and a person's individual soul. Conversely, a Hindu may follow the Dvaita philosophy which stresses that Brahman and the soul are not the same. But each denomination fundamentally believes in different methods of self-realization and in different aspects of the one supreme God. However, each denomination respects and accepts all others, and conflict of any kind is rare.

Vaishnavism, Saivism, and Shaktism, respectively believe in a monotheistic ideal of Lord Vishnu (often as Lord Krishna), Lord Shiva, or Devi; this view does not exclude other personal gods, as they are understood to be aspects of the chosen ideal. For instance, to many devotees of Krishna, Shiva is seen as having sprung from Krishna's creative force. Ganesha worshippers would connect themselves with Shiva as Shiva is the father of Ganesha, making him a Shaiv deity. Often, the monad Brahman is seen as the one source, with all other gods emanating from there. Thus, with all Hindus, there is a strong belief in all paths being true religions that lead to one God or source, whatever one chooses to call the ultimate truth. As the Vedas - the most important Hindu scriptures state: "Truth is one; the wise call it by various names" (transliterated from Sanskrit: Ekam Sat Viprah Bahuda Vadanti.)

Smartism, is monist as well as a monotheist and understands different deities as representing various aspects and principles of one supreme entity, Brahman or parabrahman. Teachers such as Swami Vivekananda, who brought Hinduism to the West, held beliefs like those found in Smartism, although he usually referred to his religion as Vedanta. Other denominations of Hinduism do not strictly hold this belief.

A Smartist would have no problem worshiping Shiva or Vishnu together as he views the different aspects of God as leading to the same One God. It is the Smarta view that dominates the view of Hinduism in the West. By contrast, a Vaishnavite considers Vishnu as the one true God, worthy of worship and other forms as subordinate. See for example, an illustration of the Vaishnavite view of Vishnu as the one true God. Accordingly, many Vaishnavites, for example, believe that only Vishnu can grant moksha.. Similarly, many Shaivites also hold similar beliefs for Shiva.

Polytheism

There are some Hindus who consider the various deities not as forms of the one Ishvara, but as independently existing entities, and may thus be properly considered polytheists.

Although the panentheistic tendency in Hinduism allowed only a subordinate rank to the old polytheistic gods, they continued to occupy an important place in the affections of individual Hindus and were still represented as exercising considerable influence on the destinies of man. The most prominent of them were regarded as the appointed "loka palas", or guardians of the world; and as such they were made to preside over the four cardinal and (according to some authorities) the intermediate points of the compass.

Thus Indra, the chief of the devas, was regarded as the regent of the east; Agni, the fire, was in the same way associated with the southeast; Yama, lord of death and justice with the south; Surya, the sun, with the southwest; Varuna, originally the representative of the all-embracing heaven (atmosphere), now the god of the ocean, with the west; Vayu (or Pavana), the wind, with the northwest; Kubera, the god of wealth, with the north; and Soma with the northeast. In some traditions, Ishana—an aspect of Shiva—is regarded as the regent of the northeast and Nirrti the regent of the southwest.

In the institutes of Manu the loka palas are represented as standing in close relation to the ruling king, who is said to be composed of particles of these his tutelary deities. The retinue of Indra consists chiefly of the Devas, gandharvas, a class of genii, considered in the epics as the celestial musicians; and apsaras, lovely nymphs, who are frequently employed by the gods to make the pious devotee desist from carrying his austere practices to an extent that might render him dangerous to their power. Narada, an ancient sage (probably a personification of the cloud, the water-giver), is considered as the messenger between the gods and men, and as having sprung from the forehead of Brahma. The interesting office of the god of love is held by Kamadeva, also called Ananga, the bodyless, because, as the scriptures relate, having once tried by the power of his mischievous arrow to make Siva fall in love with Parvati, whilst he was engaged in devotional practices, the urchin was reduced to ashes by a glance of the angry god. Two other divine figures of some importance are considered as sons of Siva and Parvati, viz. Karttikeya or Skanda, the leader of the heavenly armies, who was supposed to have been fostered by the six Knittikas or Pleiades; and Ganesha (lord of troops), the elephant-headed god of wisdom, and at the same time the leader of the dii minorum gentium.

Mother Goddesses

Goddesses are worshiped when God is thought of as the Universal Mother. Particular forms of the Universal Mother include Lakshmi, Sarasvati, Parvati, Durga, and Kali. Shaktism recognizes Shakti as the supreme goddess. The concept of Mahadevi as the supreme goddess emerged in historical religious literature as a term to define the powerful and influential nature of female deities in India. Throughout history, goddesses have been portrayed as the mother of the universe, through whose powers the universe is created and destroyed. The gradual changes in belief through time shape the concept of Mahadevi and express how the different Goddesses, though very different in personality, all carry the power of the universe on their shoulders. Jagaddhatri and Mariamman are other significant female deities.

HINDU CALENDAR

The Hindu calendar used in ancient times has undergone many changes in the process of regionalization, and today there are several regional Indian calendars, as well as an Indian national calendar.

Most of these calendars are inherited from a system first enunciated in *Vedanga Jyotisha* of Lagadha, a late BCE adjunct to the Vedas, standardized in the *Surya Siddhanta* (3rd century CE) and subsequently reformed by astronomers such as Aryabhata (499 CE), Varahamihira (6th c. CE), and Bhaskara (12th c. CE). There are differences and regional variations abound in these computations, but the following is a general overview of Hindu lunisolar calendar.

Day

The Hindu calendrical day starts with local sunrise. It is allotted five "properties", called *anga*-s. They are:

1. the *tithi* active at sunrise
2. the *vaasara* or weekday
3. the *nakshatra* in which the moon resides at sunrise
4. the *yoga* active at sunrise
5. the *karana* active at sunrise.

Together these are called the *panchânga*-s where *pancha* means "five" in Sanskrit. An explanation of the terms follows.

Vaasara

Vaasara, often abbreviated as *vaara* in Sanskrit-derived languages, refers to the days of the week and bear striking similarities with the names in many cultures:

Following are the Hindi and English analogues in parentheses

1. Ravi vâsara (Sunday; ravi = sun)
2. Soma vâsara (Monday; soma = moon)

3. Mangala vâsara (Tuesday; mangala = Mars)
4. Budha vâsara (Wednesday; budh = Mercury)
5. Guru vâsara (Thursday; vrihaspati/guru = Jupiter)
6. Shukra vâsara (Friday; shukra = Venus)
7. Shani vâsara (Saturday; shani = Saturn)

There are many variations of these names in the regional languages, mostly using alternate names of the celestial bodies involved.

Nakshatra

The ecliptic is divided into 27 nakshatras, which are variously called lunar houses or asterisms. These reflect the moon's cycle against the fixed stars, 27 days and 7¾ hours, the fractional part being compensated by an intercalary 28th *nakshatra*. Nakshatra computation appears to have been well known at the time of the Rig Veda (2nd–1st millennium BCE).

The ecliptic is divided into the *nakshatra*s eastwards starting from a reference point which is traditionally a point on the ecliptic directly opposite the star Spica called *Chitrâ* in Sanskrit. (Other slightly-different definitions exist.) It is called **Meshâdi** or the "start of Aries"; this is when the equinox — where the ecliptic meets the equator — was in Aries (today it is in Pisces, 28 degrees before Aries starts). The difference between Meshâdi and the present equinox is known as ayanângsha or fraction of ecliptic. Given the 25,800 year cycle for the precession of the equinoxes, the equinox was directly opposite Spica in 285 CE, around the date of the Surya Siddhanta.

Yoga

First one computes the angular distance along the ecliptic of each object, taking the ecliptic to start at *Mesha* or Aries (*Meshâdi*, as defined above): this is called the longitude of that object. The longitude of the sun and the longitude of the moon are added, and normalized to a value ranging between 0° to 360° (if greater than 360, one subtracts 360.) This sum is divided into 27 parts. Each part will now equal 800' (where ' is the symbol of the arcminute which means 1/60 of a degree.) These parts are called the *yoga*-s. They are labeled:

1. Vishkambha
2. Prîti
3. Âyushmân
4. Saubhâgya
5. Shobhana
6. Atiganda
7. Sukarman
8. Dhriti
9. Shûla
10. Ganda
11. Vriddhi
12. Dhruva
13. Vyâghâta
14. Harshana
15. Vajra
16. Siddhi
17. Vyatîpâta
18. Varigha
19. Parigha
20. Shiva
21. Siddha
22. Sâdhya
23. Shubha

24. Shukla
25. Brâhma
26. Mâhendra
27. Vaidhriti

Again, minor variations may exist. The *yoga* that is active during sunrise of a day is the *yoga* for the day.

Karana

A *karana* is half of a tithi. To be precise, a *karana* is the time required for the angular distance between the sun and the moon to increase in steps of 6° starting from 0°. (Compare with the definition of a tithi above.)

Since the *tithi*-s are thirty in number, one would expect there to be sixty *karana*-s. But there are only eleven. There are four "fixed" *karana*-s and seven "repeating" *karana*-s. The four "fixed" *karana*-s are:

1. Kimstughna
2. Shakuni
3. Chatushpâd
4. Nâgava

The seven "repeating" *karana*-s are:

1. Bava
2. Bâlava
3. Kaulava
4. Taitula
5. Garajâ
6. Vanijâ
7. Vishti (Bhadrâ)

- Now the first half of the first *tithi* (of the bright fortnight) is always *Kimstughna karana*. Hence this *karana* is "fixed".
- Next, the seven repeating *karana*-s repeat eight times to cover the next 56 half-*tithi*-s. Thus these are the "repeating" *karana*-s.
- The three remaining half-*tithi*-s take the remaining "fixed" *karana*-s in order. Thus these are also "fixed".
- Thus one gets sixty *karana*-s from eleven.

The *karana* active during sunrise of a day is the *karana* for the day.

(Rashi) Saur Maas (solar months)	*Ritu (season)*	*Gregorian months*	*Zodiac*
Mesh	Vasant (spring)	March/April	Aries
Vrushabh		April/May	Taurus
Mithun	Grishma (summer)	May/June	Gemini
Kark		June/July	Cancer
Simha	Varsha (monsoon)	July/Aug	Leo
Kanya		Aug/Sept	Virgo
Tula	Sharad (autumn)	Sept/Oct	Libra
Vrushchik		Oct/Nov	Scorpius
Dhanu	Hemant (autumn-winter)	Nov/Dec.	Sagittarius
Makar		Dec/Jan	Capricornus
Kumbha	Shishir (Winter-Spring)	Jan/Feb	Aquarius
Meen		Feb/Mar	Pisces

Months of the Lunisolar Calendar

When a new moon occurs before sunrise on a day, that day is said to be the first day of the lunar month. So it is evident that the end of the lunar month will coincide with a new moon. A lunar month has 29 or 30 days (according to the movement of the moon).

The *tithi* at sunrise of a day is the only label of the day. There is no running day number from the first day to the last day of the month. This has some unique results, as explained below:

Sometimes two successive days have the same *tithi*. In such a case, the latter is called an *adhika tithi* where *adhika* means "extra". Sometimes, one *tithi* may never touch a sunrise, and hence no day will be labeled by that *tithi*. It is then said to be a *tithi kshaya* where *kshaya* means "loss".

Naming Lunar Months

There are twelve lunar month names:

1. Chaitra
2. Vaishâkh
3. Jyaishtha
4. Âshâdha
5. Shrâvana
6. Bhâdrapad
7. Âshwin
8. Kârtik
9. Mârgashîrsha
10. Paush
11. Mâgh
12. Phâlgun

Determining which name a lunar month takes is somewhat indirect. It is based on the *râshi* into which the **sun** transits within a lunar month, i.e. before the new moon ending the month.

There are twelve *râshi* names, there are twelve lunar month names. When the sun transits into the *Mesha râshi* in a lunar month, then the name of the lunar month is *Chaitra*. When the sun transits into *Vrishabha*, then the lunar month is *Vaishâkh*. So on.

The Sanskrit grammatical derivation of the lunar month names *Chaitra* etc is: the (lunar) month which has its central full moon occurring at or near the *nakshatra Chitrâ* is called *Chaitra*. Similarly, for the *nakshatra*-s *Vishâkhâ, Jyeshthâ, (Pûrva) Ashâdhâ, Shravan, Bhâdrapad, Ashvinî* (old name *Ashvayuj*), *Krittikâ, Mrigashîrsha, Pushya, Meghâ* and *(Pûrva/Uttara) Phalgunî* the names *Vaishâkh* etc are derived.

The lunar months are split into two pakshas of 15 days. The waxing paksha is called shuklapaksha, *light half*, and the waning paksha the krishnapaksha, *dark half*. There are two different systems for making the lunar calendar:

- *amanta* or *mukhya mana system* - a month begins with a new moon, mostly followed in the southern states
- *purnimanta* or *gauna mana system* - a month begins with a full moon, followed more in the North.

Extra Months

When the sun does not at all transit into any *râshi* but simply keeps moving within a *râshi* in a lunar month (i.e. before a new moon), then that lunar month will be named according to the first upcoming transit. It will also take the epithet of *adhik* or "extra". For example, if a lunar month elapsed without a solar transit and the next transit is into *Mesha*, then this month without transit is labeled *adhik Chaitra*.

The next month will be labeled according to its transit as usual and will get the epithet *nija* ("original") or *shuddha* ("clean"). [Note that an *adhik mâsa* (month) is the first of two whereas an *adhika tithi* is the second of two.]

An *adhik mâsa* occurs once every two or three years (meaning, with a gap of one or two years without *adhik mâsa*-s). Extra Month, or adhik mas *mâsa* (mas = lunar month) or purushottam mas (It is known so to give it a religious name, purushottam = krishna) falls every 32.5 months. Thus 12 Hindu mas (mâsa) is equal to approximate 356 days, while solar year have 365 or 366 (in leap year) which create differece of 9 to 10 days, which is subset every 3rd year. But no adhik mas falls during Kartik to Maha.

Lost months

If the sun transits into two *râshi*-s within a lunar month, then the month will have to be labeled by both transits and will take the epithet *kshay* or "loss". There is considered to be a "loss" because in this case, there is only one month labeled by both transits. If the sun had transited into only one *raashi* in a lunar month as is usual, there would have been two separate months labeled by the two transits in question.

For example, if the sun transits into *Mesh* and *Vrishabh* in a lunar month, then it will be called *Chaitra-Vaishaakh kshaya*. There will be no separate months labeled *Chaitra* and *Vaishâkh*.

A *kshay mâsa* occurs very rarely. Known gaps between occurrence of *kshaya mâsas* are 19 and 141 years. The last was in 1983. January 15 through February 12 were *Pausha-Mâgha kshay*. February 13 onwards was *(adhik) Phâlguna*.

Special Case

If there is no solar transit in one lunar month but there are two transits in the next lunar month.

- the first month will be labeled by the first transit of the second month and take the epithet *adhik* and
- the next month will be labeled by both its transits as is usual for a *kshay mâsa*

This is a very very rare occurrence. The last was in 1315. October 8 to November 5 were *adhik Kârtik*. November 6 to December 5 were *Kârtik-Mârgashîrsh kshaya*. December 6 onwards was *Paush*.

Religious Observances in Case of Extra and Lost Months

Among normal months, *adhika* months, and *kshaya* months, the earlier are considered "better" for religious purposes. That means, if a festival should fall on the 10th *tithi* of the *Âshvayuja* month (this is called Vijayadashamî) and there are two *Âshvayuja* months caused by the existence of an *adhika Âshvayuja*, the first *adhika* month will not see the festival, and the festival will be observed only in the second *nija* month. However, if the second month is *âshvayuja kshaya* then the festival will be observed in the first *adhika* month itself.

When two months are rolled into one in the case of a *kshaya mâsa*, the festivals of both months will also be rolled into this *kshaya mâsa*. For example, the festival of Mahâshivarâtri which is to be observed on the fourteenth *tithi* of the *Mâgha krishna paksha* was, in 1983, observed on the corresponding *tithi* of *Pausha-Mâgha kshaya krishna paksha*, since in that year, *Pausha* and *Mâgha* were rolled into one, as mentioned above. When two months are rolled into one in the case of a *kshaya mâsa*, the festivals of both months will also be rolled into this *kshaya mâsa*.

Year of the Lunisolar Calendar

The new year day is the first day of the *shukla paksha* of *Chaitra*. In the case of *adhika* or *kshaya* months relating to

Chaitra, the aforementioned religious rules apply giving rise to the following results:

- If an *adhika Chaitra* is followed by a *nija Chaitra,* the new year starts with the *nija Chaitra.*
- If an *adhika Chaitra* is followed by a *Chaitra-Vaishâkha kshaya,* the new year starts with the *adhika Chaitra.*
- If a *Chaitra-Vaishâkha kshaya* occurs with no *adhika Chaitra* before it, then it starts the new year.
- If a *Phâlguna-Chaitra kshaya* occurs, it starts the new year.

Another kind of Lunisolar Calendar

There is another kind of lunisolar calendar which differs from the former in the way the months are named. This section describes the differences involved, and may be skipped if the article is already too complicated for the reader. It is only included for completeness.

When a full moon (instead of new moon) occurs before sunrise on a day, that day is said to be the first day of the lunar month. In this case, the end of the lunar month will coincide with a full moon. This is called the *pûrnimânta mâna* or "full-moon-ending reckoning", as against the *amânta mâna* or "new-moon-ending reckoning" used before.

This definition leads to a lot of complications:

- The first *paksha* of the month will be *krishna* and the second will be *shukla.*
- The new year is still on the first day of the *Chaitra shukla paksha.* The next *paksha*-s will be the *Vaishâkha krishna, Vaishâkha shukla, Jyaishtha krishna* and so on, till *Phâlguna krishna, Phâlguna shukla* and *Chaitra krishna,* which is now the last *paksha* of the year.

- The *shukla paksha* of a given month, say *Chaitra,* comprises the same actual days in both systems, as can be deduces from a careful analysis of the rules. However, the *Chaitra krishna paksha*-s defined by the two systems will be on different days, since the *Chaitra krishna paksha* precedes the *Chaitra shukla paksha* is the *pûrnimânta* system but follows it in the *amânta* system.

- Though the regular months are defined by the full moon, the *adhika* and *kshaya* lunar months are still defined by the new moon. That is, even if the *pûrnimânta* system is followed, *adhika* or *kshaya* months will start with the first sunrise after the new moon, and end with the new moon.

- The *adhika* month will therefore get sandwiched between the two *paksha*-s of the *nija* months. For example, a *Shrâvana adhika mâsa* will be inserted as follows:

  1. *nija Shrâvana krishna paksha*
  2. *adhika Shrâvana shukla paksha*
  3. *adhika Shrâvana krishna paksha* and
  4. *nija Shrâvana shukla paksha*

  after which *Bhâdrapada krishna paksha* will come as usual.

- If there is an *adhika Chaitra,* then it will follow the *(nija) Chaitra krishna paksha* at the end of the year. Only with the *nija Chaitra shukla paksha* will the new year start. The only exception is when it is followed by a *kshaya,* and that will be mentioned later.

- The *kshaya* month is more complicated. If in the *amânta* system there is a *Pausha-Mâgha kshaya,* then in the *pûrnimânta* system there will be the following *paksha*-s:

  1. *Pausha krishna paksha*
  2. *Pausha-Maagha kshaya shukla paksha*

3. *Maagha-Phaalguna kshaya krishna paksha* and a
4. *Phâlguna shukla paksha.*

- The special *kshaya* case where an *adhika mâsa* precedes a *kshaya mâsa* gets even more convoluted. First, we should remember that the *Âshvayuja shukla paksha* is the same in both the systems. After this come the following *paksha*-s:

1. *nija Kârtika krishna paksha*
2. *adhika Kârtika shukla paksha*
3. *adhika Kârtika krishna paksha*
4. *Kârtika-Mâgashîrsha kshaya shukla paksha*
5. *Mâgashîrsha-Pausha kshaya krishna paksha*
6. *Pausha shukla paksha*

followed by the *Mâgha krishna paksha* etc as usual.

- The considerations for the new year are:

1. If there is a *Chaitra-Vaishâkha kshaya shukla paksha*:
    1. if an *adhika Chaitra* precedes it, then the *adhika Chaitra shukla paksha* starts the new year
    2. if not, the *kshaya shukla paksha* starts the new year
2. If there is a *Phâlguna-Chaitra kshaya shukla paksha* then it starts the new year

It must be noted, however, that none of these above complications cause a change in the day of religious observances. Since only the name of the *krishna paksha*-s of the months will change in the two systems, festivals which fall on the *krishna paksha* will be defined by the appropriate changed name. That is, the Mahâshivarâtri, defined in the *amânta mâna* to be observed on the fourteenth of the *Mâgha krishna paksha* will now (in the *pûrnimânta mâna*) be defined by the *Phâlguna krishna paksha.*

Correspondence of the Lunisolar Calendar to the Solar Calendar

A lunisolar calendar is always a calendar based on the moon's celestial motion, which in a way keeps itself close to a solar calendar based on the sun's (apparent) celestial motion. That is, the lunisolar calendar's new year is to kept always close (within certain limits) to a solar calendar's new year.

Since the Hindu lunar month names are based on solar transits, and the month of *Chaitra* will, as defined above, always be close to the solar month of *Mesha,* the Hindu lunisolar calendar will always keep in track with the Hindu solar calendar.

The Hindu solar calendar by contrast starts on April 14-15 each year. This signifies the sun's "entry" into Mesha rasi and is celebrated as the New Year in Assam, Bengal, Orissa, Manipur, Kerala, Punjab, Tamil Nadu and Tripura. The first month of the year is called "Chitterai" in Tamil, "Medam" in Malayalam and Baisakh in Bengali/Punjabi. This solar new year is celebrated on the same day in Burma, Cambodia, Laos, Nepal and Thailand due to Hindu influence on those countries.

Year Numbering

The epoch (starting point or first day of the zeroth year) of the current era of Hindu calendar (both solar and lunisolar) is February 18 3102 BCE in the proleptic Julian calendar or January 23 3102 BCE in the proleptic Gregorian calendar. Both the solar and lunisolar calendars started on this date. After that, each year is labeled by the number of years **elapsed** since the epoch.

This is a unique feature of the Hindu calendar. All other systems use the current ordinal number of the year as the year label. But just as a person's true age is measured by the number of years that have elapsed starting from the date of the person's birth, the Hindu calendar measures the number of years elapsed. As of May 18, 2005, 5106 years had elapsed in the Hindu calendar. However, the lunisolar calendar year usually starts earlier than the solar calendar year, so the exact year will not begin on the same day every year.

Other systems of numbering the Hindu years can be read about at the Samvat article.

Year Names

Apart from the numbering system outlined above, there is also a cycle of 60 calendar year names, called Samvatsaras, which started at the first year (at elapsed years zero) and runs continuously:

1. Prabhava
2. Vibhava
3. Shukla
4. Pramoda
5. Prajâpati
6. Ângirasa
7. Shrîmukha
8. Bhâva
9. Yuva
10. Dhâtri
11. Îshvara
12. Bahudhânya
13. Pramâdhi
14. Vikrama
15. Vrisha
16. Chitrabhânu

17. Svabhânu
18. Târana
19. Pârthiva
20. Vyaya (2006-2007 AD/CE)
21. Sarvajeeth (2007-2008 AD/CE)
22. Sarvadhâri (2008-2009 AD/CE)
23. Virodhi
24. Vikrita
25. Khara
26. Nandana
27. Vijaya
28. Jaya
29. Manmadha
30. Durmukhi
31. Hevilambi
32. Vilambi
33. Vikâri
34. Shârvari
35. Plava
36. Shubhakruti
37. Sobhakruthi
38. Krodhi
39. Vishvâvasu
40. Parâbhava
41. Plavanga
42. Kîlaka
43. Saumya
44. Sâdhârana

45. Virodhikruthi
46. Paridhâvi
47. Pramâdicha
48. Ânanda
49. Râkshasa
50. Anala
51. Pingala
52. Kâlayukthi
53. Siddhârthi
54. Raudra
55. Durmathi
56. Dundubhi
57. Rudhirodgâri
58. Raktâkshi
59. Krodhana
60. Akshaya

Eras

Hinduism has of four eras or ages, of which we are currently in the last. The four are:

1. Krita Yuga or Satya Yuga
2. Treta Yuga
3. Dvâpara Yuga
4. Kali Yuga

They are often translated into English as the golden, silver, bronze and Iron Ages. (Yuga means era or age.) The ages see a gradual decline of dharma, wisdom, knowledge, intellectual capability, life span and emotional and physical strength. The epoch provided above is the start of the *Kali Yuga*. The *Kali Yuga* is 432,000 years long. The *Dvâpara, Tretâ* and *Krita (Satya) Yuga*-s are two, three and four times the length of the *Kali Yuga* respectively. Thus they together constitute 4,320,000 years. This is called a *Chaturyuga*.

A thousand and a thousand (i.e. two thousand) *chaturyuga*-s are said to be one day and night of the creator Brahmâ. He (the creator) lives for 100 years of 360 such days and at the end, he is said to dissolve, along with his entire Creation, into the Eternal Soul or *Paramâtman*.

A non-vedic view of the timespan of a yuga is given by Swami Sri Yukteswar Giri, the guru of Paramahansa Yogananda. This is detailed in his book, The Holy Science. According to this view, one complete yuga cycle is equal to one complete "precession of the equinox", a period of approximately 24,000 years. The ascending phase consists of a 1200 year Kali, 2400 year Dwapara, 3600 year Treta and 4800 year Krita (Satya) yuga. The descending phase reverses this order, thus both ascending and descending phases equal 24,000 years. According to calculations given in the book, the most recent yuga change was in 1699, when the Earth passed from Kali Yuga (the lowest material age) to Dvâpara Yuga (the second age associated with electrical, atomic and finer forces). We are in an ascending spiral right now, and will pass into the Tretâ Yuga in 4100 AD. According to the book, the motion of the stars moving across the sky (a.k.a.precession) is the observable of the Sun's motion around another star. The quality of human intellect depends on the distance of the Sun and Earth from a certain point in space known as the Grand Center, Magnetic Center or VishGunâbhi Vishnu. The closer the Sun is to it, the more subtle energy the Solar System receives, and the greater is the level of human spiritual and overall development. As the Sun moves around its companion star, it brings us closer to or drives us farther away from Vishnunabi, resulting in the rising and falling ages here on Earth.

Yukteswar tells us that the calendars of the higher ages were based on the Yugas, with each era named after its Yuga. Hence, the year 3000 BC/BCE was known as descending Dwapara 102 (because the last descending Dwapara yuga began 102 years earlier in 3102 BC/BCE). He stated that this method was used up until the recent Dark Ages, when knowledge of the connection with the yugas and the precession cycle was lost; "The mistake crept into the almanacs for the first time during the reign of Raja Parikshit, just after the completion of the last descending Dwapara Yuga. At that time Maharaja Yudhisthira, noticing the appearance of the dark Kali Yuga, made over his throne to his grandson, the said Raja Parikshit. Maharaja Yudhisthira, together with all the wise men of his court, retired to the Himalaya Mountains... thus there was no one who could understand the principle of correctly calculating the ages of the several Yugas". Thus, Yukeswar assumed that Raja Parikship was not trained in any vedic principles even though he alone ruled the world many year. Thus, he interpreted that Yugas are not calculated correctly. Consequently, he gave the theory that when the Dwapara was over and the Kali era began no one knew enough to restart the calendar count. They knew they were in a Kali Yuga (which is why the old Hindu calendar now begins with K.Y.) but the beginning of this calendar (which in 2006 stands at 5108) can still be traced to 3102 BC/BCE, (3102+2006=5108) the start of the last descending Dwapara Yuga. To this day there is still much confusion why the Kali starts at this date or what the correct length of the Yugas should be. Yukteswar suggests that a return to basing the Yuga calendar on the motion of the equinox would be a positive step.

History

The Hindu Calendar descends from the Vedic times. There are many references to calendrics in the Vedas. The

Vedânga (adjunct to Veda) called Jyautisha (literally, "celestial body study") prescribed all the aspects of the Hindu calendars. After the Vedic period, there were many scholars such as Âryabhata (5th century CE), Varâhamihira (6th century) and Bhâskara (12th century) who were experts in Jyautisha and contributed to the development of the Hindu Calendar.

The most widely used authoritative text for the Hindu Calendars is the *Sûrya Siddhânta,* a text of uncertain age, though some place it at 10th century.

The traditional Vedic calendar used to start with the month of agrahayan (agra=first + ayan = travel of the sun, equinox) or Mârgashirsha. This is the month where the Sun crosses the equator, i.e. the vernal equinox. This month was called mârgashirsha after the fifth nakshatra (around lambda orionis). Due to the precession of the Earth's axis, the vernal equinox is now in Pisces, and corresponds to the month of chaitra. This shift over the years is what has led to various calendar reforms in different regions to assert different months as the start month for the year. Thus, some calendars (e.g. Vikram) start with Chaitra, which is the present-day month of the vernal equinox, as the first month. Others may start with Vaisakha (e.g. Bangabda). The shift in the vernal equinox by nearly four months from agrahaayana to chaitra in sidereal terms seems to indicate that the original naming conventions may date to the fourth or fifth millennium BCE, since the period of precession in the Earth's axis is about 25,800 years.

Regional Variants

The Indian Calendar Reform Committee, appointed in 1952 (shortly after Indian independence), identified more than thirty well-developed calendars, all variants of the *Surya Siddhanta* calendar outlined here, in systematic use across different parts of India. These include the widespread *Vikrama* and *Shalivahana* calendars and regional variations thereof.

The Tamil calendar, a solar calendar, is used in Tamil Nadu and Kollavarsham Calendar used in Kerala.

Vikrama and Shalivahana Calendars

The two calendars most widely used in India today are the *Vikrama* calendar followed in Western and Northern India and Nepal, and the Shalivahana or *Saka* calendar which is followed in South India and Maharashtra.

Both the *Vikrama* and the *Shalivahana* eras are lunisolar calendars, and feature annual cycles of twelve lunar months, each month divided into two phases: the 'bright half' (*shukla*) and the 'dark half' (*bahula*); these correspond respectively to the periods of the 'waxing' and the 'waning' of the moon. Thus, the period beginning from the first day after the new moon and ending on the full moon day constitutes the *shukla paksha* or 'bright half' of the month; the period beginning from the day after the full moon until and including the next new moon day constitutes the *bahula paksha* or 'dark half' of the month.

The names of the 12 months, as also their sequence, are the same in both calendars; however, the new year is celebrated at separate points during the year and the "year zero" for the two calendars is different. In the Vikrama calendar, the zero year corresponds to 58 BCE, while in the Shalivahana calendar, it corresponds to 78 CE. The Vikrama calendar begins with the month of *Baishakh* (April), or *Kartak* (October/November) in Gujarat. The Shalivahana calendar begins with the month of *Chaitra* (March) and the Ugadi/Gudi Padwa festivals mark the new year.

Another little-known difference between the two calendars exists: while each month in the *Shalivahana* calendar begins with the 'bright half' and is followed by the 'dark half', the opposite obtains in the *Vikrama* calendar. Thus, each month of the *Shalivahana* calendar ends with the no-moon day and the new month begins on the day after that, while the full-moon day brings each month of the *Vikrama* calendar to a close (This is an exception in Gujarati Calendar, its month (and hence new year) starts on a sunrise of the day after new moon, and ends on the new moon, though it follows Vikram Samvat).

National Calendars in South and South East Asia

A variant of the *Shalivahana* Calendar was reformed and standardized as the Indian National calendar in 1957. This official calendar follows the *Shalivahana* calendar in beginning from the month of *Chaitra* and counting years with 78 CE being year zero. It features a constant number of days in every month (with leap years).

The Bengali Calendar, or Bangla calendar (introduced 1584), is widely used in eastern India in the state of West Bengal, Tripura and Assam. A reformation of this calendar was introduced in present-day Bangladesh in 1966, with constant days in each month and a leap year system; this serves as the national calendar for Bangladesh. Nepal follows the Bikram Sambat. Parallel months and roughly the same periods apply to the Buddhist calendars used in Burma, Cambodia, Laos, Sri Lanka and Thailand.

Correspondence between Calendars

As an indicator of this variation, Whitaker's Almanac reports that the Gregorian year 2000 AD/CE corresponds, respectively with:

1. Year 5101 in the Kaliyuga calendar;
2. Year 2544 in the Buddha Nirvana calendar;
3. Year 2543 in the Buddhist Era (BE) of the Thai solar calendar
4. Year 2057 in the Bikram Samvat calendar;

5. Year 1922 in the Saka calendar;
6. Year 1921 (shown in terms of 5-yearly cycles) of the Vedanga Jyotisa calendar;
7. Year 1407 in the Bengali calendar;
8. Year 514 in the Gaurabda Gaudiya calendar;
9. Year 1176 in the Kolla Varsham calendar.

●●

3

Hindu Denominations

Hinduism comprises numerous sects or denominations. The denominations are roughly comparable to different religions. The main divisions in current Hinduism are Shaivism, Shaktism, Vaishnavism, and Smartism. These four denominations share rituals, beliefs, and traditions, but each denomination has a different philosophy on how to achieve life's ultimate goal (moksa, liberation).

An established philosophical school within a denomination is called a *sampradaya* and a traditional lineage of teachers from any sampradaya is a *parampara.*

The presence of different denominations and schools within Hinduism should not be viewed as a schism, as there was no original unity. On the contrary, there is at present no great animosity between the different "religions" which constitute Hinduism, and among Hindu followers as a whole, there is a strong belief that there are many paths leading to the One God or the Source, whatever one chooses to call that ultimate Truth. Whether Shiva is same as Vishnu or different from Vishnu, is a matter of dispute among adherents but now most keep their disputes private.

Instead, there is a healthy cross-pollination of ideas and logical debate that serves to refine each school's philosophy. It is not uncommon, or disallowed, for an individual to follow one school but take the point of view of another school for a certain issue.

Vaishnavism

Vaishnavism is the monotheistic tradition worshiping Vishnu (or his forms of Krishna and Rama) as the supreme or *svayam bhagavan.*

The different Vaishnava schools (sampradayas) and the principle teachers (acharyas) connected with them are as follows:

- Rudra Sampradaya: principle acharya -Vallabhacharya
- Brahma Sampradaya associated with Vishnu, who is the para-brahma (Universal Creator), not to be confused with the other Brahma, who is the four-faced god in Hindu religion: principle acharya - Madhvacharya. Gaudiya Vaishnavism is associated with this sampradaya and is associated with Chaitanya Mahaprabhu, International Society for Krishna Consciousness belongs to this sampradaya.
- Srivaishnava Sampradaya associated with Laksmi: principle acharyas - Ramanujacharya,Vedanta Desikan, is the oldest Vaishnav sect in India. This sampraday was followed by Vyasa, Parasara, Bodhayana. The linage of Acharya is Lord Narayana, next Lakshmi and then Vishweksenar, Nammalwar, Nathamuni, Uyyakondar, Manakal Nambi, Alavandar, Periya Nambi, Ramanujacharya and finally Vedanta Desikan. This sampradaya eradicated the caste system in their temples and made Hinduism a secular religion.
- Kumara Sampradaya is the tradition associated with Four Kumaras: principle acharya - Nimbarka, hence Nimbarka Sampradaya
- Vaikhanasa tradition: principle acharya - Vaikhanasa
- Swaminarayan Sampraday - This stems from the Sri Sampradaya

Saivism

Saivites are those who primarily worship Siva as the supreme god, both immanent and transcendent.

Saivism embraces at the same time monism (specifically nondualism) and dualism. It focuses on yoga, meditation, and love for all beings.

Major theological schools of Saivism include Kashmir Saivism, Saiva Siddhanta and Virasaivism.

To Saivites Shiva is both with and without form; he is the Supreme Dancer, Nataraja; and is linga, without beginning or end.

Shaktism

Shaktas worship Shakti, the divine Mother, in her many forms like (Kali, Durga, Laxmi, Saraswati etc.).

Shakta form was one of the oldest forms of Hindu religion (evidences even from Indus valley civilization), but with evolution of civilization and emergence of various doctrines, various other forms of Hindu philosophy emerged. Shaivism and Shakta forms are really inseparable, as is the description of Shiva and Shakti/Sati/Parvati. Vaishanvism has also its connections with Shakta philosophy as Goddess Durga herself is called Narayani.

Smartism

Smarthas have free rein to choose whichever deity they wish to worship. They usually worship five deities (pancopasana) or panchadevata as personal formful manifestations of the impersonal Absolute, Brahman. Smarthas accept and worship the six manifestations of God, (Ganesha, Shiva, Shakti, Vishnu, Surya, and Skanda) and the choice of the nature of God is up to the individual worshiper since different manifestations of God are held to be equivalent. It is a liberal and eclectic sect.

- It is the Smarta view that dominates the view of Hinduism in the West as Smarta belief includes Advaita belief and the first Hindu saint, who significantly brought Hinduism to the west was Swami Vivekananda, an adherent of Advaita. Not till much later, gurus, such as A.C. Bhaktivedanta Swami Prabhupada, and others, brought a Vaishnavite perspective to the West. By contrast with Smarta/ Advaita belief, Vaishnavism and Shaivism follows a singular concept of God, or panentheistic monotheism or panentheistic monism.

Prominent Smarta communities:

- In south India
  - o Havyaka
  - o Iyer
  - o Vaidiki Mulukanadu
  - o Vaidiki Velanadu
  - o Vaidiki Veginadu
  - o Vaidiki Telanganya
  - o Namboothiri
  - o Badaganadu
  - o Hoysala Kannada
  - o Kota brahmin
  - o Babboor Kamme
  - o Arvel Niyogi Brahmins
- In Maharashtra
  - o Karhade
  - o Deshastha
  - o Konkanastha or Chitpavan
  - o Devrukhe

- Saraswat Brahmins
  - o Gaud Saraswat Brahmins (GSB's)

Bhakti Movement

The medieval Bhakti movement has had a significant impact on the traditional denominations of Pauranic Hinduism, especially on Vaishnavism. The Alvars were Tamil poet saints of south India who lived between sixth and ninth centuries and espoused "emotional devotion" or bhakti to Visnu/Krishna in their songs of longing, ecstasy and service. Usually twelve Vaishnava saints, who, during the early medieval period of Tamil history, helped revive devotional Hinduism bhakti through their hymns of worship to Vishnu and his avatars. The collection of their hymns is known as Divya Prabhandham. The Bhakti literature that sprang from these Alvars has contributed to the establishment and sustenance of a culture that broke away from the ritual-oriented Vedic religion and rooted itself in devotion as the only path for salvation. In addition, they helped to make the Tamil religious life independent of knowledge of Sanskrit. As part of the legacy of the Alvars, five Vaishnava philosophical traditions (sampradayas) has developed at the later stages.

In Southeast Asia

A sect of Balinese Hindus flourished on the nearby island of Java until the late 16th century, when a vast majority of its adherents converted to Islam. Theologically, it is closer to Œaivism than to other major sects of Hinduism.

The term "Agama Hindu Dharma" can also refer to the traditional practices in Kalimantan, Sumatra, Sulawesi and other places in Indonesia, where people have started to identify and accept their agamas as Hinduism.

Newer Denominations

19th to 20th century Hindu revivalist organizations include:

- Arya Samaj
- Brahmo Samaj
- Parisada Hindu Dharma
- Prarthana Samaj
- Ramakrishna Mission
- Sadharan Brahmo Samaj
- Sree Narayana Dharma Paripalana
- Swadhyay Movement
- Swaminarayan Sampraday
- Sathya Sai Organisation

Hinduism was politicized in the context of the Indian independence movement that has resulted in the rise of Hindu nationalism to a significant political force in the Republic of India.

HINDU REFORM MOVEMENTS

Several contemporary groups, collectively termed Hindu reform movements, strive to introduce regeneration and reform to Hinduism. Although these movements are very individual in their exact philosophies they generally stress the spiritual, secular and logical and scientific aspects of the Vedic traditions, creating a form that is egalitarian that does not discriminate based on Jâti (caste or subcaste), gender, or race. Thus, most modern Hindu reform movements advocate a return to the ancient, egalitarian forms of Hinduism, and view aspects of modern Hinduism, such as discrimination and the caste system, as being corrupt results from colonialism and foreign influence.

Active Hindu communities are to be found in all parts of the world. In particular, countries of the former Soviet Union and Poland have thriving Hindu communities due to the missionary work of the Hare Krishnas. Most of the Hindu movements, with the exception of the Hare Krishna movement, reflect a more Smarta-like ideology.

There are groups in India that are actively engaged in getting women and those from socially disadvantaged jâtis to become priests of Vedic ritual.

One of the foremost movements in breaking the caste system and educating the downtrodden was the Lingayat movement spearheaded by Basavanna in the 12th century in Anubhava Mantapa in Kalyani of Karnataka. The less accessible Vedas were rejected and parallel Vachanas were compiled.

The new movements look up to Swami Vivekananda; Rabindranath Tagore;Ramana Maharshi; Shri Aurobindo (for his *Integral Yoga*); A.C. Bhaktivedanta Swami Prabhupada (founder of the modern Hare Krishna movement); Swami Sivananda, Swami Rama Tirtha; Narayana Guru, Paramhansa Yogananda; Shrii Shrii Anandamurti and for inspiration. More recently, the work of Maharishi Mahesh Yogi, Sathya Sai Baba, Shirdi Sai Baba, Swami Muktananda, Swami Chinmayananda, Maharishi Dayananda Saraswati, Sri Sri Ravi Shankar, and Mata Amritanandamayi has inspired millions to create new centers of spiritual development. In the intellectual field, the writings of Ananda Coomaraswamy, Ram Swarup, Stephen Knapp, Sita Ram Goel, Subhash Kak and David Frawley have been influential.

In social work, Mahatma Gandhi, Vinoba Bhave, Baba Amte and Shrii Shrii Anandamurti have been most important. Sunderlal Bahuguna created the *chipko* movement for the preservation of forestlands according to the Hindu ecological ideas.

The Rashtriya Swayamsevak Sangh or RSS was founded Keshav Baliram Hegdewar in 1925. The goal was to unite Hindus, make them rise over their caste differences and work to achieve a Hindu Rashtra; the ideology of the Sangh, closely associated with political Hinduism, came to be known as Hindutva.

In Indonesia several movements favour a return to Hinduism in Java, Sumatra, Kalimantan, and Sulawesi. Balinese Hinduism, known as Agama Hindu Dharma, has witnessed great resurgence in recent years.

Shrii Prabhat Rainjan Sarkar (founder of Ananda Marga) initiated a new renaissance in the Indian world of samgeet.

Hinduism and the West

Since the counter-culture revolution of the 1960s, there have been an increasing number of Western devotees of various Hindu lineages and practices. These have come about not only through the Hare Krishnas, but also through the Universalist teachings of such Hindu figures as Sri Ramakrishna, and the yoga teachings of B.K.S. Iyengar. The growing number of Indian immigrants relocating into the West, and the subsequent building of Hindu temples to meet the spiritual needs of these newly established Hindu communities, has also resulted in Westerns having ready access to traditional teachings. Many Western converts were introduced to Hinduism after attending the Western temples and then embracing the tradition. There can also be no doubt that the fitness revolution's ecstatic love-affair with yoga in the 1990s has helped spur on new interest in the teachings of Hinduism in the West.

More and more texts are being written by Western-born Hindu converts specifically for a new Western audience, the vast bulk of which have little to no experience with Sanskrit which renders traditional literature all but useless. Some of the more notable instructional texts are the Shaivistic teaching series of the Western-born Satguru Sivaya Subramuniyaswami's Himalayan Academy, which includes a book on how to convert to Hinduism.

Along with the traditional Hindu lineages that are opening their doors to Westerners, there are also many non-traditional spiritualities that are also embracing the beliefs and practices of Hinduism to varying extents. The Unitarian Universalist Church often makes room in their schedule to host events tied to Hindu holidays and celebrations, during which non-Hindus can learn more about the tradition and begin to take part in the observances. There are also several Neopagan and Wiccan traditions, such as SHARANYA, which teach traditional Shakta Tantra within a Western, Wicca-influenced context.

The German Indologist Axel Michaels in his 1998 book about Hinduism distinguished *founding, proselytizing religions,* "guru-ism" as religious groups originating in India, but also widespread in the West, founded by charismatic persons with a corpus of esoteric writings of gurus predominantly in English: Maharishi Mahesh Yogi and Transcendental Meditation, Sathya Sai Baba and the Sathya Sai Organization, Bhaktivedanta Swami Prabhupada and ISKCON, Guru Maharaj Ji and the Divine Light Mission, Rajneesh Chandra Mohan and the Sannyasi movement in Poona, et cetera. These *founding, proselytizing religions,* "guru-ism" are according to the book one of the three subgroups of *founded religions* of Hinduism. The other two being *sectarian religions* and *syncretically founded religions*. The *founded religions* in turn are, according to the book, one of the three Hindu religions that comprise Hinduism. The other two Hindu religions that comprise Hinduism are *Brahmanic-Sanskritic Hinduism,* and *folk religions and religions of social communities* (subcastes, castes, tribes); *Hindu folk or tribal religions*.

HINDU MYTHOLOGY

Hindu mythology is the large body of traditional narratives related to Hinduism, notably as contained in Sanskrit literature, such as the Sanskrit epics and the Puranas. As such, it is a subset of Indian mythology. Many Indians believe that these narratives are sacred and that they communicate profound truths.

Sources

The four Vedas, notably the hymns of the Rigveda, containend allusions to many themes (see Rigvedic deities, Rigvedic rivers).

In the period of Classical Sanskrit, much material is preserved in the Sanskrit epics, the Ramayana and the Mahabharata. Besides mythology proper, the voluminous epics also provide a plethora of information about ancient Indian society, philosophy, culture, religion and ways of life.

The Puranas deal with stories that are older than the epics (*Purana* is Sanskrit for "ancient"). The date of the Puranic texts as preserved however mostly post-dates the epics, dating to the Early Middle Ages.

The epics themselves are set in different Yugas (epochs) or periods of time. The Ramayana, written by the poet Valmiki, describes the life and times of Lord Rama (the seventh avatar of Lord Vishnu) and occurs in the treta yuga, while the Mahabharatha that describes the life and times of the Pandavas, occurs in the Dwapara yuga, a period associated with Lord Krishna (the eighth avatar of Lord Vishnu). In total, there are 4 Yugas. These are the Satya Yuga (or Krita Yuga), the Treta Yuga, the Dvapara Yuga and finally the Kali Yuga.

The Bhagavatham (also referred to as Srimad Bhagavatham or Bhagavatha Purana) is probably the most read and popular of the puranas. It chronicles the story of the god Vishnu and his incarnations (avataars) on earth.

Vedic Mythology

The roots of mythology that evolved from classical Hinduism come from the times of the Vedic civilization, from the ancient Vedic religion.

The characters, theology, philosophy and stories that make up ancient Vedic myths are indelibly linked with Hindu beliefs. The Vedas are said to be four in number, namely RigVeda, YajurVeda, SamaVeda, and the AtharvaVeda. Some of these texts mention mythological concepts and machines very much similar to modern day scientific theories and machines.

Epics

The two great Hindu Epics, the *Ramayana* and the *Mahabharata* tell the story of two specific incarnations of Vishnu (Rama and Krishna). These two works are known as *Itihasa*. The epics *Mahabharata* and *Ramayana* serve as both religious scriptures and a rich source of philosophy and morality for a Hindu. The epics are divided into chapters and contain various short stories and moral situations, where the character takes a certain course of action in accordance with Hindu laws and codes of righteousness. The most famous of these chapters is the Bhagavad Gita (Sanskrit: *The Lord's Song*) in the Mahabharata, in which Lord Krishna explains the concepts of duty and righteousness to the hero Arjuna before the climactic battle. These stories are deeply embedded in Hindu philosophy and serve as parables and sources of devotion for Hindus. The Mahabharata is the world's longest epic in verse, running to more than 30,000 lines.

Cosmogony

Hinduism presents a number of accounts pertaining to cosmology, and several explanations have been given as regards the origin of the universe. The most popular belief is that the universe emerged from Hiranyagarbha, meaning the *golden womb*. Hiranyagarbha floated around in water in the emptiness and the darkness of non-existence. Ultimately, this golden egg split and the cosmos was created. Swarga emerged from the golden upper part of the Hiranyagarbha, whereas Prithvi came out from the silver coloured lower half part.

The Wars

The Weapons

Apart from the traditional *human* weapons like swords, daggers, spears, clubs, shields, bows, arrows and maces, and the weapons used by the Gods (such as Indra's thunderbolt *Vajrayudha*), the texts mention the utilization of various divine weapons by various heroes, each associated with a certain God or deity. These weapons are most often gifted to semi-divine beings, human beings or the rakshasas by the Gods, sometimes as a result of penance.

There are several weapons which were believed to be used by the Gods of the Hindu mythology, some of which are Agneyastra, Brahmastra, Chakram, Garudastra, Kaumodaki, Narayanastra, Pashupata, Shiva Dhanush, Sudarshana Chakra, Trishul, Vaishnavastra, Varunastra, and Vayavastra.

Some of these weapons are explicitly classified (for example, the Shiva Dhanush is a bow, the Sudharshan Chakra is a discus. and the Trishul is a trident), but many other weapons appear to be weapons specially blessed by the Gods. For example, the Brahmastra, Agneyastra (Sanskrit: Astra = *divine weapon*, especially, one thrown at an opponent) and the other astras appear to be single use weapons requiring an intricate knowledge of use, often depicted in art, literature and adapted filmography as divinely blessed arrows.

Sometimes the astra is descriptive of the function, or of the force of nature which it invokes. The Mahabharata cites instances when the Nagastra (Sanskrit: *Nag*=snake) was used, and thousands of snakes came pouring down from the skies on unsuspecting enemies. Similarly, the Agneyastra (Agni) is used for setting the enemy ablaze, as the Varunastra (Varuna) is used for extinguishing flames, or for invoking floods. Some weapons like the Brahmastra can only be used (lethally) against a single individual.

Apart from the astras, other instances of divine or mythological weaponry include armor (Kavacha), crowns and helmets, staffs and jewellery (Kundala).

The Deluge

The story of a great flood is mentioned in ancient Hindu texts, particularly the Satapatha Brahmana. It is compared to the accounts of the Deluge found in several religions and cultures. Manu was informed of the impending flood and was protected by the Matsya Avatara of Lord Vishnu, who had manifested himself in this form to rid the world of morally depraved human beings and protect the pious, as also all animals and plants.

After the flood the Lord inspires the Manusmriti, largely based upon the Vedas, which details the moral code of conduct, of living and the division of society according to the caste system.

The Peoples of the Epics

Hindu mythology is not only about Gods and men, but classifies a host of different kinds of celestial, ethereal and earthly beings.

Sapta Rishis

Lord Brahma, out of his thought, creates seven sages, or *Sapta Rishis,* to help him in his act of creation. *Sapta Rishis* (*sapta* means seven and *rishis* mean sages in Sanskrit). They are *Bhrigu, Angira, Atri, Gautama, Kashyapa, Vashishta,* and *Agastya.* The other meaning of Saptarishis is constellation of Great Bear (Ursa Major).

Pitrs

The Pitrs, or fathers, were the first humans. Pitrs comes from the word Pita(In Hindi and Sanskrit) or Father. So it is about paternity and paternal relations.

Worlds

Hindu mythology defines fourteen worlds (not to be confused with planets) - seven higher worlds (heavens) and seven lower ones (hells). (The earth is considered the lowest of the seven higher worlds.) The higher worlds are the seven *vyahrtis*, viz. *bhu, bhuvas, svar, mahas, janas, tapas*, and *satya* (the world that is ruled by Brahma); and the lower ones (the "seven hells" or *paatalas*) are *atala, vitala, sutala, rasaataala, talatala, mahaatala, paatala*.

All the worlds except the earth are used as temporary places of stay as follows: upon one's death on earth, the god of death (officially called 'Yama Dharma Raajaa' - Yama, the lord of justice) tallies the person's good/bad deeds while on earth and decides if the soul goes to a heaven and/or a hell, for how long, and in what capacity. Some versions of the mythology state that good and bad deeds neutralize each other and the soul therefore is born in either a heaven or a hell, but not both, whereas according to another school of thought, the good and bad deeds don't cancel out each other. In either case, the soul acquires a body as appropriate to the worlds it enters. At the end of the soul's time in those worlds, it returns to the earth (is reborn as a life form on the earth). It is considered that only from the earth, and only after a human life, can the soul reach supreme salvation, the state free from the cycle of birth and death and the place beyond the fourteen worlds where the eternal god lives.

Deities

There are many deities in Hinduism. At the top are the trimurti: Shiva (the destroyer), Vishnu (the protector), and Brahma (the creator), and their wives (goddesses in their own right): Shakti the goddess of courage and power, Lakshmi the goddess of all forms of wealth, and Saraswati the goddess of learning. The children of the Trimurti are also devas, such as Ganesha and Skanda or Kartika.

Brahma is considered the ruler of the highest of the heavens (the world called *Sathya*), so in one sense, Brahma is not beyond the fourteen worlds as Shiva and Vishnu are.

Some gods are associated with specific elements or functions: Indra (the god of thunder and lightning; he also rules the world of Swarga), Varuna (the god of the oceans), Agni (the god of fire), Kubera (the treasurer of the gods), Surya (the sun god), Vayu (the god of wind), and Soma (the moon god).

Swarga also has a set of famous heavenly dancers: Urvasi, Menaka, Rambha, and Tilottama (all female), whose job is to entertain the heavenly court, and upon orders from the heavenly kings, to distract people on the earth from accumulating too much good deeds so as to become a threat to the heavenly kings.

Other notable inhabitants of the heavens include the celestial sages, and Narada the messenger of the gods.

Yama (the god of death and justice) is said to live in Kailash along with his master Shiva. He rules the lower world of Naraka with a band of emissaries called the *Yama doota* (messengers of Yama), who bring the souls of dead persons to Yama for evaluation. Chitragupta is one of those lower level celestial beings who functions as the karmic accountant of all the actions of the human beings on earth.

Incarnations

Several gods are believed to have had incarnations (avatars). As the protector of life, one of the duties of Vishnu is to appear on the earth whenever a firm hand is required to set things right. The epic Bhagavatham is the chronology of Vishnu's ten major incarnations (there are in total twenty six incarnations): Matsya (fish), Kurma (turtle), Varaha (boar), Narasimha (lion-faced human), Vamana (an ascetic in the form of a midget), Parasurama (a militant Brahmin), Rama,

Krishna,Gautam Buddha(later buddhists separated themselves from Hindus), Kalki (a predicted warrior on a white horse who would come in this yuga) whose appearance also signals the beginning of the end of the epoch.

Bharatavarsha

The first king to conquer all of the world was Bharata, son of Dushyanta and Shakuntala. All of this world, Vishwa, is named Bharatavarsha, or *The Land of Bharata*, or *The Cherished Land*.

King Bharata's conquests are described to have stretched over all of modern India, and Pakistan, Bangladesh and Nepal, as well as the ancient Gandhara region of Afghanistan. No account has been known to exceed these geographical boundaries.

CRITICISM OF HINDUISM

Some aspects of Hinduism have been criticised, from both within the Hindu community and externally. Early Hindu reformers, such as Raja Ram Mohan Roy, questioned practices such as Sati and discrimination based on the caste system.

Varna System

The Hindu system of varnas identified four varnas in Indian society. The term *varna* is sometimes used synonymously with "caste" or "class" The Sanskrit term for caste, in the sense of social categories, is *jâti*. In historical Indic traditions the varna and caste systems are not the same system, although they are related. The classical authors scarcely speak of anything other than the varnas. Indologists sometimes confuse the two. Type(*varna*) obligations were a major concern of the Dharma Sutras and Dharma Shastras, where fulfillment of one's obligation (*dharma*) with regard to class (*varna*) and stage of life (*ashrama*) was a sign of brahmanical orthopraxy.

The four varnas are in descending hierarchical sequence: Brahmin, Kshatriya, Vaishya, and Shudra or the priests, warriors, business people and laborers. There was no varna like untouchable in Hinduism. The untouchables are considered a lower section of Shudra (Dalit) and was prevalent during the general deterioration of Indian society in middle age. The Varnabahya (outcast) is the one who never lived in cities and thus never became part of the Varna system. Many tribals (Adivasis) were Varnabahya. Varnabahya is not to be confused with untouchable. The varna system resulted in a great deal of social oppression and mistreatment of the lowest ranked castes, the Shudras (Dalits). As a result, Hinduism and the implementation of the caste system are often criticized for allowing oppression of people of lower castes, even though the original design of the caste system was not intended to harm or oppress.

Hindu religious literature, such as the Rig Veda, suggests that the original varna system was based on a flexible system, where people joined a varna and a related occupation based on their skills, qualities, and nature. However, over time, the varna system transformed into a rigid caste system, preventing the 'lower' classes (also called 'backward-caste') from rising. This caste system has gone beyond Hindus and includes Dalit or lower caste people in other religions like Islam, Christianity, Sikhism, etc in India, Pakistan and other countries in the Indian subcontinent. Discrimination against classes began as a result of this rigid fixing of the caste system. Also, religious literature suggests that the inclusion of Dalits ('untouchables') outside of the caste system was a later addition, not part of the original system.

Untouchables used to live separately within a separate subcultural context of their own, outside the inhabited limits of villages and townships. No other castes would interfere with their social life since untouchables were lower in social ranking than even those of the shudra varna. As a result,

Dalits were commonly banned from fully participating in Hindu religious life (they could not pray with the rest of the social classes or enter the religious establishments).

The inclusion of lower castes into the mainstream was argued for by Mahatma Gandhi who called them "Harijans" (people of God). The term Dalit is used now as the term Harijan is largely felt patronizing. As per Gandhi's wishes, reservation system with percentage quotas for admissions in universities and jobs has been in place for many lower castes since independence of India to bring them to the upper echelons of society. Dalit movements have been created to represent the views of Dalits and combat this traditional oppression. Caste-based discrimination is not unique to Hindus in India; converts to other religions and their descendants frequently preserve such social stratification.

Caste System

Although the Hindu scriptures and the buddhist scriptures contain some passages that can be interpreted to sanction the caste system, they also contain indications that the caste system is not an essential part of the Hindu religion and not by birth, and both sides in the debate are able to find sections in scriptures that support their views.

It is a fact that more than 70 per cent of the ancient Hindu Rishis, or enlightened masters of India, belonged to the lower castes. Valmiki and Vyasa, who wrote the epics Ramayana and Mahabharatha respectively, belonged to the lower castes.

In ancient times , one's caste was determined by one's temperament, talents and inclinations. Caste was not a barrier to the lower caste people, who rose to the level of the upper castes through their talents. This was the reason why Kshatriyas like the Buddha and Vishwamitra , became Brahmins or men of spiritual nature and why a Brahmin like Parashurama became a Kshatriya.

This is also the reason why shudras or low caste people like Valmiki , Vyasa, Vasishtha, Narada, Drona, Karna ,Thiruvalluvar were raised to the position of a Brahmin or Kshatriya , in virtue or their superior learning or valour. They would sometimes get hordes of Baluchis and at once make them Kshatriyas, and also get hordes of fishermen and make them Brahmins forthwith.

It was with the advent of the foreign invasions in India, that the caste system became rigid, and migration of people to different castes were stopped. Even then, enlightened masters from the lower castes such as Kabir, Ravi Das, Sri Narayana guru were revered by the upper castes as well.

The most ancient scriptures—the *Shruti* texts, or Vedas, place very little importance on the caste system, mentioning caste only rarely and in a cursory manner. A hymn from the Rig Veda seems to indicate that one's caste is not necessarily determined by that of one's family: "I am a bard, my father is a physician, my mother's job is to grind the corn." (Rig Veda 9.112.3).

In the Vedic period, there also seems to no discrimination against the Shudras (which later became an ensemble of the so-called low-castes) on the issue of hearing the sacred words of the Vedas and fully participating in all religious rights, something which became totally banned in the later times.

Later scriptures such as *Bhagavad Gita* and *Manusmriti* state that the four varnas are created by God. However, at the same time, the Gita says that one's varna is to be understood from one's personal qualities and one's *karma* (work), not one's birth. Some scholars believe that, in its initial period, the caste system was flexible and it was merit and job based. One could migrate from one caste to other caste by changing one's profession. This view is supported by records of sages who became Brahmins. For example, the sage Vishwamitra belonged to a Kshatriya caste, and only later became recognized as a great Brahmin sage, indicating that his caste was not determined by birth. Similarly, Valmiki, once a low-caste robber, became a great sage. Veda Vyasa, another sage, was the son of a fisherwoman. Vasishtha was a shudra and he became a sage later.

The varna system is a part of the organization of Hindu society as prescribed (not required) by the Hindu scriptures. Every society even today has intellectuals, scholars, priests (i.e. Brahmins), soldiers (i.e. Kshatriyas), businessmen (i.e. Vaishyas) and laborers (i.e. Shudras). The supposed purpose of the varna system was to ensure an efficient organization of society. It was misinterpreted by people, and that is why it is often criticized, because some people fail to interpret it correctly. The varna system was never rigid and there are significant historic instances of people moving from one varna to another. Some of the notable examples are Sage Valmiki; the author of the great epic Ramayana who was initially a wood-cutter and a robber, Sage Vyasa; the author of the epic Mahabharata, who was the son of a fisherwoman (who herself went on to marry a king later on), Sage Parashurama, a Brahmin who went on to become one of the greatest warriors etc. The greatest example is perhaps Lord Krishna, who was bought up as a cow-herd. He is depicted in many paintings as a young cow-herd playing a flute.

The Bhagavad Gita which is one of the many holy books of Hindus mentions that every living being has a soul which is a part of God and has several references against discrimination between not just humans but even animals. Chapter 5, verse 18 of Bhagawat Gita sums this up by saying that "The enlightened and wise regards with equal mind a Brahmin endowed with learning and humility, a cow, an elephant, and even a dog and an outcaste." The system of four classes incorporated in Righteousness (Dharma) is meant to provide guidance with regard to behaviour and spiritual practice to be undertaken in accordance with qualifications, that is potential and requirement, so as to acquire Bliss.

When India gained independence due to the efforts of Hindus like Gandhi, perfect equality was thrust upon the masses of India, no matter to what caste one belonged to, thus reestablishing and continuing the ancient tradition of India.

Untouchability was outlawed after India gained independence in 1947. It will take some time for the deadweight of tradition of the rigid caste system to be removed from India. But as enlightened Hinduism and Buddhism, as preached by Gandhi, Swami Vivekananda, Ramakrishna Paramahamsa, Sri Sri Ravi Shankar and others are reaching the masses, slowly these shackles are being dissolved.

Paramahansa Yogananda also opposed what he called to the un-Vedic caste system as we know it today. He taught that the caste system originated in a higher age, but became degraded through ignorance and self-interest. Yogananda said:

> "These were (originally) symbolic designations of the stages of spiritual refinement. They were not intended as social categories. And they were not intended to be hereditary. Things changed as the yugas [cycles of time] descended toward mental darkness. People in the higher castes wanted to make sure their children were accepted as members of their own caste. Thus, ego-identification caused them to freeze the ancient classifications into what is called the 'caste system.' Such was not the original intention. In obvious fact, however, the offspring of a brahmin may be a sudra by nature. And a peasant, sometimes, is a real saint."
>
> —from Conversations with Yogananda, Crystal Clarity Publishers, 2003.

There is a misconception in some minds that Hindu scriptures sanction the caste system.

In the Manu Smriti, when it comes to stance of hereditary caste system, the verse below is believed to sanction support for vocational non-hereditary caste system. As the son of Shudra can attain the rank of a brahmana, the son of brahmana can attain rank of a shudra. Even so with him who is born of a vaishya or a kshatriya. (Manu Smriti X: 65)

Vedas, the proud possession of mankind, are the foundation of Hinduism. Vedas are all-embracing, and treat the entire humanity with the same respect and dignity. Vedas speak of nobility of entire humanity (krinvanto vishvam aryam), and do not sanction any caste system or birth-based caste system. Mantra, numbered 10-13-1 in Rig Veda, addresses the entire humanity as divine children. Shrunvantu vishve amrutsya putraha.

Innumerable mantras in Vedas emphasise oneness, universal brotherhood, harmony, happiness, affection, unity and commonality of entire humanity. Vide Mantra numbered 5-60-5 in Rig Veda, the divine poet declares, "All humans are brothers; no one is big, no one is small. All are equal." Mantra numbered 16.15 in Yajur Veda reiterates that all humans are brothers; no one is superior or inferior. Mantra numbered 10-191-2 in Rig Veda calls upon humanity to be united to have a common speech and a common mind. Mantra numbered 3-30-1 in Atharva Veda enjoins upon all humans to be affectionate and to love one another as the cow loves her newly-born calf. Underlining unity and harmony still further, Mantra numbered 3-30-6 in Atharva Veda commands humankind to dine together, and be as firmly united as the spokes attached to the hub of a chariot wheel. Last mantra of Rig Veda further emphasises unity and harmony of entire humanity, "Samani Vha Aakuti, Samana Hrudyani Vha, Samanam Astu Vo Mano, Yatha Vha Su Saha Asti." ("Let your aims be one, let your hearts be one, let your minds be one, and let your unity go from strength to strength").

Bhagvad Gita, the essence of Vedas and Upanishads, has many Shlokas that echo the Vedic doctrine of one-ness of humanity. In Sholka number V (29), the Lord declares that He is the friend of all creatures ('Suhridam Sarva Bhutanam') whereas Sholka number IX (29) reiterates that the Lord has the same affection for all creatures, and whosoever remembers the Lord, resides in the Lord, and the Lord resides in him. Sholka number XVIII (61) declares that God resides in every heart (Ishwar sarva bhutanam hrudyeshe Arjun tishthti).

As per Sholka number IV (13) of Bhagvad Gita, depending upon a person's Guna (aptitude) and Karma (actions), there are four Varnas. As per this Sholka, a person's Varna is determined by his Guna and Karma, and not by his birth. Chapter XIV of Bhagvad Gita specifies three Gunas viz. Satva (purity), Rajas (passion and attachment) and Tamas (ignorance). These three Gunas are present in every human in different proportions, and determine the Varna of every person. Accordingly, depending on one's Guna and Karma, every individual is free to select his own Varna. Consequently, if their Gunas and Karmas are different, even members of the same family will belong to different Varnas. Nevertheless, notwithstanding the differences in Guna and Karma of different individuals, Vedas treat the entire humanity with the same respect; and do not sanction any caste system or birth based caste system.

STATUS OF WOMEN

The role of women in Hinduism is often disputed, and positions range from quite fair to intolerant. Hinduism is based on numerous texts, some of which date back to 2000 BCE or earlier. They are varied in authority, authenticity, content and theme, with the most authoritative being the Vedas. The position of women in Hinduism is widely dependent on the specific text and the context. Positive references are made to the ideal woman in texts such as the Ramayana and the Mahabharata. Women in vedic period were accorded very high status. The proof can be inferred from reference to thirty women seers contributing to Vedas.

Certain Hindu communities practice Matrilineality in which descent is traced through the female. The Nairs and some communities of Nambudiri Brahmins from Kerala as well as Bunts from Tulu Nadu, are matrilineal. In such communities, the woman is the family matriarch and has the right to inherit property, and having a female child is considered favorable for a family. The clan system is one in which a woman lives with her brothers and sister, as well as her mother and cousins.

Several women sages and seers are mentioned in the Upanishads, the philosophical part of the Vedas, notable among them being Gargi and Maitreyi. The Sanskrit word for female teachers as Acharyâ (as opposed to Acharya for teacher and Acharyini for teacher's wife) reveal that women were also given a place as Gurus.

The Harita Dharmasutra (of the Maitrayaniya school of Yayurveda) declares that there are two kind of women: Sadhyavadhu who marry, and the Brahmavaadini who are inclined to religion, they can wear the sacred thread, perform rituals like the agnihotra and read the Vedas. Bhavabhuti's Uttararamacharita 2.3 says that Atreyi went to Southern India where she studied the Vedas and Indian philosophy. Shankara debated with the female philosopher Ubhaya Bharati, and Madhava's Shankaradigvijaya (9.63) mentions that she was well versed in the Vedas. Tirukkoneri Dasyai (15th century) wrote a commentary on Nammalvar's Tiruvaayamoli, with reference to Vedic texts like the Taittiriya Yajurveda.

In the marriage hymn (RV 10.85.26), the wife "should address the assembly as a commander." A Rig Veda hymn says "I am the banner and the head, a mighty arbitress am I: I am victorious, and my Lord shall be submissive to my will.

(Rig Veda, Book 10. HYMN CLIX. Saci Paulomi). These are probably the earliest references to the position of women in Hindu society.

In modern times the Hindu wife has traditionally been regarded as someone who must at all costs remain chaste or pure. This is in contrast with the very different traditions that have prevailed at earlier times in 'Hindu' kingdoms, which included highly respected professional courtesans (such as Amrapali of Vesali) sacred devadasis, mathematicians and female magicians (the *basavis,* the Tantric *kulikas*). Some European scholars observed in the nineteenth century Hindu women were "naturally chaste" and "more virtuous" than other women, although what exactly they meant by that is open to dispute. In any case, as male foreigners they would have been denied access to the secret and sacred spaces that women often inhabited.

Sati

Condemned practices like Sati (widow self-immolation or "bride burning") and widow remarriage were social practices that arose in India's Middle Ages, mostly in the northern regions of India, and had nothing to do with Hindu laws and scriptures. It was a 'practice' not a law in scripture. In the later medieval ages, this practice came to be forced on the widows. However this practice was abolished from the society in the 20th century

During the Islamic onslaught into the North-Western Indian Kingdoms, the Muslims had many concubines, who were the wives of the fallen warriors. It was to avoid the shame in being subjugated to being a whore in a Muslim Harem that many women decided to die faithful wives. This was more of an act of suicide. As it has no validity in religious scriptures, it was only practiced in places where there was a dire need for the action. Rajasthan was one of the places where it was more common as due to its geographic position

Rajasthan was one of the first regions to fight Muslim invaders coming to India. Practice of Jauhar in Rajasthan was also similar and had no basis in religious scriptures.

Sati was not prevalent in ancient history. In the epic Ramayana, King Dasharatha (Rama's father) left behind three widows who never committed Sati. In the same epic the wives of Vali Ravana and of other fallen warriors did not commit Sati after the deaths of their husbands. In the Mahabharata, Kunti, the mother of Pandavas (Yudhishtira, Arjuna, Bhima) and first wife of Pandu, was a widow who never committed Sati. However, Madri, second wife of Pandu and the mother of the younger pandavas (Nakula and Sahadeva) committed sati out of free-will and left her two sons in the care of Kunti. She was thinking herself responsible for her husband's death. Her husband, Pandu, had been cursed to die the day he lusts for his wife. Earlier in his life, while on a hunting expedition, he shot an arrow into a rustling bush. It turned out that he shot a pair of deer that were mating. The surviving deer morphed back into human form and revealed itself as a sage. The sage, deeply saddened by his loss and the brazen act of the king, curses him so. In the rest of the Mahabharata, there are no references to Kaurava wives committing Sati after their husbands died in Mahabharata war.

Passages in the Atharva Veda, including 13.3.1, offer advice to the widow on mourning and her life after widowhood, including her remarriage.

In the Ramayana, Tara, in her grief at the death of husband Vali, wished to commit *sati*. Hanuman, Rama, and the dying Vali dissuade her and she finally does not immolate herself.

There is no record of Sati being practiced in the south Indian Hindu communities. Adi Shankaracharya's mother did not commit sati when her husband died. The forceful practice of sati may have risen around the time of the Gupta Empire, 400 AD.

ATHEISM IN HINDUISM

Atheism ("statement of no Lord", "doctrine of godlessness") or disbelief in God or gods has been a historically propounded viewpoint in many of the 'heterodox' and astika streams of Hindu philosophies.

Astika Atheism

The Sanskrit term *Âstika* ("pious, orthodox") is sometimes translated as "theist" and *Nâstika* as "atheist". Sanskrit *asti* means "there is", and *Âstika* per Panini 4.2.60 is derived from the verb, meaning "one who says *'asti'*, one who believes in the existence [of God, of another world, &c.]" When used as a technical term in Hindu philosophy the term Âstika refers to belief in the Vedas, not belief in the existence of God.

There are six schools of thought within Hinduism addressed as the *Shat (Astik) Darshana* (*darshana* meaning "viewpoint.") Within the Astika schools of Hindu philosophy, the Samkhya and the early Mimamsa school did not accept a God in their respective systems.

The atheistic viewpoint as present in the Samkhya and Mimamsa schools of Hindu philosophy takes the form of rejecting a creator-God. The Samkhya school believed in a dual existence of Prakriti ("nature") and Purusha ("spirit") and had no place for an Ishvara ("God") in its system. The early Mimamsakas believed in a *adrishta* ("unseen") that was the result of performing *karmas* ("works") and saw no need for an Ishvara in their system. Mimamsa, as a philosophy, deals exclusively with karma and thus is sometimes called *Karma-Mimamsa*. The karmas dealt with in Mimamsa concern the performance of Yajnas ("sacrifices to gods") enjoined in the Vedas.

Nastika Atheism

In Hindu philosophy, three schools of thought are commonly referred to as *nastika*: Jainism, Buddhism and

Cârvâka for rejecting the doctrine of Vedas. In this usage, *nastika* refers to the non-belief of Vedas rather than non-belief of God. However, all these schools also rejected a notion of a creationist god and so the word *nastika* became strongly associated with them.

Cârvâka, an atheistic school of Indian philosophy, traces its origins to 600 BCE, while some claim earlier references to such positions. It was a hedonistic school of thought, advocating that there is no afterlife. Cârvâka philosophy appears to have died out some time after 1400 CE. Dharmakirti, a 7th century philosopher deeply influenced by cârvâka philosophy, wrote in Pramanvartik:

> Believing that the Veda are standard (holy or divine), believing in a Creator for the world,
>
> Bathing in holy waters for gaining punya, having pride (vanity) about one's caste,
>
> Performing penance to absolve sins,
>
> Are the five symptoms of having lost ones sanity.

Buddhism and Jainism have their origins in pre-historic sramana tradition and are not hedonistic. Also worth mentioning are the Âjîvikas (now an extinct religion), whose founder, Makkhali Gosala, was a contemporary of Mahavira and Gautama Buddha (the central figures of Jainism and Buddhism, respectively). Gosala and his followers also denied the existence of a creator god.

Hindu Atheists in Recent Times

The Indian Nobel Prize-winner Amartya Sen, in an interview with Pranab Bardhan for the *California Magazine* published in the July-August 2006 edition by the University of California, Berkeley states:

> In some ways people had got used to the idea that India was spiritual and religion-oriented. That gave a leg up

to the religious interpretation of India, despite the fact that Sanskrit had a larger atheistic literature than what exists in any other classical language. Even within the Hindu tradition, there are many people who were atheist. Madhava Acharya, the remarkable 14th century philosopher, wrote this rather great book called Sarvadarshansamgraha, which discussed all the religious schools of thought within the Hindu structure. The first chapter is "Atheism" - a very strong presentation of the argument in favor of atheism and materialism.

Prominent Atheists

- Amartya Sen, Economist and 1998 Nobel laureate.
- Veer Savarkar (Hindu Atheist), who was president of Hindu Mahasabha. He is credited for developing a Hindu nationalist political ideology he termed as Hindutva (Hinduness).
- Amol Palekar - a notable Hindi and Marathi Filmmaker, openly claims to be agnostic and atheist, even though brought up in a Hindu background.
- Vijay Tendulkar - a famous Marathi writer and dramatist who was also known to be an atheist.
- Shreela Flather, Baroness Flather of Windsor and Maidenhead, the first Hindu woman in British politics. She described herself as a "Hindu atheist". Broadly, she is an atheist with affinity to secular aspects of Hindu culture such as dress and diet.
- G. A. Kulkarni - a Sahitya Akademi Award winner Marathi writer has expressed his atheist views through his correspondence with other famous literary figures like Sunitabai Deshpande, Jaywant Dalvi, Shri.Na. Pendse, et al.

- Manabendra Nath Roy, Bengali Indian revolutionary, political theorist and activist, founder of the Communist parties in Mexico and India.
- Dr. Shriram Lagoo, notable Marathi actor and rationalist activist.
- A. N. Murthy Rao - Prominent Kannada writer who wrote acclaimed book *Devaru* (God) rejecting the concept of god.
- K. Shivaram Karanth - Jnanapita award winner. He reflects his beliefs in his novel *Mookajjiya Kanasugalu*.
- Prabir Ghosh - The General Secretaty of The Science and Rationalists' Association of India
- Narendra Nayak - Founder of Dakshina Kannada Rationalist Association.

HINDUISM AND OTHER RELIGIONS

In the field of comparative religion, some have sought to discover similarities between Hinduism and other religions.

Indian Religions

Hinduism has a history of co-existence with Buddhism and Jainism (the Shramana traditions), and more recently, with Sikhism, within the Indian subcontinent. Consequently, these religious traditions share a number terms and concepts such as *dharma, karma* or *yoga*. Many Hindus believe that these other three Indian religions are the extension of Hinduism. Like RSS consider Sikhs as "keshdhari Hindus"(Hindus who keeps long hair). However these three religion consider themselves as separate religions. Sikhs in India come under personal laws of Hindus and for long time they have been demanding a separate Personal Law for themselves.

Hinduism and Christianity

Leaving the Goa Inquisition there is no history of forced conversion of Hindus to Christianity. The declaration Nostra Aetate officially established inter-religious dialogue between Catholics and Hindus. It has promoted common values between religions. There are over 17.3 million Catholics in India, which represents less than 2% of the total population and is the largest Christian Church within India.There had been good relation between Hindus and Christian since Independence.The main debate and violence today mainly concentrate on conversion issue of Hindus to Christianity. The Hindu parties accuse missionaries of giving money to poor Hindus in lieu of converting to Christianity. Where Christian missionaries says that low caste Hindus convert to Christianity because of Caste based discrimination.However, the Holy See has expressed concern with regards to religious violence in the state of Orissa, which is closely related to the ideology of Hindutva.

Hinduism and Judaism

Hindus have never practiced the system of Anti-Semitism in their whole history and few Jews who came to India had a history of comfortable life unlike their European counterparts. Relations with Judaism are partly based on a common opposition to some branches of islamism. Some have found links between Kabbalah and Eastern religions. On January 29, 1992, full diplomatic ties between the two were established and since then the bilateral relations have grown exceedingly. (see India–Israel relations). The common ideology of anti-Islamism has brought the two religions closer. Hindutva leader, Veer Savarkar had openly supported the formation of the state of Israel. The strategic ties between the India and Israel have improved and are at its peak.

Hinduism and Islam

Hinduism and Islam, from the arrival of the Arabs as far back as the 8th century AD, has had a checkered history. In Islam, Hinduism found a very different concept of god and civic society than it had encountered earlier. This coincided with the peak of Hindu vedanta revival and its idelogical reintegration of Buddhism and Jainism. During the Muslim conquests Islam gained many converts on the Indian sub-continent primarily from Hinduism or Buddhism; the two dominant local religions. The prime drivers for conversion are contested issues. Inter-marriage and immigration from other Islamic landshas have helped in instilling this idea in the people of greater India. Many of the new Muslim rulers looked down upon the idea Hinduism as having Iconodulistic religious practices and were to various degrees iconoclastic. Prominent examples of these are Mahmud of Ghazni and the Mughal emperor Aurangzeb on either end of the timeline for Islamic rulers. In addition, Muslims in India also developed a caste system that divided the Arab-descended "Ashraf" Muslims and the "Ajlaf" converts, with the "Arzal" untouchables at the lowest rung The term "Arzal" stands for "degraded" and the Arzal castes are further subdivided into Bhanar, Halalkhor, Hijra, Kasbi, Lalbegi, Maugta, Mehtar etc.

In contrast there were also many Muslim kings who wished to live in harmony with the Hindus. Akbar and Ibrahim Adil Shah II of Bijapur Adil Shah dynasty are notable examples. Akbar's court was home to intellectuals and saints both Hindu and Muslim, among them the great musician Tansen, and he even went so far as to try and create a new religion (the *din ilahi*) to create a rapprochement of both creeds.

The arrival of Sufi movement conversing with other mystic traditions of Vedanta and Yoga led to the rise of the syncretic Bhakti movement. Sheikh Muhammad was a Sufi saint who embraced the Hindu God Rama as his chosen bhakti ideal. Kabir wrote poetry and preached to the people, advocating a blend of philosophy and spiritual practices challenging the religious clergy of both Islam and Hinduism and claiming to be neither Hindu, nor Muslim.

The synergy between certain Sufis and Bhaktas in many regions of India led to Muslim and Hindu laity worshiping together at a *mazar* (Sufi shrine) attended by a Vaishnav priest. However, Muslim and Hindu conflict still exists in India feuled by a history of regional politics, nationalism, continued conflict and the history of the partition movements during independence from the British Raj.

Mughal art forms, especially miniatures and even certain niches of Urdu poetry, were quick to absorb classic Hindu motifs, like the love story of Krishna and Radha. Hindustani classical music is a complex and sonorous blend of Vedic notions of sound, raga and tala and absorbed a many instruments of either Middle Eastern origin or Indian-Muslim invention.

Today while Hinduism and Islam, have irreconcilable ideological differences and tensions, they share a common historical and social experience over a thousand years to result in a common social outlook.

●●

4
Hinduism in India

Hinduism is the predominant religion of the Indian subcontinent. Hinduism is often referred to as Sanâtana Dharma, a Sanskrit phrase meaning "the eternal law", by its adherents. Generic "types" of Hinduism that attempt to accommodate a variety of complex views span folk and Vedic Hinduism to bhakti tradition, as in Vaishnavism. Hinduism also includes yogic traditions and a wide spectrum of "daily morality" based on the notion of karma and societal norms such as Hindu marriage customs.

Among its roots is the historical Vedic religion of Iron Age India, and as such Hinduism is often stated to be the "oldest living religion" or the "oldest living major tradition". Hinduism is formed of diverse traditions and has no single founder. Hinduism is the world's third largest religion after Christianity and Islam, with approximately a billion adherents, of whom approximately 905 million live in India. Other countries with large Hindu populations can be found across southern Asia.

Hinduism's vast body of scriptures are divided into Sruti ("revealed") and Smriti ("remembered") texts. These scriptures discuss theology, philosophy and mythology, and provide information on the practice of dharma (religious living). Among these texts, the *Vedas* and the *Upanishads* are the foremost in authority, importance and antiquity. Other major scriptures include the *PurâGas* and the epics *Mahâbhârata* and *Râmâyana*. The *Bhagavad Gîtâ,* a treatise from the

Mahâbhârata, spoken by Krishna, is sometimes called a summary of the spiritual teachings of the *Vedas.*

Etymology

Hindû is the Persian name for the Indus River, first encountered in the Old Persian word *Hindu* (hindu), corresponding to Vedic Sanskrit *Sindhu,* the Indus River. The Rig Veda mentions the land of the Indo-Aryans as *Sapta Sindhu* (the land of the seven rivers in northwestern South Asia, one of them being the Indus). This corresponds to *Hapta HYndu* in the *Avesta* (*Vendidad or Videvdad* 1.18)—the sacred scripture of Zoroastrianism. The term was used for those who lived in the Indian subcontinent on or beyond the "Sindhu". In Arabic, the term *al-Hind* (the Hind) also refers to 'the land of the people of modern day India'.

The Persian term (Middle Persian *Hindûk,* New Persian *Hindû*) entered India with the Delhi Sultanate and appears in South Indian and Kashmiri texts from at least 1323 CE, and increasingly so during British rule. Since the end of the 18th century the word has been used as an umbrella term for most of the religious, spiritual, and philosophical traditions of the sub-continent, usually excluding the religions of Sikhism, Buddhism, and Jainism as distinct.

The term *Hinduism* was introduced by the English people to denote the religious, philosophical, and cultural traditions native to India.

Typology

Hinduism as we know it can be subdivided into a number of major currents. Of the historical division into six darshanas, only two schools, Vedanta and Yoga survive. The main divisions of Hinduism today are Vaishnavism, Shaivism, Smartism and Shaktism.

Contemporary Hinduism is predominantly monotheistic, but Hindu tradition includes aspects that can be interpreted as panentheistic, pantheistic, polytheistic and even atheistic. Other notable characteristics include a belief in reincarnation and karma, as well as in personal duty, or dharma.

McDaniel (2007) distinguishes six generic "types" of Hinduism, in an attempt to accommodate a variety of views on a rather complex subject:

- Folk Hinduism, as based on local traditions and cults of local deities at a communal level and spanning back to prehistoric times or at least prior to written Vedas.
- Vedic Hinduism as still being practiced by traditionalist brahmins (for example shrautins).
- Vedantic Hinduism, for example Advaita (Smartism), as based on the philosophical approach of the Upanishads.
- Yogic Hinduism, especially that based on the Yoga Sutras of Patanjali.
- "Dharmic" Hinduism or "daily morality", based on the notion of Karma, and upon societal norms such as Hindu marriage customs.
- Bhakti or devotionalism, especially as in Vaishnavism.

Hinduism does not have a "unified system of belief encoded in declaration of faith or a creed", but is rather an umbrella term comprising the plurality of religious phenomena originating and based on the Vedic traditions.

The term *Hindu* in origin is a Persian word in use from the time of the Delhi Sultanate, referring to any tradition that is native to India as opposed to Islam. *Hindu* is used in the sense of "Indian pagan" in English from the 17th century, but the notion of *Hinduism* as an identifiable religious tradition qualifying as one of the world religions emerged only during the 19th century.

The characteristic of comprehensive tolerance to differences in belief, and Hinduism's dogmatic openness, makes it difficult to define as a religion according to traditional Western conceptions. Although Hinduism is a clear practical concept to the majority of its adherents, many express a problem arriving at a definition of the term, mainly because of the wide range of traditions and ideas incorporated within it or covered by it. While sometimes referred to as a religion, Hinduism is more often defined as a religious tradition. It is therefore described as both the oldest of the world's religions, and the most diverse. Most Hindu traditions revere a body of religious or sacred literature, the Vedas, although there are exceptions. Some Hindu religious traditions regard particular rituals as essential for salvation, but a variety of views on this co-exist. Some Hindu philosophies postulate a theistic ontology of creation, of sustenance, and of destruction of the universe, yet some Hindus are atheists. Hinduism is sometimes characterized by the belief in reincarnation (*samsara*), determined by the law of karma, and the idea that salvation is freedom from this cycle of repeated birth and death. However, other religions of the region, such as Buddhism and Jainism, also believe in karma, outside the scope of Hinduism. Hinduism is therefore viewed as the most complex of all of the living, historical world religions. Despite its complexity, Hinduism is not only one of the numerically largest faiths, but is also the oldest living major tradition on earth, with roots reaching back into prehistory.

A definition of Hinduism, given by the first Vice President of India, who was also a prominent theologian, Sarvepalli Radhakrishnan, states that Hinduism is not "just a faith", but in itself is related to the union of reason and intuition. Radhakrishnan explicitly states that Hinduism cannot be defined, but is only to be experienced. Similarly some academics suggest that Hinduism can be seen as a category with "fuzzy edges", rather than as a well-defined and rigid entity. Some forms of religious expression are central to Hinduism, while others are not as central but still remain within the category. Based on this, Ferro-Luzzi has developed a 'Prototype Theory approach' to the definition of Hinduism.

Problems with the single definition of what is actually meant by the term 'Hinduism' are often attributed to the fact that Hinduism does not have a single or common historical founder. Hinduism, or as some say 'Hinduisms,' does not have a single system of salvation and has different goals according to each sect or denomination. The forms of Vedic religion are seen not as an alternative to Hinduism, but as its earliest form, and there is little justification for the divisions found in much western scholarly writing between Vedism, Brahmanism, and Hinduism.

A definition of Hinduism is further complicated by the frequent use of the term "faith" as a synonym for "religion". Some academics and many practitioners refer to Hinduism using a native definition, as *Sanâtana Dharma,* a Sanskrit phrase meaning "the eternal law", or the "eternal way".

Beliefs

Hinduism refers to a religious mainstream which evolved organically and spread over a large territory marked by significant ethnic and cultural diversity. This mainstream evolved both by innovation from within, and by assimilation of external traditions or cults into the Hindu fold. The result is an enormous variety of religious traditions, ranging from innumerable small, unsophisticated cults to major religious movements with millions of adherents spread over the entire subcontinent. The identification of Hinduism as an independent religion separate from Buddhism or Jainism consequently hinges on the affirmation of its adherents that it is such.

Prominent themes in Hindu beliefs include (but are not restricted to), *Dharma* (ethics/duties), *Samsâra* (The continuing cycle of birth, life, death and rebirth), *Karma* (action and subsequent reaction), *Moksha* (liberation from *samsara*), and the various Yogas (paths or practices).

Concept of God

Hinduism is a diverse system of thought with beliefs spanning monotheism, polytheism, panentheism, pantheism, monism, and atheism, and its concept of God is complex and depends upon each particular tradition and philosophy. It is sometimes referred to as henotheistic (i.e., involving devotion to a single god while accepting the existence of others), but any such term is an overgeneralization.

Most Hindus believe that the spirit or soul — the true "self" of every person, called the *âtman* — is eternal. According to the monistic/pantheistic theologies of Hinduism (such as Advaita Vedanta school), this *Atman* is ultimately indistinct from Brahman, the supreme spirit. Hence, these schools are called non-dualist. The goal of life, according to the Advaita school, is to realize that one's *âtman* is identical to Brahman, the supreme soul. The Upanishads state that whoever becomes fully aware of the *âtman* as the innermost core of one's own self realizes an identity with Brahman and thereby reaches *moksha* (liberation or freedom).

Dualistic schools understand Brahman as a Supreme Being who possesses personality, and they worship him or her thus, as Vishnu, Brahma, Shiva, or Shakti, depending upon the sect. The *âtman* is dependent on God, while *moksha* depends on love towards God and on God's grace. When God is viewed as the supreme personal being (rather than as the infinite principle), God is called *Ishvara* ("The Lord"), *Bhagavan* ("The Auspicious One") or *Parameshwara* ("The Supreme Lord"). However interpretations of *Ishvara* vary, ranging from non-belief in *Ishvara* by followers of Mimamsakas, to identifying *Brahman* and *Ishvara* as one, as in Advaita. In the majority of traditions of Vaishnavism he is Vishnu, God, and the text of Vaishnava scriptures identify this Being as Krishna, sometimes referred to as *svayam bhagavan*. There are also schools like the Samkhya which have atheistic leanings.

Devas and Avatars

The Hindu scriptures refer to celestial entities called *Devas* (or *devî* in feminine form; *devatâ* used synonymously for Deva in Hindi), "the shining ones", which may be translated into English as "gods" or "heavenly beings". The *devas* are an integral part of Hindu culture and are depicted in art, architecture and through icons, and mythological stories about them are related in the scriptures, particularly in Indian epic poetry and the Puranas. They are, however, often distinguished from Ishvara, a supreme personal god, with many Hindus worshiping Ishvara in a particular form as their *icma devatâ,* or chosen ideal. The choice is a matter of individual preference, and of regional and family traditions.

Hindu epics and the Puranas relate several episodes of the descent of God to Earth in corporeal form to restore *dharma* to society and to guide humans to *moksha.* Such an incarnation is called an *avatar.* The most prominent avatars are of Vishnu and include Rama (the protagonist in Ramayana) and Krishna (a central figure in the epic Mahabharata).

Karma and Samsara

Karma translates literally as action, work, or deed, and can be described as the "moral law of cause and effect". According to the Upanishads an individual, known as the *jiva-atma,* develops *sanskaras* (impressions) from actions, whether physical or mental. The *linga sharira,* a body more subtle than the physical one but less subtle than the soul, retains impressions, carrying them over into the next life, establishing a unique trajectory for the individual. Thus, the concept of a universal, neutral, and never-failing karma intrinsically relates to reincarnation as well as to one's personality, characteristics, and family. Karma binds together the notions of free will and destiny.

This cycle of *action, reaction, birth, death and rebirth* is a continuum called *samsara*. The notion of reincarnation and karma is a strong premise in Hindu thought. The Bhagavad Gita states that:

As a person puts on new clothes and discards old and torn clothes,

similarly an embodied soul enters new material bodies, leaving the old bodies.(B.G. 2:22)

Samsara provides ephemeral pleasures, which lead people to desire rebirth so as to enjoy the pleasures of a perishable body. However, escaping the world of *samsara* through *moksha* is believed to ensure lasting happiness and peace. It is thought that after several reincarnations, an *atman* eventually seeks unity with the cosmic spirit (Brahman/Paramatman).

The ultimate goal of life, referred to as *moksha, nirvana* or *samadhi,* is understood in several different ways: as the realization of one's union with God; as the realization of one's eternal relationship with God; realization of the unity of all existence; perfect unselfishness and knowledge of the Self; as the attainment of perfect mental peace; and as detachment from worldly desires. Such realization liberates one from *samsara* and ends the cycle of rebirth.

The exact conceptualization of *moksha* differs among the various Hindu schools of thought. For example, Advaita Vedanta holds that after attaining *moksha* an *atman* no longer identifies itself with an individual but as identical with Brahman in all respects. The followers of Dvaita (dualistic) schools identify themselves as part of Brahman, and after attaining *moksha* expect to spend eternity in a *loka* (heaven), in the company of their chosen form of *Ishvara*. Thus, it is said that the followers of *dvaita* wish to "taste sugar", while the followers of Advaita wish to "become sugar".

Objectives of Human Life

Classical Hindu thought accepts the following objectives of human life, known as the *purucârthas*: *dharma* "righteousness, *ethikos*;" *artha* "livelihood, wealth;" *kâma* "sensual pleasure;" *mokca* "liberation, freedom (from *samsara*)".

Yoga

In whatever way a Hindu defines the goal of life, there are several methods (yogas) that sages have taught for reaching that goal. Texts dedicated to Yoga include the Bhagavad Gita, the Yoga Sutras, the Hatha Yoga Pradipika, and, as their philosophical and historical basis, the Upanishads. Paths that one can follow to achieve the spiritual goal of life (*moksha*, *samadhi* or *nirvana*) include:

- Bhakti Yoga (the path of love and devotion)
- Karma Yoga (the path of right action)
- Râja Yoga (the path of meditation)
- Jñâna Yoga (the path of wisdom)

An individual may prefer one or some yogas over others, according to his or her inclination and understanding. Some devotional schools teach that *bhakti* is the only practical path to achieve spiritual perfection for most people, based on their belief that the world is currently in the *Kali Yuga* (one of four epochs which are part of the Yuga cycle). Practice of one yoga does not exclude others. Many schools believe that the different yogas naturally blend into and aid other yogas. For example, the practice of *jnana yoga*, is thought to inevitably lead to pure love (the goal of *bhakti yoga*), and vice versa. Someone practicing deep meditation (such as in *raja yoga*) must embody the core principles of *karma yoga, jnana yoga* and *bhakti yoga,* whether directly or indirectly.

Practices

Hindu practices generally involve seeking awareness of God and sometimes also seeking blessings from Devas. Therefore, Hinduism has developed numerous practices meant to help one think of divinity in the midst of everyday life. Hindus can engage in pûjâ (worship or veneration), either at home or at a temple. At home, Hindus often create a shrine with icons dedicated to their chosen form(s) of God. Temples are usually dedicated to a primary deity along with associated subordinate deities though some commemorate multiple deities. Visiting temples is not obligatory, and many visit temples only during religious festivals. Hindus perform their worship through icons (murtis). The icon serves as a tangible link between the worshiper and God. The image is often considered a manifestation of God, since God is immanent. The Padma Purana states that the *mûrti* is not to be thought of as mere stone or wood but as a manifest form of the Divinity. A few Hindu sects, such as the Ârya Samâj, do not believe in worshiping God through icons.

Hinduism has a developed system of symbolism and iconography to represent the sacred in art, architecture, literature and worship. These symbols gain their meaning from the scriptures, mythology, or cultural traditions. The syllable *Om* (which represents the *Parabrahman*) and the Swastika sign (which symbolizes auspiciousness) have grown to represent Hinduism itself, while other markings such as *tilaka* identify a follower of the faith. Hinduism associates many symbols, which include the lotus, *chakra* and *veena*, with particular deities.

Mantras are invocations, praise and prayers that through their meaning, sound, and chanting style help a devotee focus the mind on holy thoughts or express devotion to God/the deities. Many devotees perform morning ablutions at the bank of a sacred river while chanting the *Gayatri Mantra* or

Mahamrityunjaya mantras. The epic Mahabharata extols *Japa* (ritualistic chanting) as the greatest duty in the Kali Yuga (what Hindus believe to be the current age). Many adopt *Japa* as their primary spiritual practice.

Rituals

The vast majority of Hindus engage in religious rituals on a daily basis. Most Hindus observe religious rituals at home. but observation of rituals greatly vary among regions, villages, and individuals. Devout Hindus perform daily chores such as worshiping at the dawn after bathing (usually at a family shrine, and typically includes lighting a lamp and offering foodstuffs before the images of deities), recitation from religious scripts, singing devotional hymns, meditation, chanting mantras, reciting scriptures etc. A notable feature in religious ritual is the division between purity and pollution. Religious acts presuppose some degree of impurity or defilement for the practitioner, which must be overcome or neutralised before or during ritual procedures. Purification, usually with water, is thus a typical feature of most religious action. Other characteristics include a belief in the efficacy of sacrifice and concept of merit, gained through the performance of charity or good works, that will accumulate over time and reduce sufferings in the next world. Vedic rites of fire-oblation (*yajna*) are now only occasional practices, although they are highly revered in theory. In Hindu wedding and burial ceremonies, however, the *yajña* and chanting of Vedic mantras are still the norm. The rituals, upacharas, change with time. For instance, in the past few hundred years some rituals, such as sacred dance and music offerings in the standard Sodasa Upacharas set prescribed by the Agama Shastra, were replaced by the offerings of rice and sweets.

Occasions like birth, marriage, and death involve what are often elaborate sets of religious customs. In Hinduism, life-cycle rituals include *Annaprashan* (a baby's first intake of solid food), *Upanayanam* ("sacred thread ceremony" undergone by upper-caste children at their initiation into formal education) and *Úrâddha* (ritual of treating people to feasts in the name of the deceased). For most people in India, the betrothal of the young couple and the exact date and time of the wedding are matters decided by the parents in consultation with astrologers. On death, cremation is considered obligatory for all except *sanyasis, hijra,* and children under five. Cremation is typically performed by wrapping the corpse in cloth and burning it on a pyre.

Pilgrimage and Festivals

Pilgrimage is not mandatory in Hinduism, though many adherents undertake them. Hindus recognise several Indian holy cities, including Allahabad, Haridwar, Varanasi, and Vrindavan. Notable temple cities include Puri, which hosts a major Vaishnava Jagannath temple and Rath Yatra celebration; Tirumala - Tirupati, home to the Tirumala Venkateswara Temple; and Katra, home to the Vaishno Devi temple. The four holy sites Puri, Rameswaram, Dwarka, and Badrinath (or alternatively the Himalayan towns of Badrinath, Kedarnath, Gangotri, and Yamunotri) compose the *Char Dham* (*four abodes*) pilgrimage circuit. The *Kumbh Mela* (the "pitcher festival") is one of the holiest of Hindu pilgrimages that is held every four years; the location is rotated among Allahabad, Haridwar, Nashik, and Ujjain. Another important set of pilgrimages are the *Shakti Peethas,* where the Mother Goddess is worshipped, the two principal ones being *Kalighat* and *Kamakhya*.

Hinduism has many festivals throughout the year. The Hindu calendar usually prescribe their dates. The festivals typically celebrate events from Hindu mythology, often coinciding with seasonal changes. There are festivals which are primarily celebrated by specific sects or in certain regions of the Indian subcontinent. Some widely observed Hindu festivals are Maha Shivaratri, Holi, Ram Navami, Krishna Janmastami,Ganesh Chaturthi, Dussera, Durga Puja and Diwali.

Scriptures

Hinduism is based on "the accumulated treasury of spiritual laws discovered by different persons in different times". The scriptures were transmitted orally in verse form to aid memorization, for many centuries before they were written down. Over many centuries, sages refined the teachings and expanded the canon. In post-Vedic and current Hindu belief, most Hindu scriptures are not typically interpreted literally. More importance is attached to the ethics and metaphorical meanings derived from them. Most sacred texts are in Sanskrit. The texts are classified into two classes: *Shruti* and *Smriti*.

Shruti

Shruti (lit: that which is heard) primarily refers to the *Vedas*, which form the earliest record of the Hindu scriptures. While many Hindus revere the Vedas as eternal truths revealed to ancient sages (*Zcis*), some devotees do not associate the creation of the Vedas with a god or person. They are thought of as the laws of the spiritual world, which would still exist even if they were not revealed to the sages. Hindus believe that because the spiritual truths of the Vedas are eternal, they continue to be expressed in new ways.

There are four *Vedas* (called *Zg-*, *Sâma-*, *Yajus-* and *Atharva-*). The *Rigveda* is the first and most important Veda. Each Veda is divided into four parts: the primary one, the *Veda proper*, being the *Samhitâ*, which contains sacred *mantras*. The other three parts form a three-tier ensemble of commentaries, usually in prose and are believed to be slightly later in age than the *Samhitâ*. These are: the *Brâhmanas*, *Âranyakas*, and the *Upanishads*. The first two parts were subsequently called the *Karmakâna* (ritualistic portion), while the last two form the *Jñânakâna* (knowledge portion). While the *Vedas* focus on rituals, the *Upanishads* focus on spiritual insight and philosophical teachings, and discuss Brahman and reincarnation.

Smritis

Hindu texts other than the *Shrutis* are collectively called the *Smritis* (memory). The most notable of the smritis are the epics, which consist of the *Mahâbhârata* and the *Râmâyana.* The *Bhagavad Gîtâ* is an integral part of the *Mahabharata* and one of the most popular sacred texts of Hinduism. It contains philosophical teachings from *Krishna,* an incarnation of *Vishnu,* told to the prince Arjuna on the eve of a great war. The *Bhagavad Gîtâ,* spoken by Krishna, is described as the essence of the *Vedas.* However Gita, sometimes called *Gitopanishad,* is more often placed in the Shruti, category, being Upanishadic in content. The Smritis also include the *Purânas,* which illustrate Hindu ideas through vivid narratives. There are texts with a sectarian nature such as *Devî Mahâtmya,* the *Tantras,* the *Yoga Sutras, Tirumantiram, Shiva Sutras* and the *Hindu Âgamas.* A more controversial text, the *Manusmriti,* is a prescriptive lawbook which epitomizes the societal codes of the caste system.

History

The earliest evidence for prehistoric religion in India date back to the late Neolithic in the early Harappan period (5500–2600 BCE). The beliefs and practices of the pre-classical era (1500–500 BCE) are called the "historical Vedic religion". Modern Hinduism grew out of the Vedas, the oldest of which is the Rigveda, dated to 1700–1100 BCE. The Vedas center on worship of deities such as *Indra, Varuna* and *Agni,* and on the *Soma* ritual. They performed fire-sacrifices, called *yajña,* and chanted Vedic mantras but did not build temples or icons. The oldest Vedic traditions exhibit strong similarities to Zoroastrianism and other Indo-European religions.

The major Sanskrit epics, *Ramayana* and *Mahabharata,* were compiled over a protracted period during the late centuries BCE and the early centuries CE. They contain mythological stories about the rulers and wars of ancient India, and are interspersed with religious and philosophical treatises. The later Puranas recount tales about devas and devis, their interactions with humans and their battles against demons.

Three major movements underpinned the naissance of a new epoch of Hindu thought: the advent and spread of Upanishadic, Jaina, and Buddhist philosophico-religious thought throughout the broader Indian landmass. Mahavira (24th Tirthankar of Jains) and Buddha (founder of Buddhism) taught that to achieve *moksha* or *nirvana,* one did not have to accept the authority of the Vedas or the caste system. Buddha went a step further and claimed that the existence of a Self/ soul or God was unnecessary. Buddhism peaked during the reign of Asoka the Great of the Mauryan Empire, who unified the Indian subcontinent in the 3rd century BCE. After 200 CE several schools of thought were formally codified in Indian philosophy, including Samkhya, Yoga, Nyaya, Vaisheshika, Purva-Mimamsa and Vedanta. Charvaka, the founder of an atheistic materialist school, came to the fore in North India in the sixth century BCE. Between 400 BCE and 1000 CE Hinduism expanded at the expense of Buddhism.

Sanskritic culture went into decline after the end of the Gupta period. The early medieval Puranas helped establish a religious mainstream among the pre-literate tribal societies undergoing acculturation. The tenets of Brahmanic Hinduism and of the Dharmashastras underwent a radical transformation at the hands of the Purana composers, resulting in the rise of a mainstream "Hinduism" that overshadowed all earlier traditions.

Though Islam came to India in the early 7th century with the advent of Arab traders and the conquest of Sindh, it started to become a major religion during the later Muslim conquest in the Indian subcontinent. During this period Buddhism declined rapidly and many Hindus converted to Islam. Numerous Muslim rulers such as Aurangzeb destroyed Hindu temples and persecuted non-Muslims; however some, such as Akbar, were more tolerant. Hinduism underwent profound changes, in large part due to the influence of the prominent teachers Ramanuja, Madhva, and Chaitanya. Followers of the Bhakti movement moved away from the abstract concept of Brahman, which the philosopher Adi Shankara consolidated a few centuries before, with emotional, passionate devotion towards the more accessible avatars, especially Krishna and Rama.

Indology as an academic discipline of studying Indian culture from a European perspective was established in the 19th century, led by scholars such as Max Müller and John Woodroffe. They brought Vedic, Puranic and Tantric literature and philosophy to Europe and the United States. At the same time, societies such as the Brahmo Samaj and the Theosophical Society attempted to reconcile and fuse Abrahamic and Dharmic philosophies, endeavouring to institute societal reform. This period saw the emergence of movements which, while highly innovative, were rooted in indigenous tradition. They were based on the personalities and teachings of individuals, as with Shri Ramakrishna and Ramana Maharshi. Prominent Hindu philosophers, including Sri Aurobindo and Swami Prabhupada (founder of ISKCON), translated, reformulated and presented Hinduism's foundational texts for contemporary audiences in new iterations, attracting followers and attention in India and abroad. Others such as Swami Vivekananda, Paramahansa Yogananda, B.K.S. Iyengar and Swami Rama have also been instrumental in raising the profiles of Yoga and Vedanta in the West. Today modern movements, such as ISKCON and the Swaminarayan Faith, attract a large amount of followers across the world.

SOCIETY

Denominations

Hinduism has no central doctrinal authority and many practising Hindus do not claim to belong to any particular denomination. However, academics categorize contemporary Hinduism into four major denominations: Vaishnavism, Shaivism, Shaktism and Smartism. The denominations differ primarily in the god worshipped as the Supreme One and in the traditions that accompany worship of that god.

Vaishnavas worship *Vishnu* as the supreme God; Shaivites worship *Shiva* as the supreme; Shaktas worship *Shakti* (power) personified through a female divinity or Mother Goddess, *Devi*; while Smartas believe in the essential oneness of five (panchadeva) or six (Shanmata, as Tamil Hindus add Skanda) deities as personifications of the Supreme.

The Western conception of what Hinduism is has been defined by the Smarta view; many Hindus, who may not understand or follow Advaita philosophy, in contemporary Hinduism, invariably follow the Shanmata belief worshiping many forms of God. One commentator, noting the influence of the Smarta tradition, remarked that although many Hindus may not strictly identify themselves as Smartas but, by adhering to Advaita Vedanta as a foundation for non-sectarianism, are indirect followers.

Other denominations like Ganapatya (the cult of *Ganesha*) and Saura (Sun worship) are not so widespread.

There are movements that are not easily placed in any of the above categories, such as Swami Dayananda Saraswati's *Arya Samaj*, which rejects image worship and veneration of multiple deities. It focuses on the *Vedas* and the Vedic fire sacrifices (*yajña*).

The Tantric traditions have various sects, as Banerji observes:

> Tantras are ... also divided as *âstika* or Vedic and *nâstika* or non-Vedic. In accordance with the predominance of the deity the *âstika* works are again divided as Úâkta (Shakta), Úaiva (Shaiva), Saura, GâGapatya and VaicGava (Vaishnava).

As in every religion, some view their own denomination as superior to others. However, many Hindus consider other denominations to be legitimate alternatives to their own. Heresy is therefore generally not an issue for Hindus.

Ashramas

Traditionally the life of a Hindu is divided into four *Âshramas* (phases or stages; unrelated meanings include monastery). The first part of one's life, *Brahmacharya,* the stage as a student, is spent in celibate, controlled, sober and pure contemplation under the guidance of a Guru, building up the mind for spiritual knowledge. *Grihastha* is the householder's stage, in which one marries and satisfies *kâma* and *artha* in one's married and professional life respectively. The moral obligations of a Hindu householder include supporting one's parents, children, guests and holy figures. *Vânaprastha,* the retirement stage, is gradual detachment from the material world. This may involve giving over duties to one's children, spending more time in religious practices and embarking on holy pilgrimages. Finally, in *Sannyâsa,* the stage of asceticism, one renounces all worldly attachments to secludedly find the Divine through detachment from worldly life and peacefully shed the body for Moksha.

Monasticism

Some Hindus choose to live a monastic life (Sannyâsa) in pursuit of liberation or another form of spiritual perfection. Monastics commit themselves to a life of simplicity, celibacy, detachment from worldly pursuits, and the contemplation of God. A Hindu monk is called a *sanyâsî, sâdhu,* or *swâmi.* A female renunciate is called a *sanyâsini.* Renunciates receive high respect in Hindu society because their outward renunciation of selfishness and worldliness serves as an inspiration to householders who strive for *mental* renunciation. Some monastics live in monasteries, while others wander from place to place, trusting in God alone to provide for their needs. It is considered a highly meritorious act for a householder to provide sâdhus with food or other necessaries. Sâdhus strive to treat all with respect and compassion, whether a person may be poor or rich, good or wicked, and to be indifferent to praise, blame, pleasure, and pain.

Varnas

Hindu society has traditionally been categorized into four classes, called *Varnas* (*Sanskrit*: "colour, form, appearance"):

- the *Brahmins*: teachers and priests;
- the *Kshatriyas*: warriors, nobles, and kings;
- the *Vaishyas*: farmers, merchants, and businessmen; and
- the *Shudras*: servants and labourers.

Hindus and scholars debate whether the so-called *caste system* is an integral part of Hinduism sanctioned by the scriptures or an outdated social custom. Among the scriptures, the *Shrutis* do contain verses that mention the *Varna* system, but very sparingly and descriptively (i.e., not prescriptive). Indeed, the only verse in the *Rigveda* which mentions all four *varnas* is 10.90, the *Purushasûkta*. The other *varnas*, the *Brahmâ* (i.e. Brahmins) and *Râjanya* (i.e. Kshatriyas) are mentioned separately in some other verses in the *Rigveda* (e.g. RV 10.80.1) and the other Vedas, and rarely in the Upanishads. Some—definitely including most *Smriti* texts—have interpreted these as *prescribing* the division of society in the four *varnas*. A verse from the Rig Veda indicates that a person's occupation was not necessarily determined by that of his family:

> "I am a bard, my father is a physician, my mother's job is to grind the corn." (Rig Veda 9.112.3)

In the Vedic Era, there was no prohibition against the *Shudras* listening to the Vedas or participating in any religious rite, as was the case in the later times. Some mobility and flexibility within the varnas challenge allegations of social discrimination in the caste system, as has been pointed out by several sociologists.

The *Smritis,* having interpreted the Vedic mentions of the *varnas* as prescriptive, clearly sanction the division of the society into the four *varnas,* and also mention various sub-divisions within these *varnas,* which would later emerge as the present birth-based *caste system.*

Many social reformers, including Mahatma Gandhi and B. R. Ambedkar, criticized caste discrimination. The religious teacher Sri Ramakrishna (1836-1886) taught that

> "Lovers of God do not belong to any caste . . . . A brahmin without this love is no longer a brahmin. And a pariah with the love of God is no longer a pariah. Through bhakti (devotion to God) an untouchable becomes pure and elevated."

Ahimsa and Vegetarianism

Hindus advocate the practice of *ahinsâ* (non-violence) and respect for all life because divinity is believed to permeate all beings, including plants and non-human animals. The term *ahinsâ* appears in the Upanishads, the epic Mahabharata and *Ahinsâ* is the first of the five *Yamas* (vows of self-restraint) in Patanjali's Yoga Sutras.

In accordance with *ahinsâ,* many Hindus embrace vegetarianism to respect higher forms of life. Vegetarianism is propagated by the Yajur Veda and it is recommended for a *satvic* (purifying) lifestyle. Estimates of the number of lacto vegetarians in India (includes adherents of all religions) vary between 20% and 42%. The food habits vary with the community and region, for example some castes having fewer vegetarians and coastal populations relying on seafood. Some Hindus avoid onion and garlic, which are regarded as *rajasic* foods. Some avoid meat only on specific holy days.

Observant Hindus who do eat meat almost always abstain from beef. The cow in Hindu society is traditionally identified as a caretaker and a maternal figure, and Hindu society honors the cow as a symbol of unselfish giving.

Cow-slaughter is legally banned in almost all states of India.

Conversion

Concepts of conversion, evangelization, and proselytization are absent from Hindu texts and in practice have never played a significant role, though acceptance of willing converts is becoming more common. Early in its history, in the absence of other competing religions, Hindus considered everyone they came across as Hindus and expected everyone they met to be Hindus.

Hindus today continue to be influenced by historical ideas of acceptability of conversion. Hence, many Hindus continue to believe that Hinduism is an identity that can only be had from birth, while many others continue to believe that anyone who follows Hindu beliefs and practices is a Hindu, and many believe in some form of both theories. However, as a reaction to perceived and actual threat of evangelization, prozelyzation, and conversion activities of other major religions most modern Hindus are opposed to the idea of conversion from (any) one religion to (any) other per se.

Hindus in Western countries generally accept and welcome willing converts, whereas in India acceptance of willing converts is becoming more common. With the rise of Hindu revivalist movements, reconversions to Hinduism have also risen. Reconversions are well accepted since conversion out of Hinduism is not recognized. Conversion into Hinduism through marriage is well accepted and often expected in order to enable the non-Hindu partner to fully participate in their spiritual, religious, and cultural roles within the larger Hindu family and society.

There is no formal process for converting to Hinduism, although in many traditions a ritual called *dîkshâ* ("initiation") marks the beginning of spiritual life. A ritual called *shuddhi* ("purification") sometimes marks the return to spiritual life after reconversion. Most Hindu sects do not seek converts, as they believe that the goals of spiritual life can be attained through any religion, as long as it is practiced sincerely. However, some Hindu sects and affiliates such as Arya Samaj, Saiva Siddhanta Church, BAPS, and the International Society for Krishna Consciousness accept those who have a desire to follow Hinduism.

In general, Hindu view of religious freedom is not based on the freedom to proselytize, but the right to retain one's religion and not be subject to proselyzation. Hindu leaders are advocating for changing the existing formulation of the freedom of religion clause in the Universal Declaration of Human Rights since it favors religions which proselytize.

●●

5

Marriage in Hinduism

A Hindu marriage joins two individuals for life, so that they can pursue dharma (duty), artha (possessions), kama (physical desires), and moksa (ultimate spiritual release) together. It also joins two families together. The colours are normally red and gold.

Arranging the Marriage

Traditionally, Hindu parents look for a prospective match for their son/daughter from their own community also known as *arranged* marriage. Elders in the family and parents seek the prospective match through word of mouth within the community. The use of *jathakam* (astrological chart at the time of birth) of the son/daughter to match with the help of a priest is common, but not universal. Parents also take advice from the brahmin called 'panthulu' in Telugu who has details of many people looking to get married. Some communities, like the Brahmins in Mithila, use genealogical records ("Panjikas") maintained by the specialists.

Jathakam is drawn based on the placement of the stars and planets at the time of birth. The maximum points for any match can be 36 and the minimum points for matching is 18. Any match with points under 18 is not considered as an auspicious match for a harmonial relationship. If the astrological chart of the two individuals (male and female) achieve the required threshold in points then further talks are considered for prospective marriage. Also the man and woman are given chance to talk and understand each other in the duration anywhere from 15 minutes to one hour. Once there is an agreement then an auspicious time is chosen for the wedding to take place.

The Wedding

Wedding ceremonies can be expensive, and costs are typically borne by the parents. It is not uncommon for middle- or upper-class weddings to have a guest list of over 500 people. A live instrumental band is played in some parts where as some marriages have bharat is (the bridegroom's family) dancing to music just before coming to the wedding venue. Vedic rituals are performed and the family and friends then bless the couple. Food is served to all the invitees with lots of delicacies. The wedding celebrations can take up to one week depending on the practice in that different part of India.

Types of Hindu Marriage and Rituals

Historically the so called vedic marriage was but one of the few different types of Hindu marriage customs. Love marriage was also seen in historical Hindu literature and has been variously described in many names: eg Gandharva vivaha etc. In certain poor vaishnav communities still there is a custom called kanthi-badal which is exchange of bead-garlands as a very simplified form of ritual in solitude in front of an idol of Krishna, considered a form of acceptable love marriage.

Elopement has also been described in old Hindu literature. Lord Krishna himself Eloped Rukmini on horse chariot. It is written that Rukmini's father was going to marry her to Shishupal, against her wishes. Rukimini sent a letter to Krishna informing of a place and time to pick her up.

Symbolic Rituals Worn by Married Hindu Women

The married Hindu women in different parts of India follow different customs. In some places, in especially eastern

India, they put on vermilion on the hair parting, wear a pair of conch bangles (shankha), a pair of red bangles(pala) and an iron bangle on the left hand (loha) while their husband is alive. In Tamil Nadu, a married woman is required to wear a necklace with a distinctive pendant called a thali and silver toe-rings. Both are put on her by the husband during the wedding ceremony. The pendant on the thali is custom-made and its design is different from family to family. Apart from this, the married woman also wears a red vermilion (Sindoor) dot on her forehead called a Kunguma pottu (Kunkuma) and (whenever possible) flowers in her hair and colored glass bangles. The married woman is encouraged to give up all of these when her husband dies (although some choose not to).

Modernity

Many people believe that arranged marriage is the traditional form of marriage in India and that love marriage is a modern form that a few couples opt for, usually in urban areas. Love marriage differs from an "arranged marriage" in that the couple, rather than the parents, choose their own partner. However, there are various instances from ancient scriptures of Hinduism, of romantic love marriages that were accepted in ancient times. Somewhere in the course of time, arranged marriages became predominant and love marriages became unacceptable. Despite some love marriages, the vast majority of Indians continue to have arranged marriages.The families believe that what their god has said is important, he said "All shall not fight, all shall become one, by binding together with love and happiness".

VIVAHAM

The Hindu religion has a deep significance and meaning for the institution of marriage. It is viewed as a sacrament and not a contract. Hindu families are patrilocal.

Institution of Marriage: Marriage is generally a union between a male and a female with a commitment so that they can pursue Dharma, Artha (possessions) and Kama (physical desires) together. It also joins two families. It is at once a gateway to earthly life of pleasure, progress, prosperity and joy as it is also an altar of elevation to a level of spiritual experience. So every society recognizes and controls it as it results in the procreation and nurture of future generation and thereby influences the social and cultural growth of society. According to Manusmriti or laws of Manu there are eight different types of Hindu marriages. Among the eight types all didn't have religious sanction. The last four were not religiously defined and were condemned. These are: Brahma Marriage, Daiva Marriage, Arsha Marriage, Prajapatya Marriage, Gandharva Marriage, Asura Marriage, Rakshasa Marriage, Paishacha Marriage.

Type of Marriage

Eight kinds of marriage are enumerated in Manu Smrti 3.21, viz.

1. **Brahma Vivah**: In Brahma marriage once the boy completes his Brahmacharya Ashram (student hood), he is eligible to get married. His parents then approaches the parents or guardian of a girl belonging to a good family and same Varna and ask them for the hand of their daughter for their son. The father of the girl also carefully chooses the bridegroom who is well versed in Vedas and of a noble character. This is how a Brahma marriage was arranged. There was no dowry system at that time, girl came with two garments and few ornaments only. According to Dharmashastras "Brahma Vivah" is the best marriage among all.

2. **Daiva Vivah**: If the girl is groomed with ornaments and married to a priest during a scarifies, it is called Daiva Vivah. In this type of marriage the girl's family wait for a reasonable period for a suitable man for their daughter but when nobody turns up they go looking

for a groom in such places where a sacrifice is being conducted. According to the Dharmashastra, Daiva marriage is considered inferior to Brahma marriage because it is considered degrading for the womanhood to look for groom.

3. **Arsha Vivah**: In this type of marriage the bride presents a cow and a pair of bull to the guardian of girl. Marriages of this type used to happen because the parents of the bride couldn't afford the expense of their daughter's marriage at the right time according to the brahma rite. So the girl is married off to an old sage. The cows, which were taken in exchange of the bride shows that even the groom does not have any remarkable qualities. According to sastras noble marriages had no monetary or business transactions so this kind of marriages were not considered noble.

4. **Prajapatya Vivah**: In this type of marriage, the bride's father goes in search for a groom for his daughter. The protection of the bride or daughter is handed over by the father to the bridegroom during the Panigrahan ceremony or the acceptance of the bride's hands. The actual wedding ceremony takes place after Panigrahan.

5. **Gandharva Vivah**: However when a man and a woman marry with each others consent but may not have the consent of their family or are unable to involve them due to geographical reasons, then this wedding is called Gandharva Vivah or 'love marriage'. It is not considered a right kind of marriage as it is done against the will of the parents so it is inferior kind of marriage.

6. **Asura Vivah**: In the Asura type of marriage the groom is not at all suitable for the bride. In no way he is a match for the girl but the bridegroom willingly gives as much wealth as he can afford to the bride's parents

and relatives. So the system of marriage is more like buying a product. In Arsha type cows are given in exchange for the bride but there is no compulsion like the Asura type. Even the groom is also not so rich and powerful like his counterpart in Asura type.

7. **Rakshasa Vivah**: If a bride is taken by force and then persuades her to marry. This is not considered as the right kind of marriage as you are forcing somebody to marry.

8. **Paishacha Vivah**: In this type the girl's wish is not considered whether she wants to marry or not instead she was force to marry and even the bride's family is also not given anything in cash or kind. Men would marry a woman, whom he had seduced while she was asleep, intoxicated or insane. This kind of marriage was later prohibited. It is considered as the most inferior type of marriage.

Vaak Daanam

This step is a part of Kanya Varanam, where the groom-to-be (brahmachari) sends two elders on his behalf to the father of a girl whom he wishes to marry. The elders convey the message of the brahmachari and ask for the daughter's hand. The two mantras in the form of brahmachari's appeal to intercede on his behalf come from Rg 10.32.1 ("pra sugmantha...") and 10.85.23. The first mantra begs the elders to proceed and return quickly with success back from their mission on his behalf. The second mantram ("anruksharaa Rjava:...") asks for the gods' blessings for the elders' safe journey to the house of the father of the would-be-bride. The mantra prays to Aryama and Bhaga for a marriage full of harmony. The father accedes to the request of the elders and the resulting agreement for betrothal is known as vaak daanam.

Kanyaa Daanam

Here, the brahmachari meets his prospective father-in-law.As soon as the bridegroom's party arrives, they are warmly welcomed by the bride's parents, relatives and friends. At the entrance of the hall, the threshold ceremony is performed. The officiating priest chants a few mantras of blessings and welcome. The threshold ceremony requires the bride's mother to receive and bless the groom with rice, red turmeric powder (kumkum) etc., by applying tilak (red dot and uncooked rice) on the groom's forehead. She sprinkles rice and red turmeric powder on the groom, and then blesses him with the palms of both hands - stretching them close to the groom's head. Now the priest and the bride's parents lead the bridegroom and his parents to the stage where they are given appropriate seats. All the other guests take their seats in the hall to witness the marriage ceremony.

To the accompaniment of ceremonial mantras by the officiating priest the bride's parents welcome the groom by invoking God's blessings and then offering the bridegroom a nutritious .drink called Madhuparka. This is called the Madhuparka Ceremony, the origin of which dates back thousands of years when Rishis and sages of India used it as a way of welcoming guests.

Vara Prekshanam

In this ritual, the bridegroom and the bride look at each other formally for the first time. The bridegroom worries about any doshas (defects) that the bride might have and prays to the gods Varuna, Brihaspati, Indra and Surya to remove every defect and to make her fit for harmonious and long marriage life blessed with progeny and happiness (mantra: Rg 10.85.44). The bride groom recites the mantra and wipes the eyebrows of the bride with a blade of darbha grass, as if he is chasing away all defects. The darbha grass is thrown behind the bride at the conclusion of this ceremonyThe

Bridegroom shall stand facing the east. The Bride shall stand facing the north. The bride (offering the seat or Asana, shall address the bridegroom as follows:

The bride: AUM, The noble one may accept and take the seat.

The bridegroom: AUM, I am taking my seat.

The bride shall take her seat to the right of the bridegroom. The bridegroom performs the Achamana and Angasparsha with water.

All Hindu religious ceremonies begin with two observances, namely Achaman or sipping a small quantity of water and angasparsha or touching one's limbs with one's right hand middle two fingers with a little water. Achaman is purificatory and conducive to peaceful attitude of mind. Angasparsha is intended to pray for physical strength and alertness. Achaman and Angasparsha are performed with the aid of Mantras.

Madhuparka Ceremony

Holding with his left hand a cup of Madhuparka (composed of honey, curd and ghee or clarified butter), after removing the cover and looking at the Madhuparka,

The bridegroom says:

> May the breeze be sweet as honey; may the streams flow full of honey and may the herbs and plants be laden with honey for us! May the nights be honey-sweet for us; may the mornings be honey-sweet for us and may the heavens be honey-sweet for us! May the plants be honey-sweet for us; may the sun be all honey for us and may the cows yield us honey-sweet milk!

"Honey-sweet", in this case, means pleasant, advantageous, and conducive to happiness. The bridegroom shall pour out the Madhuparka into three cups and then partake a little of it from each of the cups reciting the following Mantra:

The bridegroom: The honey is the sweetest and the best. May I have food as sweet and health-giving as this honey and may I be able to relish it!

Presentation of a Ceremonial Cow

The bride father symbolically offers to the bridegroom a cow as a present. In olden times sons-in-law received real cows as gifts, since that was the most precious asset with which a newly wedded couple could start life. This part of the tradition has been preserved by a symbolical presentation. At the conclusion of the first part of the wedding ceremony, it is customary to present gifts to the bride. The bridegroom presents the bride with gifts of clothing and jewellery thereby acknowledging his life-long duty to provide her with the necessities of life.

The father of the bride, offering to the bridegroom the present of a cow, a finger-ring or some other suitable article says:

> The father of the bride: AUM, (Please) accept these presents.
>
> The bridegroom: AUM, I accept (these presents).

Mangala Snaanam and the Wearing of the Wedding Clothes by the Bride

Five Veda mantras are recited to sanctify the bride in preparation for the subsequent stages of the marriage. This aspect of the marriage is known as mangala snanam. The sun god (Surya), water god (Varuna), and other gods are invoked to purify the bride in preparation for a harmonious married life. Next, the bride wears the marriage clothes to the accompaniment of additional Veda mantras. The bridegroom then ties a darbha rope around the waist of the bride and leads her to the place, where the sacred fire is located for conducting the rest of the marriage ceremony. The bride and the groom sit on a new mat in front of the fire. The groom recites three mantras which invoke Soma, Gandharva and Agni to confer strength, beauty, and youth on the bride.

Maangalya Dhaaranam

There is no Veda Mantram for tying the mangala sutram (auspicious thread) around the neck of the bride by the groom. The latter takes the mangala sutram in his hands and recites the following verse:

mAngalyam tantunAnena mama jIvanA hethunA |

kaNThe: badhnami subhage! sanjIva Sarada: Satam ||

(meaning: This is a sacred thread. This is essential for my long life. I tie this around your neck, O maiden having many auspicious attributes! May you live happily for a hundred years (with me).

Paani Grahanam

After maangalya dhaaranam, the groom lowers his right palm and encloses it over the right hand of the bride. He covers all the five fingers of the right hand of the bride with his right palm through this act of paani grahanam. He recites mantras in praise of Bhaga, Aryama, Savita, Indra, Agni, Suryan, Vayu and Saraswati, while holding the bride's hand. He prays for long life, progeny, prosperity and harmony with the bride during their married life. The closed fingers of the right hand of the bride is said to represent her heart. The paani grahanam ritual symbolizes the bride surrendering her heart in the hands of the groom during the occasion of the marriage.

Sapta Padi

During this ritual, the groom walks with the bride to the right side of the sacred fire. All along, he holds his wife's right hand in his right hand in the way in which he held her hand during the paani grahanam ceremony. He stops, bends down and holds the right toe of his wife with his right hand and helps her take seven steps around the fire. At the beginning of each step, he recites a Veda mantra to invoke the blessings of Maha Vishnu. Through these seven mantras, he asks Maha Vishnu to follow in the footsteps of his wife and bless her with food, strength, piety, progeny, wealth, comfort and health. At the conclusion of the seven steps, he addresses his wife with a moving statement from the Veds summarized below: Dear Wife! By taking these seven steps, you have become my dearest friend. I pledge my unfailing loyalty to you. Let us stay together for the rest of our lives. Let us not separate from each other ever. Let us be of one mind in carrying out our responsibilities as householders (grihasthas). Let us love and cherish each other and enjoy nourishing food and good health. Let us discharge our prescribed Vedic duties to our elders, ancestors, rishis, creatures, and gods. Let our aspirations be united. I will be the Saaman and may you be the Rk (Saaman here refers to the music and Rk refers to the Vedic text that is being cast into music). Let me be the upper world and let you be the Bhumi or Mother Earth. I will be the Sukla or life force and may you be the bearer of that Sukla. Let me be the mind and let you be the speech. May you follow me to conceive children and gain worldly as well as spiritual wealth. May all auspiciousness come your way. This series of Veda mantras starting with "sakhaa saptapadhaa bhava ..." and ending with "pumse putraaya ..." are rich with meaning and imagery.

Pradhaana Homam

After sapta padi, the couple take their seat on the western side of the sacred fire and conduct pradhaana homam. During the conductance of this homam, the bride must place her right hand on her husband's body so that she gets the full benefit of the homam through symbolic participation. Sixteen mantras are recited to the accompaniment of pouring a spoon of clarified butter into the sacred fire at the end of recitation of each of the mantras. These mantras salute Soma, Gandharva, Agni, Indra, Vayu, the Aswini Devas, Savita, Brihaspati, Viswa Devas and Varuna for blessing the marriage and beseeches them to confer long wedded life, health, wealth, children and freedom from all kinds of worries. One prayer — the sixth mantra — has a sense of humor and provides deep insight into human psychology. The text of this mantra is: "daSaasyam putraan dehi, patim ekaadaSam kRti". Here, the groom asks Indra to bless the couple with ten children and requests that he be blessed to become the eleventh child of his bride in his old age.

Stepping on the Grinding Stone

After pradhaana homam, the husband holds the right toe of his wife and lifts her leg and places it on a flat granite grinding stone known as "ammi" in Tamil. The ammi stands at the right side of the sacred fire. The husband recites a Veda mantra when he places the right foot of his wife on the ammi: May you stand on this firm stone. May you be rock-firm during your stay on this grinding stone. May you stand up to those who oppose you while you carry out your time-honored responsibilities as a wife sanctioned by the Vedas and tradition. May you develop tolerance to your enemies and put up a fair fight to defend your legitimate rights as the head of the household in a firm manner, equal to the steady strength of this grinding stone.

Laaja Homam

After ammi stepping, a ceremony of doing homam with parched rice is conducted. Here, the wife cups her hands and the brothers of the bride fill the cupped hands with parched rice. The husband adds a drop of ghee to the parched rice and recites five Veda mantras. At the end of each of the recitation , the parched rice is thrown into the sacred fire as havis (offering) to Agni. Through these mantras, the wife prays for long life for her husband and for a marriage filled with peace and harmony. At the end of the laaja homam, the husband unties the darbha belt around the waist of his wife with another mantra. The husband states through this mantra that he unites his wife and ties her now with the bonds of Varuna and invites her to be a full partner in his life to enjoy the blessings of wedded life.

Griha Pravesam

This ceremony relates to the journey of the wife to her husband's home. The husband carries the sacred fire (homa agni) in a earthern vessel during this journey home. There are many Veda mantras associated with this journey. These mantras pray to the appropriate Vedic gods to remove all obstacles that one can experience in a journey. The bride is requested to become the mistress of the house and is reminded of her important role among the relatives of her husband. After reaching her new home, she puts her right foot first in the house and recites the following Veda mantra: I enter this house with a happy heart. May I give birth to children, who observe the path of righteousness (dharma)! May this house that I enter today be prosperous forever and never be deficient in food. May this house be populated by people of virtue and pious thoughts.

Praavisya Homam

After griha pravesam, a fire ritual known as praavisya homam is performed by the couple to the accompaniment of thirteen Veda mantras from the Rg Veda. Jayaadi homam is also part of the praavisya homam. This homam offers the salutation of the newly married couple to Agni Deva and asks for strength and nourishment to discharge the duties of a grihasthas for the next one hundred years. After that, the bride shifts her position from the right side of her husband to his left side. At that time, once again, she recites a Veda mantra invoking the gods for blessings of children and wealth to perform the duties of a householder. At the end of the above homam, a child is placed on the lap of the bride and she offers a fruit to the child, while reciting a prescribed Veda mantra. Yet another mantram asks the assembled guests to bless the bride and then retire to their own individual homes peacefully. During the first evening of the stay in her new home, the couple see the stars known as Dhruva (pole star) and Arundhati. The husband points out the pole star and prays for the strength and stability of the household thru a Veda mantra. Next, the husband points out the Arundhati star to his wife and describes to her the story of Arundhati and her legendary chastity.

The rich and meaningful ceremony of the Hindu marriage (Kalyana Mahotsavam of the temples) is thus carried out in concert with sacred Veda Mantras. The bride and bridegroom should enunciate clearly the Veda mantras and reflect on their meanings during the different stages of the marriage ceremony. This way, they can be sure of a long, happy and prosperous married life and play their appropriate role in society to the fullest extent. Srinivasa Kalyanam is performed in the temples to remind us of these hoary Vedic traditions behind a Hindu marriage.

The giving away of the Bride (*Kanya Daan*)

Kanya means daughter or girl. *Daan* means giving away. This is an important part of the marriage ceremony in which the bride's parents give her away to the groom by entrusting her to the bridegroom. The officiating priest chants appropriate verses in Sanskrit. The people in the audience (the public) are now notified that the parents have willingly expressed their wish and consent by requesting the groom to accept their daughter as his bride. As soon as the groom indicates his acceptance the bride's parents place their daughter's right hand into the bridegroom's right hand. The parents now bestow their blessings on both the bride and the groom and pray to the Lord to shower His choicest blessings on them.

The father of the bride, placing her right hand on the right hand of the bridegroom, says:

> The father of the bride: Be pleased to accept hand of my daughter (name of the bride) of the Gotra (here the surname of the family). The bridegroom: AUM, I do accept.

The bridegroom makes an Offering of the garment and the scarf to the bride to wear. The bridegroom wears the garments and the scarf offered by the parents of the bride. Then facing each other The bride and the bridegroom speak as follows:

Ye learned people assembled at this sacred ceremony know it for certain that we two hereby accept each other as companions for life and agree to live together most cordially as husband and wife. May the hearts of us both be blended and beat in unison. May we love each other like the very breath of our lives. As the all-pervading God sustains the universe, so may we sustain each other. As a preceptor loves his disciple, so may we love each other steadfastly and faithfully. - RigVeda X.85.47

Addressing the bride, the bridegroom says:

> Distant though we were, one from the other, we stand now united. May we be of one mind and spirit! Through the grace of God, may the eyes radiate benevolence. Be thou my shield. May thou have a cheerful heart and a smiling face. May thou be a true devotee of God and

mother of heroes. May thou have at heart the welfare of all living beings! - Rig Veda X.85.44

The bride:

I pray that henceforth I may follow thy path. May my body be free from disease and defect and may I ever enjoy the bliss of your companionship!

The Nuptial Homa (*Vivah-homa*)

Vivah-homa is also called the "sacred fire ceremony". All solemn rites and ceremonies commence with the performance of Homa (sacred fire ceremony) among the followers of Vedic religion. The idea is to begin all auspicious undertakings in an atmosphere of purity and spirituality. This atmosphere is created by the burning of fragrant herbs and ghee and by the recitation of suitable Mantras.

The Achaman and Angasparsha are performed for the second time. The bride also participates.

The three Achaman mantras involve sipping of a little water three times.

The seven Angasparsha mantras involve touching water with the right hand middle two fingers apply the water to various limbs first to the right side and then the left side as follows:

1. Mouth
2. Nostrils
3. Eyes
4. Ears
5. Arms
6. Thighs
7. Sprinkling water all over the body.

Acceptance of Hand (*Pani-Grahanam*)

The bridegroom rising from his seat and facing the bride, shall raise her right hand with his left hand and then clasping it says:

I clasp thy hand and enter into the holy state of matrimony so that we may be blessed with prosperity and noble progeny. Mayst thou live with me happily throughout life! Through the grace of the all-mighty Lord, who is the Creator and Sustainer of the universe and in the presence of this august assemblage, thou art being given away in marriage so that we may together rightly perform our duties as householders. With all my strength and resources, I have clasped thy hand; and thus united, we shall together follow the path of virtue. Thou art my lawfully wedded wife and I am thy lawfully wedded husband. God, the protector and sustainer of all, has given thee to me.

From today, it devolves upon me to protect and maintain thee. Blessed with children, mayst thou live happily with me as thy husband for the full span of human life (a hundred years). Following the divine law and the words of wisdom uttered by the sages, may we make a good couple and may God vouchsafe unto us a shining life of virtue and happiness. As God nourishes and sustains all creatures through His great forces like the sun, the moon, the earth, the air etc., so may He bless my wife with healthy and virtuous progeny and may you all assembled here bless her!

- I accept thee as my partner for life.
- I will not keep away even mentally anything from thee.
- I will share with thee all I enjoy.
- We will persevere in the path of virtue, surmounting all obstacles.

Solemn Vows (*Pratigna-Karanam*)

The bridegroom taking the palm of the bride into his hand helps her to rise and then they both shall walk round the altar, the bride leading. Then facing the east take the solemn vows:

Ascending the Slab / Stepping on the Stone

This ceremony is referred to as *Shilarohanam* (*Shila*: stone ; *Arohan*: stepping upon). In it, the mother of the bride assists her to step onto a stone and counsels her to prepare herself for a new life. The stone signifies strength and trust. A married couple is likely to encounter ups and downs, joys and sorrows, prosperity and adversity, sickness and health. In spite of the difficulties facing them, they are enjoined to remain steadfast and true to each other.

The bride places her right foot on the slab (stone), assisted by her mother or her brother. The priest recites a Mantra from the Atharva Veda (AV II.13.4)

The Fried-Rice Offerings (*Laja-Homah*)

Laja means puffed rice or barley like popcorn. The bride shall place the palms of her hands over those of the bridegroom and make three offerings (ahutis) of fried rice soaked in ghee (clarified butter).

The bride:

- I adore God, the unifier of hearts. Now that I am leaving my parents' home for my husband's, I pray that He may keep us perpetually united!
- With these offerings I pray for Long life for my husband and for the prosperity of all our relations!
- (Addressing her husband) In making these offerings for your prosperity I once again pray that God may bless this union of our hearts!

Circumambulation Around the Sacred Fire (*Parikrama, Pradakshina, or Mangal fera*)

This is an auspicious and important part of the marriage ceremony. It consists in walking around the sacred fire (clockwise) four times. This aspect of the ceremony and the one that follows, namely Saptapadi (seven steps)- constitute the most important part, in as much as it legalises the marriage according to Hindu custom and tradition. These two aspects of the marriage ceremony establish an indissoluble matrimonial bond between the couple.

In the first three rounds the bridegroom leads the bride as they circle together around the sacred fire. In the fourth (last) round, the bride leads the bridegroom around the sacred fire.

In each round around the sacred fire, an appropriate mantra is recited which expresses noble sentiments in relation to their future matrimonial life. Each round culminates in both the bride and the bridegroom placing offerings or ahutis of fried rice in the sacred fire. The Hindu religion emphasises enjoyment of life as well as the discharging of family, social and national responsibilities.

During the first three rounds, God's blessings and help are sought; loyalty to each other is emphasised and; a promise to keep in mind the well-being and care of the future children is made.

In the fourth (last) round (led by the bride) the bride promises that she will lead her life according to the tenets of the Hindu religion, namely Satya and Dharma or Truth and devotion to duty, and that she will always ensure that the bridegroom can rely on her to carry out her family, religious and household duties.

The bridegroom then places his hand on the bride's head and states that henceforth she will be his wife and he will shield her against any danger or harm.

At the end of the four rounds they shall exchange seats, the bride taking her seat to the left of the bridegroom.

Seven Steps (*Saptapadi*)

Besides a religious meaning behind the seven steps, there is also a mathematical rationale on performing the 7 rounds circling the fire. A circle is 360 degrees, all the numbers between 1 and 9 divides 360 except the number 7. It becomes a non-terminating number, hence symbolizing the marriage as indivisible.

The ends of their garments (the bridegroom's scarf and upper garment of the bride) are tied together by the priest (signifying marriage knot).Then both shall stand facing the north. The bridegroom shall place his right hand upon the right shoulder of the bride.

They shall take the first step in the north easterly direction.

In taking these seven steps, the right foot shall always lead and the left foot be brought forward in line with it. Uncooked grains of rice (about a small handful) are placed in a line at equal distance at seven places. The bride and the groom take seven steps together, stepping upon first mound of rice with the right foot as the priest recites a mantra. Then stepping upon the second mount of rice with the right foot as the priest recites a mantra. (All seven steps are done the same way).

- May the first step lead to food that is both nourishing and pure.
- May the second step lead to strength (at the physical, emotional, intellectual and spiritual levels).
- May the third step lead to prosperity.
- May the fourth step lead to all round happiness.

- May the fifth step lead to progeny (noble and virtuous children).
- May the sixth step lead to long life.
- May the seventh step lead to bondage (through harmony, understanding).

The bridegroom says:

Having completed the seven steps, be thou my life long companion. Mayst thou be my associate and helper in successful performance of the duties that now devolve upon me as a householder. May we be blessed with many children who may live the full duration of human life!

After the completion of the seven steps ceremony, the couple (with knots tied to each other) take their seats. The wife now takes her rightful place on the left side of her husband as the marriage is now religiously solemnized in its entirety. Now the couple are husband and wife. The husband garlands the wife and she in turn garlands her husband.

Sprinkling of Water (*Abhishek*)

The priest (or a brother of the newly wedded wife) shall sprinkle water on the foreheads of the bride and the groom. The priest recites mantras from the Rig Veda (RV X.9.1/2/3) during the sprinkling of water.

Meditating on the Sun (*Soorya Darshanam dhyaanam va*)

Looking at or mentally visualising the sun, to give them power to lead a creative, useful and meaningful life.

The bride and the bridegroom together pray:

O God, who art the illuminator of the sun, may we, through thy grace live for a hundred years, hear for a hundred years, and speak for a hundred years. And may we never be dependent upon anybody. May we likewise live even beyond a hundred years! -Rig Veda, VII. 66. 16)

Touching the Heart (*Hriday sparsh*)

Touching the heart of the bride, the bridegroom says:

May I have hearty co-operation from these in the performance of my duties. May thou be of one mind with me. May thou be consentient to my speech. May the Lord of creation unite thee to me!

The bride:

May I have hearty co-operation from these in the performance of my duties. May thou be of one mind with me. May thou be consentient to my speech. May the Lord of creation unite thee to me!

Meditating upon the Pole Star and the Arundhati Star (*Dhruva dhyaanam darshanam va*)

The Pole Star is stationary and fixed in its position, likewise the couple is expected to be steadfast and firm in fulfilling their vows and responsibilities.

The bride:

Just as the star Arundhati is attached to the star Vasishtha, so may I be ever firmly attached to my husband! Placing his hand upon the bride's forehead

The bridegroom:

As the heavens are permanently stable, as the earth is permanently stable, as these mountains are permanently stable, and as the entire universe is permanent stable, so may my wife be permanently settled in our family! -Rig Veda X.173.4 *(Addressing the bride):* Thou are the Pole star; I see in thee stability and firmness. Mayst thou ever be steadfast in thy affection for me. The great God has united thee with me. Mayst thou live with me, blessed with children, for a hundred years!

Partaking of food (*Anna Praashanam*)

In the last symbolic rite the couple make offerings of food with chantings of Vedic Havan Mantras (oblations of food in the Sacred fire). Having done that, the couple feed a morsel of food to each other from the residue of the offerings. This being the symbolic expression of mutual love and affection.

Benediction (*Aashirvadah*)

Placing his hand upon the forehead of the bride, the bridegroom says:

> Ye men and women present here, behold this virtuous bride possessed of high attainments, and before ye disperse, give her your blessings! All the people present shall pronounce the following blessings upon the couple.

1. O Lord, may this couple be prosperous!
2. O Lord, may this couple live in perpetual happiness!
3. O Lord, may this couple be ever infused with love for each other. May this couple be blessed with children and grandchildren and live in the best of homes for the full period of their lives!
4. May you two live here together. May you never be parted. May you enjoy the full span of human life in the delightful company of your happy sons and grandsons!

Om Shantih, Shantih, Shantih.

The Hindu wedding ceremony may vary in minor details from region to region and different priests may adopt some variations.

Sacraments (*Sanskaras*)

Sacraments constitute an important part of Hindu religion. Sacraments in Hinduism are designed to build a solid foundation for righteous living. They are known as 'Sanskaras'.Their purpose is to create and develop a religious and spiritual outlook in life. The Hindu religion has instituted sixteen different Sanskaras (sacraments) meant for different phases of life from conception to marriage to old age and death. The word sanskara in Sanskrit means 'to cause indelible impressions on the mind and to develop every aspect of one's personality.' Therefore it is necessary to understand and appreciate their significance and to derive benefit from their performance. Of the sixteen sanskaras in Hinduism, the sacrament of marriage or Vivah Sanskara is the most important. Marriage influences the personality of man and woman as life partners, enabling them to take their rightful place in society.

ARRANGED MARRIAGE IN INDIA

Arranged marriages have been the tradition in Indian society for centuries. Even today an overwhelming majority of Indians in India have their marriages planned by their parents and other respected family-members. . Arranged matches were made after taking into account factors such as age, height, personal values and tastes, the backgrounds of their families (wealth, social standing) and their castes and the astrological compatibility of the couples' horoscopes.

The institution of marriage in India is considered a very important one. In general both the parents and the young people feel that since they were older and wiser than their progeny, they would be able to find a suitable match for their children with more prudence than the latter. Although most marriages are arranged, some couples in India are opting for love marriage in urban areas. Among the overseas Indians, many marriages are still arranged with the assistance of the parents. Even the so called love marriages in India generally happen with the approval of the parents, although their blessing may sometimes be reluctant.

In India, the marriage is thought to be for life, and the divorce rate is extremely low. In India, 1.1% of marriages result in a divorce compared with over 45.8% for USA. The arranged marriages generally have a much lower divorce rate. The divorce rates have risen significantly in recent years:

> "Opinion is divided over what the phenomenon means: for traditionalists the rising numbers portend the breakdown of society while, for some modernists, they speak of a healthy new empowerment for women."

An arranged marriages is effectively the result of a wide search by both the girl's family and the boy's family. They check for compatibility without using emotions. It thus incorporates some of the features of modern computer database based matchmaking like Shaadmaani.Com.

Indian Arranged Marriages

The following factors are generally considered in Indian marriages to search for compatibility:

- Values and personal expectations: should match
- Age and height: girl should generally be younger and shorter
- Looks: should be acceptable to the other
- Religion: should be same, preferrably same sect
- Mother tongue, caste: should be preferrably same
- Diet (veg/non-veg/alcohol/smoking): may differ only if acceptable to the other
- Education: comparable educational levels

- Profession: the profession should be acceptable to the other
- Financial: The boy's current and future financial situation should be acceptable to the girl.
- Astrological signs/attributes: should be compatible, if the two families believe in it.

The parents generally discuss the expectations with their son/daughter before starting to look for a match. The expectations are shared with relatives and family friends who can often bring suggestions. The Indian matrimonial sites attempt to provide databases that can be querried to find matches using similar attributes.

Hindu Dharma accords paramount importance to marriage between two people found compatible, and on an auspicious day, chosen to be compatible with the bride and the groom, with the blessings of the elders and in the presence of gods, so that the couple will flourish and walk in dharma, and any progeny conceived after such elaborate rituals would be a blessed soul and good human being.

Once the parents of both bride and groom agree with each in which all the relatives and known circle are called from both sides as a witness and to bless, then in that engagement function itself a date is fixed for marriage as per bride and grooms horoscope and astrologically auspicious day, the priest will announce to all that both the family are agreed to the acceptance of marriage of their son/daughter on the particular date. Then in the name of god both the families exchange fruits and cloths as a symbol of happy acceptance.

An auspicious day is chosen in accordance with the religious almanac and the bride and the groom's horoscopes, also if it is moon's phase (ascending is preferred by some) apart from any other logistical consideration.

The wedding is conducted in accordance with Vedic rites and rituals with the invited guests considered to be the 'society' in whose presence the girl is given away in holy matrimony to the boy.

From that moment on, he is to consider himself responsible for fulfilling her smallest of small desires to the biggest of them, to the best of his ability. He promises to be faithful to her and to worship the ground she walks on. She in turn is to treat him as her lord and master, her guide and advisor through good and bad, for the rest of her life.

PUNJABI WEDDING TRADITIONS

Punjabi wedding traditions and ceremonies are traditionally conducted in Punjabi and are a strong reflection of Punjabi culture.

The actual religious marriage ceremony - among Sikhs and Muslim the weddings are conducted in Punjabi or Urdu; among Hindus, the wedding is often conducted in Sanskrit. There are commonalities in ritual, song, dance, food, and dress. The Punjabi wedding has many rituals and ceremonies that have evolved since traditional times, including many famous Punjabi dances.

Important Wedding Songs

Songs of the bridegroom's side

- Mangane di geet: sung at the time of engagement
- Maneve de gaon: songs sung to welcome the bridegroom
- Gharouli de geet: sung for the gharoult or dowry
- Chounki charanvele de geet: songs sung when the bridegroom sits on the chounki wooden bathing seat

- o Sohhle: songs of happiness and joy
- o Ghoriyaan: sung at the time of riding to the bride s house
- o Sehra: sung at the time of tying the bridegrooms flower-veil
- o Kangāna: sung when the bride and bridegroom enter the house together for the first time.

Songs of the bride's side

- o Suhag: which is sung by the bride in praise of her parents and the happy days of her childhood and in anticipation of happy days ahead.
- o Jaggo: procession song to call the neighbours to the wedding.
- o Churra charan vele da geet: sung when the chura, ceremonial bangles are worn by the bride.
- o Janj: sung when the janj, marriage procession, is to be greeted.
- o Milni: sung at the ritual introduction of the two sides.
- o Ghenne de geet: sung when the bride is adorned with jewels.
- o Siftan: song in praise of the bridegroom
- o Chhandh: evolved from poetry, songs of joy.

Sitthniyan (crude, teasing songs)

- o Song sung when the bridegroom's procession is being welcomed.
- o Song sung when the wari, or gifts from the bridegroom's side, are being exhibited.

- o Song sung when the groom's party sits down to the meal.
- o Song sung when the daaj, dowry or the bridal gifts, are being displayed.

Others

- o LavanPhere :sung at the time of the actual wedding ritual.
- o Mahinya :sung when the girl is preparing for the wedding and is bathed by the women at home. It goes for both men and women.
- o Vedi de geet : sung while erecting the marriage pandal.
- o Khatt: sung at the time the maternal grandparents present gifts to the bride on an overturned tokra, or basket.
- o Pani vaarna: welcoming the bride to her new home.
- o Bidaigi: sung when the bride is being sent off in the doli.
- o Ghughrian: sung when the doli arrives at the groom s house.
- o Shahana: sung by mirasis in praise of the bridegroom.
- o Til Methre: sung while welcoming the bride and orienting her to the family.
- o Pattal: song sung before meal.

Wedding Rituals

Pre-Wedding Rituals:

Rokka: In this ceremony, the boy and the girl commit to enter a wedlock, and won't consider any more matrimonial proposals. Ardaas is done, followed by exchange of gifts.

Mangni: The Engagement. Usually very high profile. This when the boys' side of the family goes to the girls' side with gifts, jewellery, and other goods, to confirm the engagement.Usually even an exchange of rings takes place.

Dholki:Can be one day or many days, usually high profile in a banquet hall, ladies sings traditional songs, and it is the eastern version of the western Bridal shower. Now a days people hire DJs and have a dance party followed by dinner.

Mehndi: The Mehandi ceremony takes place in the atmosphere of a party. The bride and other ladies get mendhi (henna designs)done, on their hands and feet (most ladies get it done only on their hands but the bride gets it done on both hands and feet). For the bride the mendhi is sent by the future Mother in Law.

Ubtan: This ritual demands that the bride-to-be stay at home in her old clothes for a couple of days before her wedding. Before her bath, ubtan (a paste of powdered turmeric and mustard oil) is applied on her body by female relatives and friends. Both, the ghara ghardoli and the ubtan ceremonies are also performed for the groom at his house. Here the decorated pitcher of water (ghadoli) is brought for his bath by his bhabi (elder brother's wife).

Rut Jugga: The Rut Jugga ceremony is where the family dances and sings in the beautifully decorated wedding home. Rut Jugga is in the last hours of the night. They decorate copper vessels called "gaffers" with diyas (clay lamps) and fill them with mustard oil and light them. The bride/bridegrooms maternal aunt (mammi) carries it on her head, and another lady will have a long stick with bells, and she will be shaking it. The ladies will then go into other friends and families homes and be welcomed by sweets and drinks, they will then dance there and move on. It is a loud ceremony, filled with joy, dancing, fireworks, and food. And if the family wishes the ladies' dholki (ladies night of singing) and mendhi will follow the mayian and dinner.

Wedding Process

Sarbala/Shabbala: A young nephew or cousin also dons similar attire. He is called the sarbala/shabbala (caretaker of the groom) and accompanies him .

Sehrabandi: his relatives bless his sehra or turban.

Varna: The groom's bhabi lines his eyes with surma (kohl). After this, the groom's sisters and cousins feed and decorate his mare. varna, a ceremony that is supposed to ward off the evil eye. The cash is given away to the poor.

Milni: (means "Introductions") The Ardas is performed by the priest (Giani) followed by the formal introductions of the main male players in the families. Example is both eldest Chachas (father's younger brother) will come together and exchange garlands of flowers and money. After or during the wedding, ladies will do the same thing, but a much smaller affair.

Jaimala: After Milni, the bride and groom come in the middle of the circle where the family is standing, and place a heavily made garland made of flowers on each other to state, they accept each other and will love and live together with one and other.

Kanyadaan:

Pheress/Lavan: Depending on a Hindu Punjabi Wedding or Sikh Wedding, the Bride and Groom will walk in tow around the Guru Granth Sahib four times at the set intervals, Hindus around the Agni, (sacred fire).

Nikah: Nikah is Muslim marriage ceremony. Nikah is the contract between a bride and bridegroom and part of an Islamic marriage, a strong covenant (mithaqun Ghalithun) as expressed in Qur'an 4:21.

Walima: It is one of the two traditional parts of an Islamic wedding. The *walima* is performed after the *nikah*, or marriage ceremony.

Juta chhupai. This is when the girl's young relatives grab the groom's untended shoes and hide it away to be returned after the ceremony for a fee which is Kalecharis of gold for the bride's sisters and of silver for her cousins. This joyful custom is called juta chhupai.

'Post-Wedding Rituals:

Vidaai/Doli: Vidaai marks the departure of the bride from her parental house. As a custom, the bride throws phulian or puffed rice over her head. The ritual conveys her good wishes for her parents. Her brother's accompany the bride. Her relatives throw coins in the wake of this procession.

Rituals Observed at the Groom's House:

Pani vaarna. The groom's mother performs the traditional aarti with a pitcher of water. She makes seven attempts to drink the water from the pitcher. The groom must allow her to succeed only at the seventh attempt. The bride must, with her right foot, kick the mustard oil that is put on the sides of the entrance door before she enters the house.

Phera Dalna: the newly weds visit the bride's parents on the day after the wedding. The bride's brother usually fetches them.

MARRIAGE WEBSITES

Marriage websites, or online matrimonial sites, are a variation of the standard dating websites, with a focus on those wanting marriage rather than simply dating. Typically, matrimonial sites are used by people who prefer arranged marriage over love marriage. The term planned marriage has been used to describe marriages originating through matrimonial websites.

Matrimonial sites are specially popular in India and among Indians setled overseas. Young men and women in India generally do not feel any compulsion to date since dating has not been a part of the culture historically. In the west, the phonemonon termed "love" is considered a prerequisite for marriage. In India, however "love" is often taken to be the total mutual dedication that comes after marriage

Matrimonial sites register users, after which they are able to upload their profile onto a searchable database maintained by the website. Those users looking to find suitors can search the database with customised searches that typically include nationality, age, gender, availability of photograph and often religion, geographic location and caste (mainly for websites based in India).

Introduction to Online Matrimony

Online Matrimony is an organized web based Matrimonial/Marriage service facilitating wishful young men and women to find their suitable life partners. In India organized marriage services business is worth INR 10 billion . Online Matrimony caters to people spread across the globe to find their suitable partner living in a remote place but matching his/her specific interests and requirements. Given the varied and complex match making process of Indian system that is based on diverse aspects such as Caste, Religion,

Economic Standard, Job status, age, height, family back ground etc., Online Matrimony services have become quite successful. Over the years patrons of these services are going up. This World Wide Web based service has millions of users with millions of dollars business potential . The major Indian marriage websites are

- shaadi.com,
- jeevansathi.com,
- bharatmatrimony.com and
- shaadiyahoo.com

There are also websites that cater to specific communities. Some communites, such as Jains run some non-profit web-sites.

Misuse

Along side riding on the success and convenience of Online Matrimony services, one needs to exercise care and caution in giving out the information. Recent trends showed that there is a possibility of putting this information to misuse

The precautions that are recommended include

- Verification of individuals identity and educational qualifications.
- Verification of employment and assets owned.
- Verification of family background.
- Verification of personal habits (such as smoking, drinking or dietary habits).

The best form of verification is considered to be using reliable intermediaries, for example common relatives or friends or people belonging to the same community who may be familiar with the proposed match. Contacting neighbors and coworkers is sometimes considered to be appropriate.

Shaadi.com suggests these precautions against fraud:

- Guard your anonymity during initial contacts.
- Start slow – Use emails initially.
- Request for a photo.
- Chat on the phone.
- Meet in person only when you are ready.
- Meet in a safe place.
- Watch for warning signs like inconsistancies. Involve your family or your close friends in your search.
- Beware of money scams.
- Don't be embarrassed to report fraud to the police.

In India

India has always been rooted in tradition and religious beliefs. Traditional marriage in India depends heavily on tying partners based on certain important characteristics (religion, caste, class, social status, etc.) than a romanticized tying of partners, as is common in much of the Western world. Arranged marriages and marriages within the family has been the usual norm in Indian families. Love marriages are much less common, although this has been drastically changing over the years. The essential marriage broker is a volunteer (person who does introduction between bride's and groom's family without any monetary consideration), or a professional, who used to be involved in most arranged marriages, or a combination of a priest and a barber. In the last decade the print matrimonials gained an upper hand. With the internet boom in India, the picture of a marriage broker with a huge diary with tucked-in photographs is slowly phasing out, giving way to a gamut of online matrimonial sites.

Indian marriage requirements can, in many cases, be so specific in religion, caste, language, and location needed that the internet suits many potential Indian husbands and wives perfectly. A service provider may use registration profiles to filter preferences and may run several different portals to cater for needs like different languages.

Female Membership

The typical woman will begin joining matrimonial sites as soon as she graduates college around the age of 23. Female membership at these sites steadily increase from 18 through 26 years of age. At age 27, there is a considerable drop-off in membership as most women seek to get married by then. Women over 40 make up less than 3% of the enrollment.

Paid Vs. Free Membership

In the last decade online matrimonial and matchmaking websites have become very popular and an accepted form of arranged marriages. Various kinds of matrimonial websites exist, especially targeted towards Indians. People who wish to join such websites have the option to either use paid services, like those offered by websites like Shaadi.com and BharatMatrimony.com, or use free websites like www.101marriages.com or MyMarriageList.com etc. www.101marriages.com is as 100% free matrimonial site. Both free and paid websites offer similar services, although premium services are sometimes offered exclusively on paid websites. According to various reports, a significant portion of matchmaking in the Indian community will move to cyberspace in the next few years.

MATCHMAKING

Matchmaking is any process of introducing people for the purpose of marriage.

In some cultures, the role of the matchmaker was and is quite professionalized. The Ashkenazi Jewish shadchan, or the Hindu astrologer, were often thought to be essential advisors and also helped in finding right spouses as they had links and a relation of good faith with the families. In cultures where arranged marriages were the rule, the astrologer often claimed that the stars sanctified matches that both parents approved of, making it quite difficult for the possibly-hesitant children to easily object - and also making it easy for the astrologer to collect his fee. Tarot divination has also been employed by some matchmakers.

Social dance, especially in frontier North America, the contra dance and square dance, has also been employed in matchmaking, usually informally. However, when farming families were widely separated and kept all children on the farm working, marriage-age children could often only meet in church or in such mandated social events. Matchmakers, acting as formal chaperones or as self-employed 'busybodies' serving less clear social purposes, would attend such events and advise families of any burgeoning romances before they went too far.

The influence of such people in a culture that did not arrange marriages, and in which economic relationships (e.g. "being able to support a family", "good prospects") played a larger role in determining if a (male) suitor was acceptable, is difficult to determine. It may be fair to say only that they were able to speed up, or slow down, relationships that were already forming. In this sense they were probably not distinguishable from relatives, rivals, or others with an interest. Clergy probably played a key role in most Western cultures, as they continue to do in modern ones, especially where they are the most trusted mediators in the society. Matchmaking was certainly one of the peripheral functions of the village priest in Medieval Catholic society, as well as a Talmudic duty of rabbis in traditional Jewish communities.

Since the emergence of the mythology of romantic love in the Christian world in medieval times, the pursuit of happiness via such romantic love has often been viewed as something akin to a human right. Matchmakers trade on this belief, and the modern net dating service is just one of many examples of a dating system where technology is invoked as a magic charm with the capacity to bring happiness. These services often rely on personality tests (but genetics has even been proposed), aiming to maximize the identitfication of the best match.

The acceptance of dating systems, however, has created something of a resurgence in the role of the traditional professional matchmaker. Those who find dating systems or services useful but prefer human intelligence and personal touches can choose from a wide range of such services now available. According to Mark Brooks (an online personals and social networking expert), "you can actually find people who are compatible, and this is a major advance that is going to keep the industry alive for the upcoming 50 years". He also stated that matchmakers offer "a chance to connect" and "a chance to authenticate" prospects in ways the Web sites can't.

MATCHMAKING IN DIFFERENT CONTEXTS

In North America

There have been communities in The United States of America with matchmaking as little ago as the 1960s

In Asia

In Singapore, the Social Development Unit (SDU), run by the city-state's government, offers a combination of professional counsel and dating system technology, like many commercial dating services. Thus the role of the matchmaker has become institutionalized, as a bureaucrat, and every citizen in Singapore has access to some subset of the matchmaking services that were once reserved for royalty or upper classes.

Matchmaking Theories

A certain number of academics and practionners in sexology (and marriage counseling) have tried to 'theorise' matchmaking in order to maximise its success. Matchmaking may for instance rely on personality tests trying to determine profiles that are more likely to be compatible with one another.

Academics include Pepper Schwartz , Helen Fisher (anthropologist), , Neil Clark Warren, Hugo Schmale, or Claus Wedekind (matchmaking based on genetics).

Matchmaking in Literature, Theater and Cinema

- *La Celestina*, a play by Fernando de Rojas
- *The Matchmaker*, a play by Thornton Wilder
- *The Matchmaker* (film), a 1958 film starring Shirley Booth
- *The MatchMaker* (1997 film), a 1997 film starring Janeane Garofalo

Matchmaking in Other Contexts

The concept of matchmaking is also used in the business world and known as B2B Matchmaking, Investor Matchmaking, Business Speed Dating or Brokerage Events. In contradiction to social networking solutions, real meetings between business people are in focus. Trade fair organisations e.g. find this concept an added value for their exhibitors because it gives them the opportunity of advanced planned meetings.

●●

6

Hindu Wedding Rituals

Hindu wedding ceremonies are traditionally conducted at least partially in Sanskrit, the language in which most holy Hindu ceremonies are conducted. The local language of the people involved is also used since most Hindus cannot understand Sanskrit. They have many rituals that have evolved since traditional times and differ in many ways from the modern western wedding ceremony and also among the different regions, families, and castes such as Rajput weddings and Iyer weddings. The Hindus attach a lot of importance to marriages and the ceremonies are very colorful and extend for several days.

In India, where most Hindus live, the laws relating to marriage differ by religion. By the Hindu Marriage Act of 1955 passed by the Union Parliament of India, for all legal purposes, all Hindus of any caste, creed or sect, Sikh, Buddhists and Jains are considered as Hindus for the sake of the Hindu marriage Act — and can hence intermarry. By the Special Marriage Act, 1954, a Hindu can marry a non-Hindu employing any ceremony provided certain legal conditions are fulfilled.

The pre-wedding ceremonies include engagement (involving vagdana or oral agreement and lagna-patra written declaration), and arrival of the groom's party at the bride's residence, often in the form of a formal procession. The post-wedding ceremonies involve welcoming the bride to her new home.

Just as Hinduism is hard to grasp and contrast against the newer, book-defined, structured religions such as Christianity and Islam, India's prevalent wedding traditions are also hard to categorize purely on a religious basis. They have a closer similarity to ancient cultures such as Greek, Roman, Egyptian and Chinese.

An important thing to note is that despite the fact that the modern Hinduism is largely based on the puja form of the worship of *devas* as enshrined in the Puranas, a Hindu wedding ceremony at its core is essentially a Vedic yajna (a fire-sacrifice), in which the Aryan deities are invoked in the Indo-Aryan style. It has a deep origin in the ancient ceremony of cementing the bonds of friendship/alliance (even among people of the same sex or people of different species in mythological contexts), although today, it only survives in the context of weddings. The primary witness of a Hindu marriage is the fire-deity (or the Sacred Fire) *Agni,* and by law and tradition, no Hindu marriage is deemed complete unless in the presence of the Sacred Fire, seven encirclements have been made around it by the bride and the groom together.

Ancient system of Hindu-Vedic-marriages was fully scientific. It did not differentiate between male and female as is being done presently.

- The basis for a fulfilling and happy life

Te santu jard—istayah sampriyau royisnu sumansyamanau।
Pasyema sharadah shatam jivema sharadah shatam shrunuyam shardah shatam॥

"We should be able to live a graceful life that is full of mutual love and warmth. Our sentiments should be auspicious.
We should be able to see for a hundred years, live a healthy life of a hundred years and listen the music of spring for a hundred years."

The sage of the above mentioned vedic — aca, has emphasized that the basis of happy and fulfilling married life is the sense of unity, intimacy and love between husband and wife. Therefore they should have sex, marriage is not for self-indulgence but it should be considered a life long social and spiritual responsibility. Married life is an opportunity for two persons to grow from life partners into soul mates.

Main Rituals

All of the rituals vary based on family traditions. The names of the rituals also vary.

Prior to Marriage

Conducted at the homes (cabbage) of the parents of the bride and the groom.

Engagement

A decision made by the parents in front of the community members to have the marriage, sometimes using a document.

Barni Bandhwana

Approximately 15 days prior to the actual wedding, on an auspicious day, the pundit will perform a puja to Lord Ganesh (the remover of obstacles). During this puja, a piece of mauli (thread) is tied to the hands of the groom, and his parents. This puja is done to make a humble request to Lord Ganesh that the wedding happen without any problems, beside the occasional mishap e.g. tripping over. After that day, the family performs a puja to Lord Ganesh every day until after the wedding is complete.

Mamara

The *mamara* is an important ceremony, common to both the bride and the groom's families. This ceremony is performed by the maternal uncle of the groom/bride, who, along with his wife and family, arrives with much fanfare, and is received by the bride/groom's mother with the traditional welcome.

Sangeet Sandhya

The sangeet sandhya is an evening of musical entertainment. The bride's family puts on a show for the groom and bride. Included as part of this event is an introduction of all the family members for the bride.

Tilak Ceremony

Tilak is a mark of auspiciousness. It is put on the forehead using Kumkum, a red turmeric powder. The male members of the bride's family, like her father, brother, uncles place a tilak on the forehead of the groom. This is typically followed by giving some gifts to the groom and the groom's accompanying family members requesting them to take care of the bride later.

Mehendi Lagwana

Another name for "Vivaah" is "haath pila karna" or simply translated, making hands yellow. Mehendi (henna) is applied to the bride's hands and feet. In the right hand, a round spot is left open for Hathlewa.

During Marriage Festivities

Barat Nikasi

The groom, leaves for the wedding venue riding a decorated horse or elephant. This is a very colorful and grand ceremony. The groom is dressed in a sherwani (long jacket) and 'churidars' (fitted trousers). On his head he wears a 'sehra' (turban) with a 'kalgi' (brooch) pinned onto it. The turban usually has flowers extending from it to keep the grooms face covered during the wedding ceremony.

Before he departs, his relatives apply the ceremonial 'tilak' on his forehead and his sister feeds the horse or elephant sweetened grain. The 'baraat' (consisting of the groom seated on the horse or elephant, and relatives and friends of the groom) is headed by the dancing of the congregated folks. Accompanied by the rhythm of the north Indian dholak, the baraat reaches the place of the wedding.

Upon arriving at the venue of the wedding, the groom is welcomed by a welcome song. This is called "talota". Then the groom knocks on the door with his sword and enters.

Var Mala/Jai Mala

In most Hindu weddings, the groom is led to a small stage, known as *mandap,* where he is greeted by the bride's family. The maternal uncle, brother or brides' best friends bring the bride to the stage. The bride and the groom are handed the garlands while the priest is chanting the religious hymns. Following this, the groom and bride exchange garlands, which are the *var mala* or *jai mala,* signifying their acceptance of each other as husband and wife. Then, the groom's mother-in-law measures the groom's chest, and pokes and prods him to make sure he is tough enough to defend her daughter. She then puts *kajal* on the groom to ward off evil spirits.

Aarti

The 'baraatis' (groom's party) are received by the bride's family and at the entrance to the wedding venue. The bride's mother welcomes the groom by performing the 'aarti' (traditional Indian welcome ritual with a lamp or 'diya' placed on a platter or 'thali') to welcome her son-in-law and placing a tilak on his forehead

Baasi-Jawari

This event takes place the day of the wedding. The bride's sisters hide the groom's shoes and ask for money if he (groom) wants them back and be able to go home with the bride.

Kanya Daan

Kanya Daan, which means the giving away of one's daughter, has been derived from the Sanskrit words *Kanya* which means girl and *Daan* which means donation. Kanya Daan is a very significant ritual performed by the father of the bride in presence of a large gathering that is invited to witness the wedding. The father pours out libation of sacred water symbolizing the giving away of his daughter to the bride groom. The groom recites Vedic hymns to Kama, the god of love, for pure love and blessings.

As a condition for offering his daughter for marriage, the father of the bride requests a promise from the groom for assisting the bride in realizing the three ends:

- dharma,
- artha,
- and kama.

The groom makes the promise by repeating three times that he will not fail the bride in realizing dharma, artha and kama.

Ideally, the parents of the bride place the right hand of the bride over the right hand of the groom and place their own left hands at the bottom and the right hands (the two of them) on top, securing the Conch with gold, betel nut, flowers and a little fruit (in it) placed in bride's hand. It is at this point that the purpose of the Kanyadaan is clearly stated per scripture and the names of the parents and forefathers are stated from both sides. Wedding can not legally proceed without this Kanyadaan step in which parents of the bride agree to the wedding.

This must be remembered that in Hindu wedding, the bride and groom marry each other and the priest only assists with the Mantra. He can not declare them married as no authority is vested in him to do so. Agni, gods and the invited members of the family and friends are the witness.

Panigrahana Hathlewa

After being led to the wedding mandup, the bride and groom have their hands tied together. The priest does a puja to Lord Ganesh and then puts a coin & mehendi on the bride's right hand where the round empty spot is (where no mehendi was put) and ties his hand with the brides. This puja is done schedule in advance based on an auspicious time & date.

Gathabandhan

In this ritual priest tying a knot using the ends of the clothing worn by the bride and groom. The priest ties the end of the groom's dhoti or the kurta; whichever he is wearing, with that of the bride's saree, the knot signifying the sacred wedlock.

Laja Homa

The ritual connotes the actual core wedding ceremony, for the very meaning of the word "vivaah" is-marriage. The groom and the bride then circle the holy fire seven times, making seven promises to be fulfilled in the married life, after which they are considered to be 'married' to each other. This ritual is called "phere". Traditionally, there were three pheras. But now this has been mixed with saptapadi and now seven pheras are done for each "vachan".

Saptapadi

The *Saptapadi* (Sanskrit for *seven steps/feet,* c.f. Latin cognates *septum+pedii*) or the *saat pheras* is perhaps the most important component of Vedic Hindu weddings. The couple conduct seven circuits of the Holy Fire (*Agni*), which is considered a witness to the vows they make each other. In some regions, sashes worn by the bride and groom are tied together for this ceremony. Elsewhere, the groom holds the bride's right hand in his own right hand. Each circuit of the consecrated fire is led by either the bride or the groom, varying by community and region. Usually, the bride leads the groom in the first circuit. In North India, the first six circuits are led by the bride, and the final one by the groom. In Central India, the bride leads the first three or four circuits. With each circuit, the couple makes a specific vow to establish some aspect of a happy relationship and household for each other.

- *To provide for food always.*
- *To give you excellent health and energy.*
- *Todained in Vedas, during your life time.*
- *To give you happiness in life.*
- *To make your cows and good animals to grow in strength and in numbers.* (Animals such as horse can now be substituted with "Car")
- *To make all the seasons be beneficial to you.*
- *To make the homams (sacrifices to be done in Holy Fire) to be performed by you in your life as ordained in Vedas, successful and free from hindrances.*

A joint vow is usually made at the end of the seven steps, which varies by region. A typical vow is:

After crossing seven steps with me thus, you should become my friend. I too have become your friend now. I will never discard this friendship and you should also not do that. Let us be together always. Let us resolve to do things in life in the same manner and tread the same path. Let us lead a life by liking and loving each other, having good hearts and thoughts, and enjoying the food and our strong points together. Let us have undivided opinions. We will perform the vrithas united. Let us have same and joint desires. I will be Sama (one of the vedas); you will be

Rig (another Veda). Let me be the Heaven; you be the Earth. Let me be the Shukla (Moon) and you be its wearer. Let me be the mind and you its spokesman (Vak). With these qualities, you be my follower. You the sweet tongued, come to me to get good children and wealth.

In North Indian weddings, the bride and the groom say the following words after completing the seven steps:

"We have taken the Seven Steps. You have become mine forever. Yes, we have become partners. I have become yours. Hereafter, I cannot live without you. Do not live without me. Let us share the joys. We are word and meaning, united. You are thought and I am sound. May the night be honey-sweet for us. May the morning be honey-sweet for us. May the earth be honey-sweet for us. May the heavens be honey-sweet for us. May the plants be honey-sweet for us. May the sun be all honey for us. May the cows yield us honey-sweet milk. As the heavens are stable, as the earth is stable, as the mountains are stable, as the whole universe is stable, so may our unions be permanently settled."

Vidaai

Also called *rukhsati* in North India. This is considered to be the most emotional ritual, when the bride leaves her parents' home and makes her way to her husband's. Family and friends, who also shower her with blessings and gifts, give her a tearful farewell. The male members of the bride's family bid farewell to the groom by applying the traditional 'tilak' (vermilion) on his forehead and shower him with gifts.

In earlier times the bride use to leave in a palanquin. These days the couple leaves in a decorated car.

At their New Home

Darshan

After Vidaai, the couple first visits a temple, preferably that of Lord Rama and Sita, to seek their blessing from where they move towards Groom' house.

Dwar-Rokai

After leaving the groom's father-in-law's house, the couple come home. They are stopped at the entrance of the house by either the groom's sister or his father's sister. There, in an earthen vessel, the sister/aunt uses a mixture of salt and water to ward off evil spirits from the groom. After this, the pot is thrown on the ground and destroyed. After this, the couple enter the house.

Griha Pravesh

When the bride arrives at her new home, her mother-in-law, who welcomes her with the traditional 'Aarti'. At the entrance, she puts her right foot onto a tray of vermilion powder mixed in water or milk, symbolizing the arrival of good fortune and purity. With both her feet now covered in the red powder paste, she kicks over a vessel filled with rice and coins to denote the arrival of fertility and wealth in her marital home.

Mooh Dikhai

The family now indulges in a series of games and post-wedding rituals, amidst much laughter to make the new member feel comfortable. One such ritual is the Mooh dikhai. Literally translated, Mooh Dikhai means 'show your face', but this is a ritual, which helps to introduce the newly wed to members of her husband's family. Each member of the groom's family comes in turn to make an acquaintance with the new bride.

Pheri

In some regions of North India, the couple returns (unaccompanied by the groom's family) to the bride's parents' home the day after the wedding, usually for an afternoon meal and evening tea. The groom is introduced to the bride's side of the extended family and her friends. In the period between the engagement and the wedding, it is usually considered bad-luck for the groom to visit the bride's house, so the pheri (literally, return or turning-around; distinct from phere) marks the beginning of the groom's social integration into the bride's side of the family.

Modern Hindu Weddings

Modern Hindu weddings are often much shorter and do not involve all of the rituals of the traditional ceremony which sometimes went on for five days. Instead certain ceremonies are picked by the families of the bride and the groom depending on their family tradition, caste, jâti etc. Hence the ceremonies vary among the various ethnic groups that practice Hinduism. The wedding is normally conducted under a wedding mandap, a canopy traditionally with four pillars, and an important component of the ceremony is the sacred fire (Agni) that is witness to the ceremony. Sometimes, the bride comes to her husband's house in a doli which is a palanquin traditionally made of wood and decorated with jewels. Before the wedding party departs to the Hindu temple, the priest will sometimes place a coconut under the tire. In the old days a horse-drawn carriage was used to carry the bride and groom, and the breaking of the coconut demonstrated the road-worthiness of the horse-drawn carriage.

●●

7

Ayyavazhi's Teachings and Impact

Ayyavazhi is a dharmic belief system that originated in South India in the 19th century. It is cited as an independent monistic religion by several newspapers, government reports and academic researchers. In Indian censuses, however, the majority of its followers declare themselves as Hindus. Therefore, Ayyavazhi is also considered a Hindu sect.

Ayyavazhi is centered on the life and preachings of Ayya Vaikundar; its ideas and philosophy are based on the holy texts *Akilattirattu Ammanai* and *Arul Nool*. Accordingly, Vaikundar was the Purna avatar of Narayana. Ayyavazhi shares many ideas with Hinduism in its mythology and practice, but differs considerably in its concepts of good and evil and dharma. Ayyavazhi is classified as a dharmic belief because of its central focus on dharma.

Ayyavazhi first came to public attention in the 19th century as a Hindu sect. Vaikundar's activities and the growing number of followers caused a reformation and revolution in 19th century Travancorean and Tamil society, surprising the feudal social system of South India.

Though Ayyavazhi followers are spread across India, they are primarily present in South India, especially concentrated in Tamil Nadu and Kerala. The number of practitioners is estimated to be between 700,000 and 8,000,000, although the exact number is unknown, since Ayyavazhis are reported as Hindus during censuses.

Etymology and History

Ayya in Tamil means 'Father' and *vazhi*, 'the pathway' ; The simple derivative in the sense is *'The Pathway of (or) towards Father'* . Apart, due to the diverse synonymous versions for the phrase in Tamil, it also leads to various other theories.

Ayyavazhi began to be noticed initially by the large number of people gathering to worship Vaikundar (known historically as "Mudisoodum Perumal") (1809 C.E – 1851 C.E) at Poovandanthoppe. The Thuvayal thavasu (washing penance) of 1840 is the origin of Ayyavazhi as an alternative religio-cultural phenomena. The majority of its participants were from marginalised and poor sections of society. They began to function as a distinct and autonomous society, and gradually, they identified their path with the phrase 'Ayya vazhi'. Although the majority of these followers were from the Chanar cast, a large number of people from other castes also came to it. For Christian missionaries proselytising India, Ayyavazhi posed a great challenge. Ayyavazhi's rapid growth throughout its first century of existence was noted by Christian missionary reports from the mid-19th century.

By the middle of 19th century, Ayyavazhi had come to be recognised as a separate religion with deep roots in the regions of South Travancore and South Tirunelveli. The numbers of faithfull increased significantly from the 1840s. By the close of the 19th century, Swamithope was considered the center of Ayyavazhi. After the time of Vaikundar, Ayyavazhi was spread through his teachings. The five Seedars, disciples of Vaikundar and their descendants, traveled to several parts of the country bearing the mission of Ayyavazhi. Meanwhile, the Payyan dynasty started administrating the Swamithoppe pathi, while other Pathis came under the administration of the followers of Ayya. Following the instructions of

Akilattirattu Ammanai (Akilam), the Nizhal Thangals (small pagodas) have been established across the country for worship and the study of scripture.

Arul Nool, the first Ayyavazhi work in print was released in 1927, followed by the Akilam in 1933, almost a century after it had been written down. As a result, Ayyavazhi abandoned active oral traditions in favor of literary scriptures. Ayyavazhi headquarter reports that Ayyavazhi spread more rapidly after Indian Independence (1940s) and still more rapidly through the 1990s. Many Ayyavazhi-based social welfare organisations were established in the late 20th century. Several alternative versions of Akilam, including some controversial versions, were released during the same period. The Anbukkodimakkal Thirucchabai, a democratic bureau, was established by the religious headquarters in the early 1990s to organize and govern the religion. Organisational conferences are held in various cities in South India including Mumbai, Chennai and Thiruvananthapuram.

Considering the growth of Ayyavazhi, Ayya Vaikunda Avataram, the day of Vaikundar's incarnation, was declared a holiday by the state administration for the district of Kanyakumari in 1994, followed by the districts of Tirunelveli and Tuticorin in 2006. Currently, Bala Prajapathi Adikalar, heir to the Payyan dynasty, is considered the leader of Ayyavazhi.

Scriptures and Holy Places

The holy books of Ayyavazhi are the Akilattirattu Ammanai (commonly referred to as *Akilam*) and the Arul Nool, and they are the source of the religion's mythology. The *Akilattirattu Ammanai* was written by Hari Gopalan Seedar in 1841, as if hearing the contents of Akilam told by Narayana to his consort Lakshmi. In addition to the mythological events Akilam also provides an extensive quantity of historical facts, especially that of mid and late 2nd millennium C.E.

While the original text is damaged, the daughter versions such as the *Swamithope* version, the *Kottangadu* version as well as the *Panchalankurichi* versions, are the earliest existing palm-leaf versions of Akilam. Other released versions includes the Sentrathisai Ventraperumal, the Kalai Ilakkiya Peravai, the Vivekanandan, the highly criticised VTV and the earliest and commonly accepted Palaramachandran version. Akilam contains more than 15,000 verses in seventeen sections. It is written in poetic Tamil in a ballad form, and is composed with a unique literal-style with two sub-genres, *Viruttam* and *Natai* throughout.

The secondary scripture, Arul Nool, includes various books that are believed to be written by Arulalarkal (one possessed by divine power). It contains prayers, hymns and instructions for the way of worship in Ayyavazhi, as well as rituals prophesy and many acts. It also contains many events found in the Akilam pertaining to the life of Vaikundar. Unlike Akilam, there is no definitive history for Arul Nool. All these texts are compiled in Tamil language.

To the Ayyavazhi devotees, there are seven holy places, called Pathis, with the Pancha pathis being the most important. The temple of the Swamithope pathi is the headquarters of the Ayyavazhi.

The five Pancha pathi are: 1. the Swamithope Pathi, the venue of the great Tavam and the religion's headquarters. 2. Ambala Pathi, where Vaikundar joined six of the Seven Deities unto himself. 3. Mutta Pathi, the venue of the Second and Third Vinchais. 4. Thamaraikulam Pathi, where the Akilattirattu Ammanai was written down. 5. Poo Pathi, where Ayya joined the Earth goddess Poomadanthai to himself by symbolic marriage.

Vakaippathi, though not included in the Pancha pathis by the headquarters, is still considered as a Pathi but with lesser importance. There is disagreement among followers of

Ayyavazhi regarding the holiness of some other Pathis, such as Vaikunda Pathi and Avathara Pathi. The list of Pathis announced by the headquarters of Ayyavazhi does not include these Pathis.

Symbolism

The symbol of Ayyavazhi is a lotus carrying a flame-shaped white *Namam*. The lotus represents the 1,008-petalled *Sahasrara* (in Tamil, *Ladam*), while the Namam represents the *Aanma Jyothi* or *atman*. Both of the Ayyavazhi scriptures refer to Thirunamam (the "flame shaped symbol" present in the top of the Lotus in the Ayyavazhi symbol), but not to the lotus directly. The symbol is the ideological summary of Akilam-based philosophy. This symbol has been in use since the mid-20th century.

The mythical narration in akilam about the eight yugas is often viewed philosophically as a reference to eight chakras. The first Neetiya Yukam, is Bindu and the final state, Dharma Yukam, is Sahasrara, or absolute bliss. In this series, the energy of consciousness (Namam) of oneself is invoked, rising from Bindu (Neetiya Yukam) to the final Sahasrara (Dharma Yukam). This lotus, the highest spiritual center of enlightenment is for experiencing the absolute "bliss". The reigning power in the final Dharma Yukam (Sahasrara) is Ekam, which is a part of Vaikundar a Trinity conception, or a manifestation of the supreme absolute. Thus Ayyavazhi's symbol is derived from Akilam. The symbol, "Lotus with Thirunamam", shows "Vaikundar's experienced in Sahasrara."

In certain Hindu texts the Sahasrara chakra has 1000 petals. But in Ayyavazhi symbolism, Saharara has 1008 petals. In Ayyavazhi, there is no scriptural authority indicating the importance of 1000, but the number 1008 is commonly mentioned. Also, the incarnation year of Vaikundar is 1008 M.E (Malayalam Era). Backing these scriptural identities, the

1008-petal lotus is followed in Ayyavazhi symbolism. *Sahasrara* is symbolised as a lotus without a stem.

Ayyavazhi architecture was developed in constructing Nizhal Thangals, where the inverted lotus flower of *Sahasrara* is used to cover the roof. The lotus may also represent the heart and the flame shape (Thirunamam), the divinity. Ayyavazhi has used other symbols including Vaishnavite ' *Triple Namam* '(not used currently), and Conch.

Teachings and Impact

The majority of Ayyavazhi's key teachings can be found in the book Akilattirattu Ammanai and other teachings are collated from various books written by unknown authors, whose works feature in the Arul Nool. Like Dharma, the other teachings of Ayyavazhi are twofold, sociological and mystical. The mystical teachings are devoted to revealing divine knowledge, while social teachings are primarily concerned with eliminating inequality and discrimination in society. The teachings encourage a positive relationship with God, as opposed to one based on fear. Followers are encouraged to refer to God as *Ayya*, "dear father", to strengthen their intimacy and affection towards God.

Ayyavazhi mystics focus on supreme oneness. Among its variations, the theology always maintains this focus on oneness. The evil of Kali blocks the ultimate or supreme oneness prevailing between individual souls and the universe, creating among them a false sense of individuality and of extreme pride. This erroneous view causes the apparent sense of separation from the oneness and motivates against it. Ekam — the "over-soul" or the supreme soul — is identified as the whole of existence, changeless in nature and ubiquity. This is "one which undergoes different changes with respect to space and time" because of the evil force maya.

All of creation evolved from this Ekam, the supreme consciousness. All the qualities of Ekam are within each soul, and evolve from it. Each and every individual soul is a reflection or mirror of the absolute Supreme, Ekam, which provides the textual basis and metaphor for the mirror's role in Ayyavazhi worship. Human and all other souls are restricted and limited by the evil of Kali. This is why individual souls are not able to attain supreme bliss, and so are secondary to Ekam. Once a soul overcomes the influence of maya, it becomes one with Ekam. Its individuality is gone, and thereby it is Ekam. On the other hand, this supreme consciousness is personified as Paramatma (over-soul) by which, God is the "Husband", while all other souls are his "consorts", symbolised by Thirukkalyana Ekanai, where Vaikundar marries the individual souls. Also, the Ayyavazhi philosophy applies a common formula for the creation of human beings and the rest of the universe. Thus whatever exists externally to human beings exists also internally.

Ayyavazhi clearly and explicitly condemns the caste based inequalities in its social teachings. It heavily criticises the caste discrimination rather than the 'Caste system' itself. From its inception, Ayyavazhi has also served as an engine of social reform, particularly in the area of Travancore, which was previously noted for its unusually strong caste system. In this contest, the mingling of castes in Ayyavazhi centers was a vital element in the transformation of society.

Ayya Vaikundar was the first to succeed as a social reformer in launching political struggle, social renaissance as well as religious reformation in the country. Vaikundar was the pioneer of the social revolutionaries of Tamil Nadu and Kerala. He was also said to be the forerunner of all social reformers of India. Akilam displayed sympathy for the laboring classes, and opposed to the often excessive taxes they were forced to pay. From the beginning the followers, fortified by the teachings, have also taken a strong stand against political oppression. This is most clearly seen in Akilam, where the Thiruvithkanur king is identified as Kalineesan, (one who is a captive of Kali) and the British are identified as Venneesan (the white neesan) in the social sense. Ayyavazhi was in the forefront of movements for Human Rights and Social Equality. Ayyavazhi also effected social changes in southern India, resulting in the emergence of social and self-respect movements such as *Upper cloth agitation*, Temple entry agitation and other movements including those of Narayana Guru, Chattampi Swamikal, Vallalar and Ayyankali.

WORSHIP CENTERS

The followers of Ayyavazhi established *Pathis* and *Nizhal Thangals*, which are centers of worship and religious learning in various parts of the country. They serve as centres for propagation of the beliefs and practices of Ayyavazhi. There are thousands of *Nizhal Thangals* throughout India, mostly in South India. A research paper approved by Madurai Kamaraj University reports more than 8000 worship centres in Tamil Nadu and Kerala alone. Reports from the London Missionary Society (LMS) of the mid-19th century also speak of *Nizhal Thangals*. Since Ayyavazhi is not centrally organised, *Swamithope pathi* serves as the religious headquarters for all. The *Pathi*s earn more importance among the worship centers.

The seven *Pathi*s, obtain their significance from the fact that Vaikundar and his activities were historically associated with these centers of worship. The *Swamithope pathi*, though considered the religion's headquarters, does not officially control the rest of the religious centers. All *Pathis*, except itself, are managed by independent committees. The five *Pathis* known as Pancha pathi are considered foremost among Pathis.

Nizhal Thangals, compared with *Pathis*, are simple small structures built for worship and for learning the teachings of Vaikundar. They also served as centers of school education during the early days. Food and shelter are offered to the needy in these centres. Some of them were established when Vaikundar was alive. Among them Arul Nool, specifies seven Thangals, and these are considered primary over the others. Today, charity is one of the main activities conducted in these centers.

These centers emerged as the abode of Dharma. The Nizhal Thangals form an important institution in the socio-religious life of the people of Ayyavazhi. Panividai may be conducted up to three times daily, but all worship centers provide Panividai at least once daily.

ETHICS

The ethics of Ayyavazhi, integrated with the meta-narrative mythology, are found throughout the primary scripture, *Akilattirattu Ammanai*. Regarding ethics, Arul Nool is an accumulation of the core concepts found in Akilam. In Akilam, the ethical abstracts are pointed out as "told by God" at several places at different situations to lesser god-heads, devas, saints, etc. when ever asked by them.

Neetham is the primary virtue of Ayyavazhi. This shows how society, its people, the ruling king, etc., lived in absolute harmony with nature, placing the power of Almighty in all their works, deeds and activities during early ages. In return, nature and the divine beings protect the society which follows the Neetham. Chastity and life in ultimate union with nature form the central theme, an ethical form that is to be followed. As in Akilam, Vinchai is the rules and regulations provided by God (Narayana) to Vaikundar. There are three such Vinchais. Acts found there also fit to humans to improve their moral code. The first *Vinchai of Tiruchendur* forms the largest ethical accumulation found in Akilam.

To an extent, the Dharmic teachings in Ayyavazhi are also considered as ethics. Charity in social ethics and "attempting to realise the ultimate truth of oneness" in spirituality are the ethical codes under the banner of Ayyavazhi dharma. Akilam also gives separate ethics for Devas also. It is notable that the Ayyavazhi ethics undergo a vast deviation from the incarnation of Vaikundar since a universal change took place then. Over all, as the foremost ethical code, people are advocated to overcome the evil force kalimayai with the weapons of love, forbearance and peace, since Kaliyan as maya rules the minds of people.

Arul Nool constitutes the major role in forming the rules and regulations of Ayyavazhi, including ethics. It gives separately the social as well as divine ethics. The Sivakanda Athikara Pathiram here is the section especially dedicated to teach the ethics. The rituals, especially circumambulations, are to be followed to wash-out the sin committed related to immoral thinking.

RELIGIOUS STUDIES

It is difficult to give a clear-cut listing to Ayyavazhi concepts because of the relation the Ayyavazhi scriptures maintains with the Hindu scriptures. Akilam primarily says the central themes of the existing scriptures (that of Hindu) had gone awry by the advent of Vaikundar. It also narrates that Akilam was given to mankind as an alternative because Kaliyan destroyed the original Vedas and Shastras, and at the beginning of Kali Yuga, several additions were given to the previous scriptures by him. Both of these view points give the views of Akilam on Hindu scriptures, and place them as reasons for rejecting them.

The philosophy, terms and mythology of the Ayyavazhi scriptures are the basis of religious study on Ayyavazhi theology. But several terms quoted in Akilam couldn't be understood wholly unless by referring to the descriptive details of those terms in Hindu scriptures. For example, if the 96 tatvas are understood, then the Kaliyan is understood. Therefore theologians and philosophers today turn to Hindu scriptures to further their understanding of the tatvas as properties of the human body, which are not elaborated upon in Akilam. However, to understand Akilam and its philosophy, one should have a basic knowledge over the Hindu ideas and concepts. Since Akilam have no different view in this matter from Hindu scriptures, it was left to be gathered from there.

On mythical studies, Akilam covers almost the entire main mythology of Hinduism, including Mahabharata, Ramayana, Kantha Purana and Vishnu Purana, but with limited details. It includes only the main events that are directly linked to the main-stream story flow. But to undergo a detailed study on each, the appropriate Hindu scriptures that include those events in detail need to be referred. Akilam provides all these collectively in brief with an overall story line, which make it unique. Many philosophical concepts from Hinduism are found in Akilam; some of them are completely accepted, some are regenerated, while others are rejected.

Generally it was considered that once a particular concept is not found well-described in Ayyavazhi scriptures, such as Akilattirattu Ammanai or Arul Nool (as detail as in Hindu scriptures), and instead simply was quoted, then that particular conception is accepted as in Hindu scriptures for religious studies. But once Akilam has different views over something from that of the existing (Hindu) scriptures, then it would be found deeply described in Akilam itself and hence no need for referring other scriptures.

God

The theology of Ayyavazhi differs considerably from other monistic religions. It speaks of Ekam, the Oneness from which all that exists formed, and also an ultimate oneness that exists behind all differences. The Ekam, which is articulated as the supreme divine power itself, is supposed to remain unaffected by maya deep inside every changeable matters as an absolute constant. In theological terms, God is, in the highest sense, formless, infinite, genderless and beyond time and space. The term Ekam in Tamil language give simply the meanings, "one", "absolute", "the whole which exists" and "the incomparable"; all give some sort of direct monistic definition about God from Ayyavazhi theology.

Narrating through mythology, The *Sivam* and the *Sakthi* are the first to get evolved from Ekam. The *Natham*(voice), Trimurthi, other lesser gods and the entire universe further evolved. The Trimurthi are greater among the personified Devas. Siva, one among the Trimurthi, was the supreme power until Kali Yuga. Vishnu is the supreme from the advent of Kali Yuga. Then, from the incarnation of Vaikundar, again the powers of all god-heads, including that of Vishnu, is transformed to Vaikundar. Ekam, the supreme oneness as one among the Trinity takes a place within Vaikundar for the present age. Therefore, Vaikundar is said to be the only worshippable and supreme power. However, a quote from Akilam thirteen says this supreme oneness (Ekam) itself is created by Vaikundar, who is a personified God. In this regard, Ayyavazhi being centered on Vaikundar, is more monotheistic rather than monistic. No other god-heads, even the Father of Vaikundar, Narayana, have gained an equal or greater status than Vaikundar. Vaikundar is a turine power who includes the qualities of the Santror, Narayana and Ekam within himself.

In Ayyavazhi mythology, Kroni, a primordial evil manifestation, was fragmented into six and each fragments took birth and plays an anti-Vishnu roles throughout the successive six yugas. He was finally destroyed by a final judgment which is followed by the god-ruled Dharma Yukam. This narration gives some dualistic dimension to Ayyavazhi theology. But since the focus of Arul Nool, the accumulation of Ayyavazhi teachings is extremely monistic and since the final fragment of Kroni itself is called *Kalimayai* (a conception rather than a physical or material incarnation), it was commonly accepted that the 'Maya' is symbolised in such a way that contrasts the dualistic view on Ayyavazhi. Apart from all these, there are also separate quotes in Ayyavazhi scriptures which give pantheistic and panentheistic definition to Ayyavazhi theology.

Festivals and Rituals

Basically, there are two yearly festivals for Ayyavazhi. The Ayya Vaikunda Avataram is celebrated on the twentieth day of the Tamil month *Masi* (March - April). This is the only Ayyavazhi festival to be celebrated as per the Solar calendar. The mass procession conducted on this day from Nagercoil to Swamithoppe is a popular one in this part of the country. The Thiru Edu-Vasippu is a festival of seventeen days celebrated in the Tamil month of Karthigai (November - December). This celebration of textual reciting as a festival itself is a unique feature to Ayyavazhi. Apart from this, there is a tri-yearly celebration of Kodiyettru Thirunal in Swamithope. Another unique feature is the celebration of every day as a festival in Swamithope,(exclusive to Swamithope) called as *'Nitham Thirunal'* .

In addition to the philosophical concepts and mythology, the rituals of Ayyavazhi evolved in their own way. Most of the rituals have different operational and historical meanings. Historically, the rituals were used or viewed as an attempt to break the caste-based inequalities prevailed in the society of the time, and to strengthen and uplift the sociologically downtrodden and ill-treated. Examples of this include the charity on food as *'Anna Dharmam'* , physical as well as spiritual cleanliness through Thuvayal Thavasu, eliminating untouchability through Thottunamam, self-respect and courage through headgear, and unifying various castes through Muthirikkinaru.

But they too reveal, however, high philosophical ideas preached in a ritual language.The Muthirikkinaru and Thirunamam are treated religiously as if the *Patham* and *Namam* of them have the power to heal all sorts of mental as well as physical illness. Thuvayal thavasu is suggested as a training to reach the ultimate aim of Dharma Yukam. The use of the crown reveals that "all are kings", visualising an ideology similar to *advaita*. Also, Ayyavazhi scriptures succeeded very much in helping to understand these philosophical ideas to the common mass which is very much unusual. The individual rituals, the ecstatic religiosity and the ritual healing, which are the features of Ayyavazhi worship, contributed to the formation of an idea of emancipation and a social discourse. Rituals attempt to uplift and treat the disenfranchised. Another important thing to be noted is the alternative phrases religiously used in Ayyavazhi universe different from Hinduism, to represent certain practices.

Inclusiveness and Exclusivity

The formula of inclusiveness and exclusivity, as applied in the religio-cultural universe of Ayyavazhi, is unique because both the theories are mixed up in Ayyavazhi scriptures. The inclusive theory accepts the views of different religions for a certain period of time, and from then onwards exclusively rejects all of them in its narrative.

Ayyavazhi accepts different god-heads of several religions, like the concept of Allah and almost all the god-heads of Hinduism. It also says that the one and the same God incarnates in different parts of the world at different time for rescuing the people from sufferings. But due to the advent of Kaliyan and because of the cruel nature of his boons, for the first time, the supreme power Ekam incarnates in the world as Vaikundar, and so all the lesser god-heads and previous scriptures had lost their substances. So after the time of the Vaikunda avatar, Vaikundar was said to be the only worshippable God and hence, the theology of Ayyavazhi was channeled towards exclusivism. The manner in which Akilam treats the scriptures of different religions is complicated. For instance, while there is no direct reference to the terms 'Christ' or 'Bible' anywhere in any of the Ayyavazhi texts, there is an indirect reference in Akilam thirteen which is supposed to be an implication that Christ was an incarnation of Narayana, but it was widely thought that it did not recognise the Bible composition. It seems the view of Akilam on Bible is "it was created with the intention of man and not that of God". Likewise, Akilam accepts the term "Allah", but seemingly rejects the religion of Islam and its ideas. In common, creation of religions and shaping individualities for them are heavily criticised. The concepts 'God' and 'Religion' are kept poles apart in Akilam, and it seems to maintain an ideology something like *'Accept God; Reject religion'* .

Ayyavazhi accepts various incarnations in Hinduism, but necessarily rejects the so called *' Hindu '* scriptures. It initially accepts Vedas. Later since Kaliyan had bought the Vedas as boon they too lost their substance by the advent of Kaliyan, and so had gone invalid. It also says that he (Kaliyan) had performed several additions and had hidden some of their content. And hence God incarnated as Vaikundar. So for the present age, Akilam is said to be the only *'Book of Perfection'* . By this Ayyavazhi rejects all other scriptures and follows only its own. Akilam highly condemns the creation of religions especially exclusivistic religious and theological ideas. It shows them as the foremost *Kali mayai* (evil of Kali). The scriptures teach sensibly and symbolically that God and his activities are beyond the reach of religions. It also preaches about universal oneness.

Mythology

The mythology of Ayyavazhi narrates that the essence of this vision is an account of a history - a past, a present and a future - meant by weaving together of empirical facts, historical events as well as mythical accounts. It moves around three axiomatic typologies, namely Santror, Kali Yukam and Dharma Yukam, placing their base on the concepts and events of previous yugas that are associated also with Hindu mythology. The basic concepts give a symbolic vision which is at once religious and social.

It is closely linked to that of Hinduism. Akilam talks about the previous yugas and the evolution of Kroni through them. Events, mythical characters, and concepts are shared with Hinduism, though they may be engendered in different form. The number of Yugas and Avatars differs in Ayyavazhi from Hinduism. The personification of the entity of Evil for the current yuga, Kaliyan, is unique to Ayyavazhi. Akilam says that the true concepts were destroyed, so that all previous scriptures had lost their substances due to the advent of Kali.

The book also speaks of God incarnating in the world in the Kali Yukam (the present age) to destroy the evil spirit, the final and the most serious manifestation of Kroni. God incarnates as Vaikundar, and since Vaikundar lived recently, he was well-known in history. So in the second part of the mythology many mythical as well as historical facts were woven together. Most of the events such as Muthirikkinaru, Wearing of Headgear during worship, Thuvayal Thavasu all were noted in history.

Though there are quotes in Arul Nool to accredit the ten Avatars of Vishnu, it seems that they are not seen in equal status with these incarnations. It was considered secondary to the primary avatars, who are associated with the destructions of the fragments of Kroni. This view is not inconsistent with Hinduism, as only Narasimha, Rama and Krishna are considered the primary avatars who are still worshipped. The other avatars are considered secondary avatars who are not worshipped.

Santror and Dharma Yukam

The Santror is the subject of the religious vision of Ayyavazhi. There is both a religious and a social category in its connotation. In the social sense, it is believed that the term Santror fits rightly to the early "Chanars", who were called by the Arabs as "Al Hind", and known in Biblical times as the "People of Five Rivers"; they are now scattered with more than 250 branches throughout the world. But in turn, in ideological sense and from the literary meaning of the term "Santror" in Tamil, it represents one who is noble and lives with dignity and supreme knowledge, giving an inclusive character and universal reach. Historians account that in ancient dravidian cultures, zealous devotees of God were called as 'Chanars'. A quote from Akilam too reads, "Chanars (Santror) are those who have the ability to see 'the invisible' constantly."

The Santror are given a historical background in Ayyavazhi mythology as seven boys who were made to born in the mythical garden Ayodha Amirtha Vanam *(supposed to be between present-day Srirangam,Tamil Nadu and Triconamalee,Srilanka)* by using the seven seeds from seven upper worlds, by Thirumal, to the seven virgins. Theologians interpret that these 'Seven boys' refer to the ancestors of the whole human race, and hence the term "Santror" refers to the entire human race. Their lineage started at the end phase of Dvapara Yukam and continued through the Kali Yukam into the Dharma Yukam. It is believed that Kali is being destroyed continuously by the activities of the Santror in the Path of Vaikundar, and so the Dharma Yukam unfolds eventually. In this sense they have a considerable roll in the destruction of Kali, the foremost evil.

The Ayyavazhi proposes an emancipatory utopia under the banner of Dharma Yukam. The basis of the belief is that Ayya Vaikundar had come to establish and rule as the everlasting king over the Dharma Yukam in the place of Kali Yukam after sentencing Kroni to hell by a final judgment from the Lion-throne of *Dwaraka pathi,* the rising mythical landmass (which was sunken at the end of Dwapara Yuga by Krishna) located south east of present-day Kanyakumari. The Dharma Yukam is narrated as beyond the limits of time and space. It is often related to Moksha – the personal liberation, and to the state of 'Oneness' too.

Relation with Hinduism

The Hindu and Ayyavazhi ideologies are closely tied to each other. The place where Ayyavazhi and Hinduism depart from each other is at the advent of Kali Yuga. Akilam says that until Kali Yuga, the Vedas and all other Hindu scriptures remain with divinity. Each of the gods in Hinduism also remain with all their powers. But from the beginning of Kali Yuga they and all their virtues collapsed. Kaliyan was a part of the mundane primordial manifestation who spread maya or illusion upon the existing scriptures and Devas. In Kali Yuga, all true scriptures are bound to maya and are unhelpful.

On the other hand, there in Kailash, Siva believing the words of devas, created Kaliyan without discussing to Vishnu, he who had the responsibility to destroy the Kaliyan as per the previous deeds. So Vishnu refused to take birth in the world to destroy Kaliyan. So Siva and Brahma surrendered all their powers to Vishnu. Until this event, Siva was the supreme power as per Akilam. This is a theological idea similar to Shaivism, where Siva is supreme to all. Now onwards, however, Vishnu is the supreme power. Here the ideology changes similar to that of Vaishnavism. This supremacy of Vishnu remains like this from the beginning of Kali Yuga until the incarnation of Vaikundar, from where it changes further.

During the incarnation, Vishnu himself can not incarnate directly in the world to destroy Kaliyan, since he had bought as boon the power of Devas, including Vishnu's, and spread it all over the world as maya. So God needs to be incarnated with a new set of rules and with unique importance. A total universal transformation of the power relation of god-heads, the rules of scriptures, the dharma, etc., took place, and Vaikundar was given birth by taking in the power of Ekam, by Lakshmi and Vishnu conjoining together inside the sea.

And from now onwards all the powers were handled over from Vishnu to Vaikundar inside the sea. Siva, Vishnu and Brahma therefore form a part within Vaikundar. This ideology about Trimurthi (three are equal in power) is similar to that of Smartism. Vishnu alone forms a double role; one, within Vaikundar, and the other, as the father of him, remain inside the sea and regulating Vaikundar through Vinchais. After Vaikundar was given birth to, by assuming the Power of Ekam, Vaikundar was supreme to Vishnu and all other God-heads, though Narayana playing the role of Father to Vaikundar. However, Vaikundar had to obey the order of Vishnu, since Vaikundar was given birth to perform the duties of Vishnu, which he could not do. Vaikundar (and scriptures given by him) is the manifestation of the supreme Ekam so, in Ayyavazhi spirituality, he is the only worshippable universal power

Regarding scriptures, the first part of Akilam is summed-up events of the previous yugas, which are present in Hindu scriptures. The second part says about the universal transformation and the uniqueness of Vaikundar and his incarnational activities. So as a summary, till the beginning of Kali yuga, what is Hinduism, that is Ayyavazhi. From then onwards for a series of reasons, Akilam says that Hindu scriptures and its ideology had lost its purity and was destroyed, and so the Dharma was re-configured in the name of Akilam and Vaikundar and the Hindu ideas were re-formed.

Phenomenology

Akilam points out its basis as a regeneration of Dharma in the form of an entirely new ideology. But today, most of the followers of Ayyavazhi address Vaikundar merely as the incarnation of Vishnu. Likewise, most of the Nizhal Thangals were called *Narayana Swami Pathi* or *Narayana Swami Temple,* similar to Hindu Vaishnavism. Most of the followers also worship Hindu deities such as Kali, Hanuman and other folk deities in spite of the anti-polytheistic ideas based on Ayyavazhi scripture.

Some followers of Ayyavazhi include Vaikundar as part of the ten avatars of Vishnu as Kalki, while some denominations strongly advocate moksha, the personal liberation, though it is not stated directly in Akilam. Some even reject the Trinity conception in Ayyavazhi and believe Narayana to be the supreme universal power. The unique monotheistic belief which is the central theme of Akilam is completely unknown among most of the followers today. Deviating far away from the strict monotheistic teachings of Akilam, some thangals provides *panividais* for other lesser gods too.

The spread of Ayyavazhi among the common people was mainly due to the practice of Shamanism. Being similar to Hindus in almost all aspects Ayyavazhi followers are hard to be identified. The only sign to distinguish the practitioners of Ayyavazhi is the fact that they wore the Thirunamam (a sign on their forehead). The Nizhal Thangals are identified among the other temples by the fact that idols are replaced by mirrors in the Palliyarai. Only the recitations of a handful of scholars educated in the Ayyavazhi scriptures point out the real facts and concepts of Akilam and the philosophical and ideological deviation of Ayyavazhi from Hinduism. Not even the Payyans from the headquarters able to portray the Akilam-based ideology clearly. All these philosophical, ideological and religious variations in the society of Ayyavazhi make them hard to be identified and differentiated as a separate belief and instead taken as a Hindu sect.

Social Structure

Ayyavazhi worship was marked by its simplicity. The absence of idol worship and priestly mediation, and inclusion of alternate type of centres of worship, the Pathis and Nizhal Thangals, were other characteristics of Ayyavazhi worship. Rituals of Ayyavazhi are a reform or revolutionary activity, focusing upon social equality, deviating from Hinduism. The rituals are also characterised and bound by religious beliefs that give them an alternative spiritual meaning. Its scriptures cover basic elements and ideas throughout Hinduism. They refer to Shastras, Agamas, Vedas and Puranas. But address them all to be gone awry by the Advent of Vaikundar, from where Ayyavazhi scriptures forms negative ideas over all other traditions. Though Ayyavazhi shares many god-heads with Hinduism, it weaves unique ideology and power assumption for them. Ayyavazhi can be portrayed as a *Hindu renaissance*. Ayyavazhi is viewed as a reform movement too, as it brought many social changes there in the Tamil and keralite society during the 19th century.

The religious structure evolved in the path of Ayyavazhi scriptures and, as a result, it transfigured itself as an alternative religio-cultural system in the social category. The Ayyavazhis addressed their system as *"Path of God"* with the phrase *"Ayya Vazhi"*. On one hand, they believe that their tradition had come to replace all old traditions (religions), but on the other hand, they believe that Ayyavazhi is the synopsis of the world's religious knowledge. On one hand, they believe that Vaikundar unified all deities within him; on the other, as all the previous had gone awry by the advent of Vaikundar. Apart from this, Ayyavazhi has separate theology, mythology, holy places, worship centres, and ethics of its own.

Though many new papers, academic researchers and some of its followers consider it as a separate religion, many of the followers are even of the opinion that this is but a Hindu sect rather than an autonomous religion. They indulge in the mystic practices of possessions and divinations similar to the tribal religions of Tamil Nadu. Also, many of its core beliefs are similar to some Hindu sects such as Advaita and Smartism.

Regarding demographics, Ayyavazhi followers are highly concentrated in South India though found across India, comparatively in less numbers. In Kanyakumari and Tirunelveli districts of Tamil Nadu, it is very hard to find a village without a worship centre of Ayyavazhi. Apart from the listings from the religious headquarters (though it is evident that Ayyavazhi followers are spread across the India from university papers) there are no official figures for the number of followers of Ayyavazhi because they are considered Hindus in the census.

●●

8

Hinduism and Islam

Hinduism and Islam are two of the world's largest religions. Orthodox Hinduism is the socio-religious way of life of the Hindu people of the Indian subcontinent, their diaspora, and some other regions which had Hindu influence in the ancient and medieval times. Islam is a monotheistic religion in which the supreme deity is Allah and the last prophet being Muhammad ibn Abdullah. Orthodox Hinduism mostly shares common terms with the *dhârmic* religions, including Buddhism, Jainism and Sikhism. Islam shares common terms with the *Abrahamic* religions (those religions claiming prophet Abraham), i.e. Judaism and Christianity. The scriptures of Islam are the Qurân, which is primary book because it is considered the word of God, and the several Shia and Sunni Hadîths, which are secondary in authority, and deal with the life and acts of Islamic Prophet Muhammad. The scriptures of Orthodox Hinduism are the *Shrutis* (the four Vedas and their three tier of commentaries), which are considered authentic, most authoritative and Divine Revelation. Furthermore, Hinduism is also based on the *Smritis* (including the Ramâyana, the Bhagavad Gîtâ and the Purânas), which are considered by be of secondary authority and human creation.

Nevertheless, Hinduism and Islam do have many similarities, as well as differences, as discussed below.

Theology and Concept of God

Islam follows a strictly monotheistic faith. There is One God in Islam, and only One, and this principle of monotheism is called Tawhîd, and there can be no compromise on Tawhîd.

In contrast, Hinduism's belief in God can be variously categorized as monotheism, monism, henotheism or polytheism. To understand the concept of God in Hinduism, it is necessary to know that Orthodox Hinduism has six systems of philosophy, viz.:

1. Sânkhya
2. Yoga
3. Nyâya
4. Vaishechika
5. Pûrva Mîmânsâ
6. Vedânta

The last one, *Vedânta* is further split into sub-branches, of which the most popular is Advaita Vedanta propounded by Sage Adi Shankara in the Early-Medieval India. Each philosophical system and sub-system has its own distinct concept of God. This leads to a variety of concepts of God in Hinduism.

Hindu and Islamic Social Systems

During the Muslim conquests, Islam gained many converts on the Indian sub-continent primarily from Hinduism or Buddhism; the two dominant local religions. Inter-marriage and immigration from other Islamic lands have helped in instilling this idea in the people of greater India. Many of the new Muslim rulers looked down upon the idea Hinduism as having Iconodulistic religious practices and were to various degrees iconoclastic. Prominent examples of these are Mahmud of Ghazni and the Mughal emperor Aurangzeb on either end of the timeline for Islamic rulers. In addition, Muslims in India also developed a caste system that divided the Foreign-descended "Ashraf" Muslims and the "Ajlaf" converts, with the "Arzal" untouchables at the lowest rung The term "Arzal" stands for "degraded" and the Arzal castes are further subdivided into Bhanar, Halalkhor, Hijra, Kasbi, Lalbegi, Maugta, Mehtar etc.

In contrast there were also many Muslim kings who wished to live in harmony with the Hindus for interests of the Islamic empire. Akbar and Ibrahim Adil Shah II of Bijapur Adil Shah dynasty are notable examples. Akbar's court was home to intellectuals and saints both Hindu and Muslim, among them the great musician Tansen who converted to Islam, and he (Akbar) even went so far as to try and create a new religion (the *din ilahi*) to create a rapprochement of both creeds for creating a stable empire. 'Todar Mal' who was highly regarded Hindu minister (vizir) of Akbar. Shaikh Ahmad Sirhindi, does not credit Akbar for saving the temple instead gives credit to the "infidels" for building their own temple by demolishing the mosque. Frustration in the sub-continent grew as a result of this leading to the gradual decline of the Muslim mughal empire replaced by the Sikhs, Marathas, the Vijayanagara kingdom and later the British.

In the last 60 years after Indian independence, the Muslims have had to live without the preferential treatment that was offered to them during the days of the sultanates and even during the British Raj's positive discrimination against the Muslims as a part of the divide and rule policy. The communal tensions between the Hindus and the Muslims have erupted many a times during this period. Notable incidents of this phenomenon include the demolition of the Babri Masjid and the Gujrat Riots of 2002.

Kabir wrote poetry and preached to the people, advocating a blend of philosophy and spiritual practices. Sufism as a whole is primarily concerned with direct personal experience, and as such may be compared to various esoteric forms of mysticism such as Bhakti form of Hinduism,

Hesychasm, Zen Buddhism, Kabbalah, Gnosticism and Christian mysticism.

The synergy between certain Sufis and Bhaktas in many regions of India led to Muslim and Hindu laity worshiping together at a *mazar* (Sufi shrine). However, Muslim and Sikh conflict erupted in India fueled by a history of regional politics, nationalism, continued conflict and the partition movements during independence from the British Raj in 1947.

However the main proponents of this new synergy included Saints like Rumi, Shirdi Sai Baba and Kabir today it can be said it exits in the form of the Qawwali

Qawwali is a form of devotional Sufi music common in Afghanistan, India, Iran, Pakistan, Tajikistan and Turkey. It is known for its secular strains. Some of its modern-day masters have included Nusrat Fateh Ali Khan and the Sabri Brothers. Amir Khusro, a disciple of Nizamuddin Auliya, of the Chishti Order, is credited with inventing Qawwali in the 14th century.

Mughal art forms, especially miniatures and even certain niches of Urdu poetry, were quick to absorb classic Hindu motifs, like the love story of Krishna and Radha. Hindustani classical music is a complex and sonorous blend of Vedic notions of sound, raga and tala and absorbed a many instruments of either Middle Eastern origin or Indian-Muslim invention such as the ghazal

INDIAN MUSLIM NATIONALISM

Indian Muslim nationalism refers to the political and cultural expression of nationalism, founded upon the religious tenets and identity of Islam, of the Muslims of the Indian subcontinent.

Rising from the first days of Islamic empires in the Indian Subcontinent, this article endeavors to explore and trace Muslim nationalism through medieval India and into the events of the 20th and early 21st century, within the modern nations of India, Pakistan and Bangladesh.

The Indian subcontinent's Muslim population numbers around 450 million.

Historical Foundations

The historical foundations of Muslim nationalist thinking derives inspiration from the years of the Delhi Sultanate and the Mughal Empire in northern India. Those were the years when Muslim kingdoms were among powerful military groups in India, and an Islamic society that descended from the Middle East, Persia and the Central Asia and from areas which became modern day Afghanistan spread the religion amongst Indians.

Ideological Foundations

The first Muslim uprising began with the Muslim Sultan- The Tiger of Mysore, Tipu Sultan in 1766, whose famous armed resistance of Mysore, using bamboo Rockets, was the catalyst for the demise of the British from India and earned him the title *Father of the Indian Rocket*. In fact, the battle against the British in Mysore, 1766 seems to be at the pinnacle of unrest in the colonised lands of all the European colonisers.

The first organized expressions began with Muslim scholars and reformers like Syed Ahmed Khan, Syed Ameer Ali and the Aga Khan who had an influential major hand in the Anti-British Resistance movements during the "Indian Revolution".

Expression of Muslim separatism and nationhood emerged from modern Islam's pre-eminent poet and philosopher, Sir Allama Muhammad Iqbal and political activists like Choudhary Rahmat Ali.

In Politics

Some prominent Muslims politically sought a base for themselves, separate from Hindus and other Indian nationalists, who espoused the Indian National Congress. Muslim scholars, religious leaders and politicians founded the All India Muslim League in 1906.

Muslims comprised 25% to 30% of (pre-partition) India's collective population. Some Muslim leaders felt that their cultural and economic contributions to India's heritage and life merited a significant role for Muslims in a future independent India's governance and politics.

But after the rise of Hindu nationalism, a movement led by Allama Iqbal and ultimately Muhammad Ali Jinnah, who originally fought for Muslim rights within India, later felt a separate homeland must be obtained for India's Muslims in order to achieve prosperity. They espoused the *Two-Nation Theory*, that India was in fact home to the Muslim and Hindu nations, who were distinct in every way.

Another section of Muslim society, led by Khan Abdul Ghaffar Khan, Dr. Mukhtar Ahmed Ansari and Maulana Azad felt that participation in the Indian Independence Movement and the Indian National Congress was a patriotic duty of all Muslims.

Religious leaders like Maulana Maudoodi did not prefer a single nation over two or vice versa, but sought to propagate the religion and create an Islamic republic in India.

Partition of India

Muhammad Ali Jinnah led the Muslim League's call for Pakistan. Some historians have come to believe that Jinnah did not actually want the partition of the Indian subcontinent, but used it as a potent weapon to secure greater political power for Indian Muslims. However, as time went on, communal tensions rose and so partition won increasing support among many Muslims in Muslim-majority areas of the Indian subcontinent.

On August 14, 1947, Pakistan was created out of the Muslim majority provinces of British India, Sind, the west of Punjab, Baluchistan and the North West Frontier Province, and in formerly in the east with Bengal. Communal violence broke out and millions of people were forced to flee their homes and many lost their lives. Hindus and Sikhs fled from Pakistan to India and Muslims fled from India to Pakistan.

However, because Muslim communities existed throughout the Indian subcontinent, partition actually left tens of millions of Muslims within the boundaries of the secular Indian state. Currently, approximately 13.4% of the population of India is Muslim.

The Muslim League idea of a Muslim Nationalism encompassing all of the Muslims of the Indian subcontinent seemed to lose out to ethnic nationalism in 1971, when East Pakistan, a Bengali dominated province, fought with support and the subsequent war with India helped them win their independence from Pakistan, and became the independent country of Bangladesh.

Pakistani Nationalism

Pakistan has more than 160 million Muslims. It is also the fastest growing population among the 10 most populated countries with greater than 2% population growth each year and is expected to become the most populated Muslim country in the world within 10 years.

Pakistani Nationalism has varied from the original idea in the early 1900s to the status quo, usually varying by socio-economic class and political ideology. Originally, it was a concept defined by the Western regions of British India and their religious affiliation of Islam. During the late years of

British rule and leading up to Partition, it had three distinct supporters:

1) Realists, such as Mohammad Ali Jinnah, who driven by political inflexibility demonstrated by the Congress Party, feared a systematic disenfranchisement of Muslims (and not necessarily Islam). This also included many members of the Parsi, and Nizari Ismaili communities.

2) Technocratic Elitists, such as the majority of Aligarh students who were driven by a fear of being engulfed in "false secularism" that would assimilate their beliefs and values into a common system that defied Islamic tenets while hoping to create a state where their higher education and wealth would keep them in power over the other Muslims of India.

3) Idealists, primarily lower Orthodoxy (Barelvi), that feared the dominative power of the upper Orthodoxy (Deoband) and saw Pakistan as a safe haven to prevent their domination by State-controlled propaganda. Although many upper Orthodoxy also supported the state in the interests of an Islamic Republic.

Through the years this situation varied, however all parties secular and religious see Pakistan as a member of the global community, and Pakistanis as global citizens hailing from many different backgrounds including (and with great pride): Iran, Arabia, and India. Their primary purpose it to represent themselves as honest hard-working Muslims and provide safe haven to the millions of Muslim refugees from around the world such as Afghanistan and Burma.

In more recent times and through the efforts of Pervez Musharraf, there has been a distinctive U-turn on this policy, as the West sees this "Muslim melting pot" a manifest of Muslim Transnationalism which secular fundamentalists in the West see as a threat to Western society. Unfortunately, this effort has created strong rifts in Pakistani society with Westernized, classes benefitting from government patronage and support for their lifestyles have enjoyed the fruits of an economic boom while even the slightly religious classes of Pakistan have suffered from discriminatory treatment due to their unwillingness to change their lifestyles to European ones.

Many Pakistanis believe in the implementation of Shariah, in a way that respects their religion and does not compromise its ideals and tenets to appease outsiders. This includes controversial legislation such as Hudood, which even many strict Muslims realize, requires strong institutions to properly enforce. For the controversial nature of these ordinances, see the separate entry on them. There is a small smattering of secularists who, primarily educated in the West, believe in the separation of Church and State, and their power and influence is greater due to their knowledge of English and interest in politics.

Today Pakistan is a thriving nation-state but not without its fair share of problems. It is second only to Malaysia in terms of economic diversification, and is one of the "Next Eleven" nations that will drive the world economy, as determined by Goldman Sachs.

Bangladeshi Nationalism

Bangladesh is home to more than 135 million Muslims. It is the third-largest Muslim community in the world. Originally the Eastern wing of Pakistan, it gained independence in 1971 following a bloody civil war that claimed the lives of many people.

The founding of Bangladesh is open to controversy. While many Indian analysts see it as proof positive of the failure of the two-nation concept as purported by Mohammad

Ali Jinnah, its formation is more due to socio-economics and political feudalism than a strong desire by the members of the state to step away from the idea of a Muslim homeland.

After the founding of Pakistan, the dominant political parties within the Western block were controlled by Urdu-speaking Indian migrants (especially those from Aligarh), who were seen as the leaders of Muslims in British India and (right or wrong) the "champions" of Pakistan. Because of their fluency in the lingua franca of Muslim South Asia, Urdu, and desire to transplant the tried-and-true institutions of the old Indian state to newly-created Pakistan, Urdu became the National language. This caused great concern among native Western and Eastern Pakistanis, the majority of whom spoke languages such as Bengali, Punjabi, Kashmiri, Pashto, and Gujarati rather than Urdu. On the other hand, due to its neutrality, it was seen as the perfect language to build the nation-state upon.

Unfortunately, Urdu itself came under attack, to the chagrin of some prominent Bengalis who spoke it and believed in it as a means of bridging the many gaps throughout the newly-created Pakistan. Some Technocrats and Elitists saw Urdu as a means by which to retain power, keeping non-speakers out, alienating most Bengalis. This, along with the economic disparity between West and East Pakistan that saw massive transfers of capital from the East to the West, created a situation where Bengalis felt increasingly isolated and unable to participate in the new nation-state. Few West Pakistanis saw this and continued to participate in both sides of the country (many Memons and Gujaratis were living and building businesses in East Pakistan). This led to the creation of Bengali political parties that espoused greater regional autonomy and recognition of Bengali as a second National Language.

Following a stunning victory whereby Bengali parties captured the majority of the seats in the elections of 1970, the elite enclaves of Western Pakistani Muslims, primarily residing in Karachi and Lahore at that time, feared ethnic domination and sectarianism. With the rise of ethnic politics, it would be very easy for other ethnicities to feel threatened, and besides, they argued, it would be counter-intuitive to the idea of one Muslim state where ethnicity is irrelevant and greater importance should be placed on the common heritage of Islam.

The Western Pakistani response was bloodthirsty, killing hundreds and thousands or according to some millions of innocent Bengalis in an effort to suppress who they deemed were insurgents. In the end, Bangladesh was created and millions of residents of the former West and East wings were displaced. Most non-Bengalis, fearing persecution, attempted to flee to Western Pakistan. A significant number of Biharis, who identify with Pakistan, continue to live in Bangladesh with no status and no recognition from the Bangladeshi government, while a strong number of Bengalis continue to live in Pakistan and are mostly integrated into the fabric of a culturally diverse Pakistan.

Muslim Nationalism in India

According to official government statistics, India has 110 million Muslims spread across many states including Uttar Pradesh, Bihar, West Bengal, Assam, Kerala, Gujarat and Andhra Pradesh. It is the third-largest home to Muslims after Indonesia and Pakistan, and the second-largest home to Shia Muslims (after Iran).

Since partition, there has been a great deal of conflict within the various Muslim communities as to how to best function within the complex political and cultural mosaic that defines Indian politics in India today.

All in all, Muslim perseverance in sustaining their continued advancement along with Government efforts to focus on Pakistan as the primary problem for Indian Muslims in achieving true minority rights has created a sometimes extreme support for Indian nationalism, giving the Indian State much-needed credibility in projecting a strong secular image throughout the rest of the world.

The creation of Pakistan has created a deep identity crisis for Muslim Indian. Hindus in India bitterly resent the fact that their motherland was, allegedly, divided by Muslims to gain their own land. This bitterness more often turns against Indian Muslims. Thus Muslim Indians although patriotic, resent their patriotism being questioned. Recent terrorist attacks like Mumbai Bomb Blast, Varanasi Temple bombing, Delhi Bomb Blasts , Akshardham Temple attack place the Muslim Indian community in an awkward situation as the attacks occur due to some local support.

But in the recent past, many modern educated Muslims have come forward and denounced the brand of Islam taught in the madrasas, and reaffirmed their patriotism. Also, Muslims are present in all the major fields. The Indian film industry popularly known as Bollywood has many popular Muslim stars. The Indian cricket team, has its share of Muslim players who play with zeal and patriotism as any other players. The players have performed with distinction especially in matches against Pakistan.

The Jamiat Ulema-e-Hind, a leading Indian Islamic organization has propounded a theological basis for Indian Muslim's nationalistic philosophy. Their thesis is that Muslims and non-Muslims have entered upon a mutual contract in India since independence, to establish a secular state. The Constitution of India represents this contract. This is known in Urdu as a *mu'ahadah*. Accordingly as the Muslim community's elected representatives supported and swore allegiance to this *mu'ahadah* so the specific duty of Muslims is to keep loyalty to the Constitution. This *mu'ahadah* is similar to a previous similar contract signed between the Muslims and the Jews in Medina.

Given this situation, the intermediate economic state of the Muslims in India has created a transitory composition of its population. Tens of thousands of Bangladeshis migrate to India each year, and while India also bans immigration into India (owing to its own overpopulation), this has set the tone for relatively hostile relations between the two countries, and has a profound impact on Muslim Nationalism.

●●

9
Indian Religions and Philosophy

Indian religions are the related religious traditions that originated in the Indian subcontinent, namely Hinduism, Jainism, Buddhism, Sikhism and Ayyavazhi, inclusive of their sub-schools and various related traditions. They form a subgroup of the larger class of "Eastern religions". Indian religions have similarities in core beliefs, modes of worship, and associated practices, mainly due to their common history of origin and mutual influence.

The documented history of Indian religions begins with historical Vedic religion, the religious practices of the early Indo-Aryans, which were collected and later redacted into the *Samhitas*, four canonical collections of hymns or mantras composed in archaic Sanskrit. These texts are the central *shruti* (revealed) texts of Hinduism. The period of the composition, redaction and commentary of these texts is known as the Vedic period, which lasted from roughly 1500 to 500 BCE.

The late Vedic period (9th to 6th centuries BCE) marks the beginning of the Upanisadic or Vedantic period. This period heralded the beginning of much of what became classical Hinduism, with the composition of the Upanishads, later the Sanskrit epics, still later followed by the Puranas.

Jainism and Buddhism arose from the sramana culture. Buddhism was historically founded by Siddhartha Gautama, a Kshatriya prince-turned-ascetic, and was spread beyond

India through missionaries. It later experienced a decline in India, but survived in Nepal and Sri Lanka, and remains more widespread in Southeast and East Asia. Jainism was established by a lineage of 24 enlightened beings culminating with Parsva (9th century BCE) and Mahavira (6th century BCE).

Certain scholarship holds that the practices, emblems and architecture now commonly associated with the Hindu pantheon and Jainism may go back as far as Late Harappan times to the period 2000-1500 BCE.

Hinduism is divided into numerous denominations, primarily Shaivism, Shaktism, Vaishnavism, Smarta and much smaller groups like the conservative Shrauta. Hindu reform movements and Ayyavazhi are more recent. About 90% of Hindus reside in the Republic of India, accounting for 83% of its population.

Sikhism was founded in the 15th century on the teachings of Guru Nanak and the nine successive Sikh Gurus in Northern India. The vast majority of its adherents originate in the Punjab region.

Common Traits

Sometimes summarised as "Dharmic" religions or dharmic traditions, (though the 'subtler' meaning of *Dharma* or *dhamma* differs per religion); Hinduism, Buddhism, Jainism and Sikhism share certain key concepts, which are interpreted differently by different groups and individuals. Common traits can also be observed in both the ritual and the literary sphere. For example, the head-anointing ritual of *abhiseka* is of importance in three of these distinct traditions, excluding Sikhism. Other noteworthy rituals are the cremation of the dead, the wearing of vermilion on the head by married women, and various marital rituals. In literature, many classical narratives and purana have Hindu, Buddhist or Jain versions.

All four traditions have notions of *karma, dharma, samsara, moksha* and various *yogas*. Of course, these terms may be perceived differently by different religions. For instance, for a Hindu, *dharma* is his duty. For a Jain, *dharma* is righteousness, his conduct. For a Buddhist, *dharma* is usually taken to be the Buddha's teachings. Similarly, for a Hindu, yoga is the cessation of all thoughts/activities of the mind. For Jains yoga is sum total all physical, verbal and mental activities.

Rama is a heroic figure in all of these religions. In Hinduism he is the God-incarnate in the form of a princely king; in Buddhism, he is a Bodhisattva-incarnate; in Jainism, he is the perfect human being. Among the Buddhist Ramayanas are: *Vessantarajataka,* Reamker, Ramakien, Phra Lak Phra Lam, Hikayat Seri Rama etc. There also exists the *Khamti Ramayana* among the Khamti tribe of Asom wherein Rama is an avatar of a Bodhisattva who incarnates to punish the demon king Ravana (B.Datta 1993). The *Tai Ramayana* is another book retelling the divine story in Asom.

Prehistory

Evidence attesting to prehistoric religion in the Indian subcontinent derives from scattered Mesolithic rock paintings such as at Bhimbetka, depicting dances and rituals. Neolithic agriculturalists inhabiting the Indus River Valley buried their dead in a manner suggestive of spiritual practices that incorporated notions of an afterlife and belief in magic. Other South Asian Stone Age sites, such as the Bhimbetka rock shelters in central Madhya Pradesh and the Kupgal petroglyphs of eastern Karnataka, contain rock art portraying religious rites and evidence of possible ritualised music. The Harappan people of the Indus Valley Civilization, which lasted from 3300–1300 BCE (mature period, 2600-1900 BCE) and was centered around the Indus and Ghaggar-Hakra river valleys, may have worshiped an important mother goddess symbolising fertility, a concept that has recently been challenged.

Excavations of Indus Valley Civilization sites show small tablets with animals and altars, indicating rituals associated with animal sacrifice.

Vedic Tradition

Vedic Period

The Vedic Period is most significant for the composition of the four Vedas, Brahmanas and the older Upanishads (both presented as discussions on the rituals, mantras and concepts found in the four Vedas), which today are some of the most important canonical texts of Hinduism, and are the codification of much of what developed into the core beliefs of Hinduism.

The Vedas reflect the liturgy and ritual of Late Bronze Age to Early Iron Age Indo-Aryan speaking peoples in India. Religious practices were dominated by the Vedic priesthood administering domestic rituals/rites and solemn sacrifices. The Brahmanas, Aranyakas and some of the older Upanishads (such as BAU, ChU, JUB) are also placed in this period. Many elements of Vedic religion reach back to early Bronze Age Proto-Indo-Iranian times. The Vedic period is held to have ended around 500 BCE.

Specific rituals and sacrifices of the Vedic religion include:

- The *Soma* cult described in the Rigveda, descended from a common Indo-Iranian practice.
- Fire rituals, also a common Indo-Iranian practice :
  - o The *Agnihotra* or oblation to Agni.
  - o The *Agnistoma* or Soma sacrifice (including animal sacrifice) .
  - o The *Agnicayana,* the sophisticated ritual of piling the Uttara fire altar.
- The Darsapaurnamasa, the fortnightly New and Full Moon sacrifice

- The Caturmasya or seasonal sacrifices (every four months)
- a large number of sacrifices for special wishes (Kâmyecmi)
- The *Ashvamedha* or horse sacrifice.
- The *Purushamedha*, or sacrifice of a man, imitating that of the cosmic Purusha and Ashvamedha
- The rites referred to in the Atharvaveda are concerned with medicine and healing practices, as well as some charms and sorcery (white and black magic).
- The domestic (grihya) rituals deal with the rites of passage from conception to death and beyond.

Vedanta

The period of *Vedanta* (Sanskrit : end of Vedas), typically thought to have begun around 600 BCE, marked the end of the evolution of the main Vedic texts; it also accompanied the transformation of the semi-nomadic nature of the Indo-Aryan tribes to agriculture-based polities, as they increasingly formed permanent settlements in the Indo-Gangetic plain and other parts of Northern India. This period was foreshadowed by the Brahmanas that interpreted the four canonical Vedas in various fashions, which finally led to the Upanishads. While the ritualistic status of the four Vedas remained undiminished, the early Upanishads mainly relate to spiritual insights. At this time, the concepts of reincarnation, samsara, karma, and moksha began to be accepted in ancient India outside the sphere of the priestly establishment i.e. the Brahmana class. Some scholars think that these new concepts developed by aborigines outside the caste system, others detect Sramana or even Ksatriya influence. These concepts were eventually accepted by Brahmin orthodoxy, and were to form much of the core philosophies of the later epics and Hinduism, as well as, against a different philosophical and religious background, in Buddhism and Jainism.

Astika and Nastika Categorization

Astika and *nastika* are sometimes used to categorise Indian religions. Those religions that believe that God is the central actor in this world are termed as *astika*. Those religions that do not believe that God is the prime mover and actor are classified as *nastika* religions. From this point of view the Vedic religion (and Hinduism) is an *astika* religion, whereas Buddhism and Jainism are *nastika* religions.

Another definition of the terms *astika* and *nastika*, followed by Adi Shankara, classifies religions and persons as *astika* and *nastika* according to whether they accept the authority of the main Hindu texts, the Vedas, as supreme revealed scriptures, or not. By this definition, Nyaya, Vaisheshika, Samkhya, Yoga, Purva Mimamsa and Vedanta are classified as *astika* schools, while Charvaka is classified as a *nastika* school. By this definition, both Buddhism and Jainism are classified as *nastika* religions since they do not accept the authority of the Vedas.

Shramana Tradition

Vedic Brahmanism of Iron Age India co-existed and closely interacted with the parallel non-Vedic shramana traditions. These were not direct outgrowths of Vedism, but separate movements that influenced it and were influenced by it. The shramanas were wandering ascetics. Buddhism and Jainism are a continuation of the Shramana tradition, and the early Upanishadic movement was influenced by it. The 24th Jain Tirthankar, Mahavira (599–527 BCE), stressed five vows, including *ahimsa* (non-violence), *satya* (truthfulness), *asteya* (non-stealing) and *aparigraha* (non-attachment).

The historical Gautama Buddha, who was a Buddha, was born into the Shakya clan of Angirasa and Gautama

Rishi lineage, just before the kingdom of Magadha (which lasted from 546–324 BCE) rose to power. His family was native to Kapilavastu and Lumbini, in what is now southern Nepal.

The Ajivikas and Samkhyas, both of which did not survive, also belonged to the sramana tradition.

Rise and Spread of Jainism and Buddhism

Both Jainism and Buddhism spread throughout India during the period of the Magadha empire. Scholars Jeffrey Brodd and Gregory Sobolewski write that *"Jainism shares many of the basic doctrines of Hinduism and Buddhism."* Jainism has declined since the 12th century in many regions, but continues to be an influential religion in Gujarat, Rajasthan, Madhya Pradesh, Maharashtra and Karnataka.

Buddhism in India spread during the reign of Asoka the Great of the Mauryan Empire, who patronised Buddhist teachings and unified the Indian subcontinent in the 3rd century BCE. He sent missionaries abroad, allowing Buddhism to spread across Asia. Indian Buddhism started declining following the rise of Puranic Hinduism during the Gupta dynasty, but continued to have a significant presence in some regions of India until the 12th century. Scholar James Bird writes, *"But when primitive Buddhism originated from Hindu schools of philosophy, it differed as widely from that of later times, as did the Brahmanism of the Vedas from that of the Puranas and Tantras."*

Period after 200 BCE

After 200 CE several schools of thought were formally codified in Indian philosophy, including Samkhya, Yoga, Nyaya, Vaisheshika, Purva-Mimamsa and Vedanta. Hinduism, otherwise a highly polytheistic, pantheistic or monotheistic religion, also tolerated atheistic schools. The thoroughly materialistic and anti-religious philosophical Cârvâka school that originated around the 6th century BCE is the most explicitly atheistic school of Indian philosophy. Cârvâka is classified as a *nastika* ("heterodox") system; it is not included among the six schools of Hinduism generally regarded as orthodox. It is noteworthy as evidence of a materialistic movement within Hinduism. Our understanding of Cârvâka philosophy is fragmentary, based largely on criticism of the ideas by other schools, and it is no longer a living tradition. Other Indian philosophies generally regarded as atheistic include Classical Samkhya and Purva Mimamsa.

Between 400 CE and 1000 CE Hinduism expanded as the decline of Buddhism in India continued. Buddhism subsequently became effectively extinct in India but survived in Nepal and Sri Lanka.

There were several Buddhistic kings who worshiped Vishnu, such as the Gupta, Pala, Malla, Somavanshi, and Sattvahana. Buddhism survived followed by Hindus. *National Geographic* edition reads, *"The flow between faiths was such that for hundreds of years, almost all Buddhist temples, including the ones at Ajanta, were built under the rule and patronage of Hindu kings."*

POST-VEDIC DEVELOPMENT OF HINDUISM

The end of the Vedantic period around the 2nd century AD spawned a number of branches that furthered Vedantic philosophy, and which ended up being seminaries in their own right. The output generated by these specialized tributaries was automatically considered a part of the Hindu or even Indian philosophy. Prominent amongst these developers were Yoga, Dvaita, Advaita and the medieval Bhakti movement. The modern day popular movements were the ones founded by Swami Vivekananda, Sri Aurobindo, Raja Ram Mohan Roy among others.

In the latter Vedantic period, several texts were also composed as summaries/attachments to the Upanishads. These texts collectively called as Puranas allowed for a divine and mythical interpretation of the world, not unlike the ancient Hellenic or Roman religions. Legends and epics with a multitude of gods and goddesses with human-like characteristics were composed. Two of Hinduism's most revered *epics,* the Mahabharata and Ramayana were compositions of this period. Devotion to particular deities was reflected from the composition of texts composed to their worship. For example the *Ganapati Purana* was written for devotion to Ganapati (or Ganesh). Popular deities of this era were Shiva, Vishnu, Durga, Surya, Skanda, and Ganesh (including the forms/incarnations of these deities.)

Bhakti Movement

The Bhakti Movement began with the emphasis on the worship of God, regardless of one's status - whether priestly or laypeople, men or women, higher social status or lower social status.

The movements were mainly centered around the forms of Vishnu (Rama and Krishna) and Shiva. There were however popular devotees of this era of Durga.

Vaishnavism

The most well-known devotees are the Alwars from southern India. The most popular Vaishnava teacher of the south was Ramanuja, while of the north it was Ramananda.

Several important icons were women. For example, within the Mahanubhava sect, the women outnumbered the men, and administration was many times composed mainly of women. Mirabai is the most popular female saint in India.

Sri Vallabha Acharya (1479 - 1531) is a very important figure from this era. He founded the Shuddha Advaita (*Pure Non-dualism*) school of Vedanta thought.

Shaivism

The most well-known devotees are the Nayanars from southern India. The most popular Shaiva teacher of the south was Basava, while of the north it was Gorakhnath.

Female saints include figures like Akkamadevi, Lalleshvari and Molla.

Recent Groups

The modern era has given rise to dozens of Hindu saints with international influence. For example, Brahma Baba established the Brahma Kumaris, one of the largest new Hindu religious movements teaches the discipline of Raja Yoga to millions. Representing traditional Gaudiya Vaishnavism, Prabhupada founded the Hare Krishna movement, also international with many followers. In late 18th century India, Swaminarayan founded the Swaminarayan Sampraday. Anandamurti, founder of the Ananda Marga, has influenced many worldwide. Through all these new Hindu denominations traveling international, many Hindu practices such as yoga, meditation, mantra, divination, vegetarianism have become absorbed by new coverts and others influenced.

Sikhism

Sikhism originated in fifteenth century Northern India with the teachings of Nanak and nine successive gurus. The principal belief in Sikhism is faith in *Vâhigurû*— represented by the sacred symbol of *çk ôaEkâr* [meaning one god]. Sikhism's traditions and teachings are distinctly associated with the history, society and culture of the Punjab. Adherents of Sikhism are known as Sikhs (*students* or *disciples*) and number over 23 million across the world.

Although it began as a relatively neutral faith system that proposed to include the best practices of Hinduism and

Islam, over time its Gurus led followers in various rebellions and battles against the Islamic Mughal rulers of the time, most notably against Aurangzeb.

Status in the Republic of India

In a judicial reminder, the Indian Supreme Court observed Sikhism and Jainism to be sub-sects or *special* faiths within the larger Hindu fold, and that Jainism is a denomination within the Hindu fold. Although the government of British India counted Jains in India as a major religious community right from the first Census conducted in 1873, after independence in 1947 Sikhs and Jains were not treated as national minorities. In 2005 the Supreme Court of India declined to issue a writ of Mandamus granting Jains the status of a religious minority throughout India. The Court however left it to the respective states to decide on the minority status of Jain religion.

However, some individual states have over the past few decades differed on whether Jains, Buddhists and Sikhs are religious minorities or not, by either pronouncing judgments or passing legislation. One example is the judgment passed by the Supreme Court in 2006, in a case pertaining to the state of Uttar Pradesh, which declared Jainism to be undisputably distinct from Hinduism, but mentioned that, "The question as to whether the Jains are part of the Hindu religion is open to debate. However, the Supreme Court also noted various court cases that have held Jainism to be a distinct religion.

Another example is the Gujarat Freedom of Religion Bill, that is an amendment to a legislation that sought to define Jains and Buddhists as denominations within Hinduism. Ultimately on July 31, 2007, finding it not in conformity with the concept of freedom of religion as embodied in Article 25 (1) of the Constitution, Governor Naval Kishore Sharma returned back the Gujarat Freedom of Religion (Amendment) Bill, 2006 citing the widespread protests by the Jains as well as Supreme Court's extrajudicial observation that Jainism is a "special religion formed on the basis of quintessence of Hindu religion by the Supreme Court"

INDIAN PHILOSOPHY

The term Indian philosophy, may refer to any of several traditions of philosophical thought that originated in the Indian subcontinent, including Hindu philosophy, Buddhist philosophy, and Jain philosophy. Having the same or rather intertwined origins, all of these philosophies have a common underlying theme of Dharma, and similarly attempt to explain the attainment of emancipation. They have been formalized and promulgated chiefly between 1,000 BC to a few centuries A.D, with residual commentaries and reformations continuing up to as late as the 20th century by Aurobindo and ISKCON among others, who provided stylized interpretations.

The characteristic of these schools is that they may belong to one "masthead" and disagree with each other, or be in agreement while professing allegiance to different banners. An example of the latter is the non-Vedic Jain and the Vedic Samkhya schools, both of which have similar ideas on pluralism; an example of the former would be the Dvaita and the Advaita schools, both of whom are Vedic. However, every school has subtle differences.

Competition between the various schools was intense during their formative years, especially between 800 BC to 200 AD. Some like the Jain, Buddhist, Shaiva and Advaita schools survived, while others like Samkhya and Ajivika did not.

The Sanskrit term for "philosopher" is *dârúanika,* one who is familiar with the systems of philosophy, or *darœanas*.

Common Themes

Indian thinkers viewed philosophy as a practical necessity that needed to be cultivated in order to understand how life can best be led. It became a custom for Indian writers to explain at the beginning of philosophical works how it serves human ends (purucârtha). They centered philosophy on an assumption that there is a unitary underlying order, which is all pervasive and omniscient. The efforts by various schools were concentrated on explaining this order. All major phenomena like those observed in nature, fate, occurrences, etc. were outcomes of this order.

The earliest mention of this appears in the Rig Veda, which speaks of the Brahman, or the universally transcendent and "ethereal" building block of all the world. It is described as dimensionless, timeless and beyond reach of the known frontiers of happiness and knowledge.

The idea of [ta, translated as "righteousness" or "the cosmic and social order" by Gavin Flood, also plays an important role.

Periods

pre-1500 BC - the *Vedas* and *Upanishads*

pre-500 BC - the Jaina, the Buddha, the *Bhagavad Gita,* the *Manu Smriti*

pre-300 BC - the rise of the orthodox Darshanas

200 AD - Nagarjuna and the rise of Mahayana Buddhism

600 AD - Shankaracharya and the rise of Vedanta

post-900 AD - rise of other Vedantic schools: Visishtadvaita, Dvaita, etc.

Schools

Classical Indian philosophy can be roughly categorised into "orthodox" (astika) schools of Hindu philosophy, and "heterodox" (nâstika) schools that do not accept the authorities of the Vedas.

Orthodox Schools (Astika)

Many Hindu intellectual traditions were codified during the medieval period of Brahmanic-Sanskritic scholasticism into a standard list of six orthodox (astika) schools (darshanas), the "Six Philosophies" (*cad-darœana*), all of which cite Vedic authority as their source:

- Nyaya, the school of logic
- Vaisheshika, the atomist school
- Samkhya, the enumeration school
- Yoga, the school of Patanjali (which assumes the metaphysics of Samkhya)
- Purva Mimamsa (or simply Mimamsa), the tradition of Vedic exegesis, with emphasis on Vedic ritual, and
- Vedanta (also called Uttara Mimamsa), the Upanishadic tradition, with emphasis on Vedic philosophy.

These are often coupled into three groups for both historical and conceptual reasons: Nyaya-Vaishesika, Samkhya-Yoga, and Mimamsa-Vedanta.

The six systems mentioned here are not the only orthodox systems, they are the chief ones, and there are other orthodox schools such as the "Grammarian" school.

The Vedanta school is further divided into six sub-schools: Advaita (monism/nondualism), Visishtadvaita (monism of the qualified whole), Dvaita (dualism), Dvaitadvaita (dualism-nondualism), Suddhadvaita, and Achintya Bheda Abheda schools.

Heterodox Schools (Nastika)

Schools that do not accept the authority of the Vedas are defined by Brahmins to be unorthodox (nastika) systems.

Jain Philosophy

Jainism came into formal being after Mahavira synthesized philosophies and promulgations, during the period around 550 BC, in the region that is present day Bihar in northern India. This period marked an ideological renaissance, in which the patriarchal Vedic dominance was challenged by various groups. Buddhism also arose during this period.

Jains however believe that the Jaina philosophy was in fact revived by Mahavira, whom they consider as the 24th and final Jain Tirthankars (enlightened seers), a line that stretches to time immemorial. The 23rd seer, Parsva may be dated to around 900 B.C.

Jainism may not be a part of the Vedic Religion (Hinduism), , even as there is constitutional ambiguity over its status. Jain tirthankars find exclusive mention in the Vedas and the Hindu epics. During the Vedantic age, India had two broad philosophical streams of thought: The Shramana philosophical schools, represented by Buddhism Jainism, and the long defunct Samkhya and Ajinkya on one hand, and the Brahmana/Vedantic/Puranic schools represented by Vedanta, Vaishnava and other movements on the other. Both streams are known to have have mutually influenced each other.

The Hindu scholar, Lokmanya Tilak credited Jainism with influencing Hinduism in the area of the cessation of animal sacrifice in Vedic rituals. Bal Gangadhar Tilak has described Jainism as the originator of Ahimsa and wrote in a letter printed in Bombay Samachar, Mumbai:10 Dec, 1904: "In ancient times, innumerable animals were butchered in sacrifices. Evidence in support of this is found in various poetic compositions such as the Meghaduta. But the credit for the disappearance of this terrible massacre from the Brahminical religion goes to Jainism."

Swami Vivekananda also credited Jainsim as one of the influencing forces behind the Indian culture.

A *Jain* is a follower of *Jinas*, spiritual 'victors' (*Jina* is Sanskrit for 'victor'), human beings who have rediscovered the *dharma*, become fully liberated and taught the spiritual path for the benefit of beings. Jains follow the teachings of 24 special Jinas who are known as *Tirthankars* ('ford-builders'). The 24th and most recent *Tirthankar*, Lord Mahavira, lived in c.6th century BC, which was a period of cultural revolution all over the world. Socrates was born in Greece, Zoroaster in Persia, Lao Tse and Confucious in China and Mahavira and Buddha in India. The 23rd Thirthankar of Jains, Lord Parsvanatha is recognised now as a historical person, lived during 872 to 772 B.C.. . Jaina tradition is unanimous in making Rishabha, as the First Tirthankar.

One of the main characteristics of Jain belief is the emphasis on the immediate consequences of one's physical and mental behavior. Because Jains believe that everything is in some sense alive with many living beings possessing a soul, great care and awareness is required in going about one's business in the world. Jainism is a religious tradition in which all life is considered to be worthy of respect and Jain teaching emphasises this equality of all life advocating the non-harming of even the smallest creatures.

Non-violence (Ahimsa) is the basis of right View, the condition of right Knowledge and the kernel of right Conduct in Jainism.

Jainism encourages spiritual independence (in the sense of relying on and cultivating one's own personal wisdom) and self-control which is considered vital for one's spiritual development. The goal, as with other Indian religions, is *moksha* which in Jainism is realization of the soul's true nature, a condition of omniscience (Kevala Jnana). Anekantavada is one of the principles of Jainism positing that reality is perceived differently from different points of view, and that no single point of view is completely true. Jain doctrine states that only Kevalis, those who have infinite knowledge, can know the true answer, and that all others would only know a part of the answer. Anekantavada is related to the Western philosophical doctrine of Subjectivism.

Buddhist Philosophy

Buddhist philosophy is a system of beliefs based on the teachings of Siddhartha Gautama, an Indian prince later known as the Buddha.

From its inception, Buddhism has had a strong philosophical component. Buddhism is founded on the rejection of certain orthodox Hindu philosophical concepts. The Buddha criticized all concepts of metaphysical being and non-being as misleading views caused by reification, and this critique is inextricable from the founding of Buddhism.

Buddhism shares many philosophical views with other Indian systems, such as belief in karma, a cause-and-effect relationship between all that has been done and all that will be done. Events that occur are held to be the direct result of previous events. However, a major difference is the Buddhist rejection of a permanent, self-existent soul (atman). This view is a central one in Hindu thought but is rejected by all Buddhists.

Cârvâka

Cârvâka is characterized as a materialistic and atheistic school of thought. While this branch of Indian philosophy is not considered to be part of the six orthodox schools of Hinduism, it is noteworthy as evidence of a materialistic movement within Hinduism.

Modern Philosophy

Modern Indian philosophy was developed during British period (1750- 1947). The philosophers in this era gave contemporary meaning to traditional philosophy. Swami Vivekananda, Rabindranath Tagore, Sri Aurobindo, Anandkumar Swami, Ramana Maharshi and Sarvepalli Radhakrishnan interpreted traditional Indian philosophy in terms of contemporary significance. Osho and J. Krishnamurti developed their own schools of thought.

Political Philosophy

The Arthashastra, attributed to the Mauryan minister Chanakya, is one of the early Indian texts devoted to political philosophy. It is dated to 4th century BCE and discusses ideas of statecraft and economic policy.

The political philosophy most closely associated with India is the one of ahimsa (non-violence) and Satyagraha, popularized by Mahatma Gandhi during the Indian struggle for independence. It was influenced by the Indian Dharmic philosophy (particularly the Bhagvata Gita) and Jesus Christ, as well as, secular writings of authors such as Leo Tolstoy, Henry David Thoreau and John Ruskin. In turn it influenced the later movements for independence and civil rights, especially those led by Nelson Mandela and Martin Luther King, Jr.

●●

10

Hindu Cuisine and Costumes

The cuisine of India is characterized by sophisticated and subtle use of various spices, herbs and other vegetables grown in India and also for the widespread practice of vegetarianism across many sections of its society. Each family of Indian cuisine is characterized by a wide assortment of dishes and cooking techniques. As a consequence, it varies from region to region, reflecting the varied demographics of the ethnically diverse Indian subcontinent.

India's religious beliefs and culture have played an influential role in the evolution of its cuisine. However, India's cuisine also evolved with the subcontinent's cross-cultural interactions with the neighboring Middle East and Central Asia as well as the Mediterranean, making it a unique blend of various cuisines from across Asia. The spice trade between India and Europe is often cited as the main catalyst for Europe's *Age of Discovery*. The colonial period introduced European cooking styles to India adding to the flexibility and diversity of Indian cuisine. Indian cuisine has had a remarkable influence on cuisines across the world, especially those from Southeast Asia. In particular, curry, which originated in India, is used to flavor food across Asia.

History and Influences

As a land that has experienced extensive immigration and intermingling through many millennia, India's cuisine has benefited from numerous food influences. The diverse climate in the region, ranging from deep tropical to alpine, has also helped considerably broaden the set of ingredients readily available to the many schools of cookery in India. In many cases, food has become a marker of religious and social identity, with varying taboos and preferences (for instance, a segment of the Jain population will not consume any roots or subterranean vegetables). One strong influence over Indian foods is the longstanding vegetarianism within sections of India's Hindu, Buddhist and Jain communities. People who follow a strict vegetarian diet make up 20–42% of the population in India, while less than 30% are regular meat-eaters.

Around 7,000 BC, sesame, eggplant, and humped cattle had been domesticated in the Indus Valley. By 3000 BC, turmeric, cardamom, black pepper and mustard were harvested in India. Many recipes first emerged during the initial Vedic period, when India was still heavily forested and agriculture was complemented with game hunting and forest produce. In Vedic times, a normal diet consisted of fruit, vegetables, meat, grain, dairy products and honey. Over time, some segments of the population embraced vegetarianism, due to ancient Hindu philosophy of *ahimsa*. This practice gained more popularity due to cooperative climate where variety of fruits, vegetables, and grains could easily be grown throughout the year. Buddhism, among several other beliefs and practices borrowed vegetarianism from Hinduism to embrace Ahimsa. A food classification system that categorised any item as saatvic, raajsic or taamsic developed in Ayurveda. Each was deemed to have a powerful effect on the body and the mind

Later, invasions from Central Asia, Arabia, the Mughal empire, and Persia, and others had a deep and fundamental effect on Indian cooking. Influence from traders such as the Arab and Portuguese diversified subcontinental tastes and meals. As with other cuisines, Indian cuisine has absorbed New World vegetables such as tomato, chilli, and potato, as staples. These are actually relatively recent additions.

Islamic rule introduced rich gravies, pilafs and non-vegetarian fare such as kebabs, resulting in Mughlai cuisine (Mughal in origin), as well as such fruits as apricots, melons, peaches, and plums. The Mughals were great patrons of cooking. Lavish dishes were prepared during the reigns of Jahangir and Shah Jahan. The Nizams of Hyderabad state meanwhile developed and perfected their own style of cooking with the most notable dish being the Biryani.

During this period the Portuguese and British introduced foods from the New World such as potatoes, tomatoes, squash, and chilies as well as cooking techniques like baking.

Elements

The staples of Indian cuisine are rice, *atta* (whole wheat flour), and a variety of pulses, the most important of which are *masoor* (most often red lentil), *chana* (bengal gram), *toor* (pigeon pea or yellow gram), *urad* (black gram) and *mung* (green gram). *Pulses* may be used whole, dehusked, for example dhuli moong or dhuli urad, or split. Pulses are used extensively in the form of dal (split). Some of the pulses like *chana* and "Mung" are also processed into flour (*besan*).

Most Indian curries are cooked in vegetable oil. In North and West India, groundnut oil has traditionally been most popular for cooking, while in Eastern India, mustard oil is more commonly used. In South India, coconut oil and Gingelly Oil is common. In recent decades, sunflower oil and soybean oil have gained popularity all over India. Hydrogenated vegetable oil, known as Vanaspati ghee, is also a popular cooking medium that replaces Desi ghee, clarified butter (the milk solids have been removed).

The most important/frequently used spices in Indian cuisine are chilli pepper, black mustard seed (*rai*), cumin (jeera), turmeric (haldi, manjal), fenugreek (methi), asafoetida (*hing, perungayam*), ginger (adrak, inji), coriander (dhania), and garlic (lassan, poondu). Popular spice mixes are garam masala which is usually a powder of five or more dried spices, commonly including cardamom, cinnamon, and clove. Each region, and sometimes each individual chef, has a distinctive blend of Garam Masala. Goda Masala is a popular spice mix in Maharashtra. Some leaves are commonly used like *tejpat* (cassia leaf), coriander leaf, fenugreek leaf and mint leaf. The common use of curry leaves is typical of all South Indian cuisine. In sweet dishes, cardamom, nutmeg, saffron, and rose petal essence are used.

The term "curry" is usually understood to mean "gravy" in India, rather than "spices."

Geographical Varieties

Northern

North Indian cuisine is distinguished by the proportionally high use of dairy products; milk, paneer, ghee (clarified butter), and yoghurt (yogurt, yoghourt) are all common ingredients. Gravies are typically dairy-based. Other common ingredients include chilies, saffron, and nuts.

North Indian cooking features the use of the "tawa" (griddle) for baking flat breads like roti and paratha, and "tandoor" (a large and cylindrical charcoal-fired oven) for baking breads such as naan, and kulcha; main courses like tandoori chicken also cook in the tandoor. Other breads like puri and bhatoora, which are deep fried in oil, are also common. Goat and lamb meats are favored ingredients of many northern Indian recipes.

The samosa is a popular North Indian snack, and now commonly found in other parts of India, Central Asia, North America, Britain, Africa and the Middle East. A common variety is filled with boiled, fried, or mashed potato. Other fillings include minced meat, cheese (*paneer*), mushroom (*khumbi*), and chick pea.

The staple food of most of North India is a variety of lentils, vegetables, and roti (wheat based bread). The varieties used and the method of preparation can vary from place to place. Popular snacks, side-dishes and drinks include mirchi bada, buknu, bhujiya, chaat, kachori, imarti, several types of pickles (known as achar), murabba, sharbat, aam panna and aam papad. Popular sweets are known as *mithai* (means sweetmeat in Hindi), such as gulab jamun, jalebi, peda, petha, rewadi, gajak, bal mithai, singori, kulfi, falooda, khaja, ras malai, gulkand, and several varieties of laddu, barfi and halwa.

Some common North Indian foods such as the various kebabs and most of the meat dishes originated with Muslims' incursions into the country. Considering their shared historic and cultural heritage, Pakistani cuisine and North Indian cuisine are very similar.

Eastern

East Indian cuisine is famous for its desserts, especially sweets such as rasagolla, chumchum, sandesh, rasabali, chhena poda, chhena gaja, chhena jalebi and kheeri. Many of the sweet dishes now popular in Northern India initially originated in the Bengal and Orissa regions. Apart from sweets, East India cuisine offers delights of posta (poppy seeds).

Traditional cuisines of Orissa, Bengal, and Assam are delicately spiced. General ingredients used in Oriya, Bengali, and Assamese curries are mustard seeds, cumin seeds, nigella, green chillies, cumin paste and the spice mix panch phoron or panch phutana. Mustard paste, curd, nuts, poppy seed paste and cashew paste are preferably cooked in mustard oil. Curries are classified into bata (paste), bhaja (fries), chochchoree (less spicy vapourized curries) and jhol (thin spicy curries).These are eaten with plain boiled rice or ghonto (spiced rice). Traditional breakfasts includes pantabhat or pakhaal, as well as cereals such as puffed rice or pressed rice, in milk, often with fruits. The cuisine of Bangladesh is very similar to eastern Indian cuisine, particularly that of West Bengal. Fish and shellfish are commonly consumed in the eastern part of India. The popular vegetable dishes of Orissa are Dalma and Santula. The most popular vegetable dish of Bengal is Sukto. Deep fried, shallow fried and mashed vegetables are also very popular. As in southern India, rice is the staple grain in Eastern India too. A regular meal consists of lentils, a primary non vegetarian side dish usually made of fish and a few other secondary side dishes made of vegetables.

Southern

South Indian cuisine is distinguished by a greater emphasis on rice as the staple grain, the ubiquity of sambar and rasam (also called *chaaru/saaru* and *rasam*), a variety of pickles, and the liberal use of coconut and particularly coconut oil and curry leaves. Curries called Kozhambu are also popular and are typically vegetable stews cooked with spices, tamarind and other ingredients. The dosa, poori, idli, vada, bonda and bajji are typical South Indian favorites. These are generally consumed as part of breakfast. Other popular dishes include Kesaribath, Upma/Uppittu, Bisibele Bath, Rice Bath, Tomato Bath, Pongal, Poori & Saagu, Pulao, Puliyogarai and Thengai Sadham. Hyderabadi biryani, a popular type of biryani, reflects the diversity of south Indian cuisine. South Indian cuisine obtains its distinct flavours by the use of tamarind, coconuts, lentils, rice and a variety of vegetables.Udupi cuisine is one of the popular cuisine of South India.

Andhra, Chettinad, Tamil, Hyderabadi, Mangalorean, and Kerala cuisines each have distinct tastes and methods of cooking . In fact each of the South Indian states has a different way of preparing sambar; a connoisseur of South Indian food will very easily tell the difference between sambar from Kerala, sambar from Tamil cuisine, Sambaru from Karnataka and *pappu chaaru* in Andhra cuisine.Some popular dishes include the Biriyani, Ghee Rice with meat curry, seafood (prawns, mussels, mackerel) and paper thin Pathiris from Malabar area.

Western

Western India has three major food groups: Gujarati, Maharashtrian and Goan. Maharashtrian cuisine has mainly two sections defined by the geographical sections. The coastal regions, geographically similar to Goa depend more on rice, coconut, and fish. The hilly regions of the Western Ghats and Deccan plateau regions use groundnut in place of coconut and depend more on jowar (sorghum) and bajra (millet) as staples. Saraswat cuisine forms an important part of coastal Konkani Indian cuisine. Gujarati cuisine is predominantly vegetarian. Many Gujarati dishes have a hint of sweetness due to use of sugar or brown sugar. Goan cuisine is influenced by the Portuguese colonization of Goa.

North Eastern

The food of the North East is very different from other parts of India. This area's cuisine is more influenced by its neighbours, namely Burma and the People's Republic of China. For example it uses less of the well known spices that are popular in other parts of India. Yak is a popular meat in this region of India.

Popularity and Influence Outside India

Indian cuisine is one of the most popular cuisines across the globe. The cuisine is popular not only among the large Indian diaspora but also among the mainstream population of North America and Europe. In 2003, there were as many as 10,000 restaurants serving Indian cuisine in England alone. A survey held in 2007 revealed that more than 1,200 Indian food products have been introduced in the United States since 2000. According to Britain's Food Standards Agency, the Indian food industry in the United Kingdom is worth £3.2

billion, accounts for two-thirds of all eating out and serves about 2.5 million British customers every week.

Apart from Europe and North America, Indian cuisine is popular in South East Asia too because of its strong historical influence on the region's local cuisines. Indian cuisine has had considerable influence on Malaysian cooking styles and also enjoys strong popularity in Singapore. Indian influence on Malay cuisine dates back to 19-century. Other cuisines which borrow Indian cooking styles include Vietnamese cuisine, Indonesian cuisine and Thai cuisine. The spread of vegetarianism in other parts of Asia is often credited to ancient Indian Buddhist practices. Indian cuisine is also fairly popular in the Arab world because of its similarity and influence on Arab cuisine.

The popularity of *curry*, which originated in India, across Asia has often led to the dish being labeled as the "pan-Asian" dish. *Curry's* international appeal has also been compared to that of pizza. Though the *tandoor* did not originate in India, Indian tandoori dishes, such as *chicken tikka* made with Indian ingredients, enjoy widespread popularity. Historically, Indian spices and herbs were one of the most sought after trade commodities. The spice trade between India and Europe led to the rise and dominance of Arab traders to such an extent that European explorers, such as Vasco da Gama and Christopher Columbus, set out to find new trade routes with India leading to the *Age of Discovery*.

Beverages

Tea is a staple beverage throughout India; the finest varieties are grown in Darjeeling and Assam. It is generally prepared as *masala chai*, wherein the tea leaves are boiled in a mix of water, spices such as cardamom, cloves, cinnamon, and ginger, and large quantities of milk to create a thick, sweet, milky concoction. Different varieties and flavors of tea are prepared to suit different tastes all over the country.

Another popular beverage, coffee, is largely served in South India. One of the finest varieties of *Coffea arabica* is grown around Mysore, Karnataka, and is marketed under the trade name "Mysore Nuggets". Indian filter coffee, or *kaapi,* is also especially popular in South India. Other beverages include *nimbu pani* (lemonade), *lassi, chaach, badam doodh* (almond milk with nuts and cardamom), *sharbat* and coconut water. In Southern India there is a beverage served cold known as Panner Soda or Gholi Soda which is a mixture of carbonated water, rose water, and sugar. Another beverage from the South is rose milk, which is served cold.

India also has many indigenous alcoholic beverages, including palm wine, fenny and Indian beer. There's also bhang, prepared using cannabis, and typically consumed, especially in North India, during Holi and Vaisakhi. However the practice of drinking a specific beverage with a meal, or wine and food matching, is not traditional or common in India.

Although the above listed beverages are popular, people often prefer to consume drinking water with their food, because drinking water is considered to not overshadow the taste of the food. In fact it is customary to offer drinking water to guests before serving any hot or cold drinks.

Etiquette

Several customs are associated with the manner of food consumption. Traditionally, meals are eaten while seated either on the floor or on very low stools or cushions. Food is most often eaten without cutlery, using instead the fingers of the right hand. However, these traditional ways of dining are being influenced by eating styles from other parts of the world.

Traditional serving styles vary from region to region in India. A universal aspect of presentation is the thali, a large plate with samplings of different regional dishes accompanied by raita, breads such as naan, puri, or roti, and rice. In South India, a cleaned banana leaf is often used as a hygienic, visually interesting and environmentally friendly, alternative to plates.

Amongst upper class North Indians, cutlery, which has been adopted since Roman influence in the 16th century, is now in common use; the Roman's exports of pepper lead to the introduction of cutlery in Asia. Amongst the middle class communities throughout India spoons and forks have been adopted. The roti (Indian bread) is folded into a spoon-like formation and the curry is picked up with it, without letting the curry touch the hands.

SARIS

Saris was a Palestinian Arab village that was depopulated during the major offensive launched by the Haganah on 6 April 1948. Called Operation Nachshon, and launched before the British had left Palestine, its objective was to capture villages between Jerusalem and the coastal plain.

During Ottoman rule in Palestine, in 1596, Saris was a village in the *nahiya* (subdistrict) of Jerusalem under the *liwa'* (district) of Jerusalem and it had a population of 292. The villagers paid taxes on a number of crops, including wheat, barley, olives fruit and carob, as well as on goats, beehives and vineyards.

In the late 19th century, Saris was described as being located on top of a hill, with olive trees growing below the village. In 1944/45 its population was 560, with 3,677 dunums (over 900 acres) used for cereals and 366 dunums (H"90 acres) of orchards and irregated land.

1948, and After

On 13 April, before the village was attacked, Israel Galili wrote to Yosef Weitz of the JNF asking for a settlement to be established at Saris 'as soon as possible.'

The Scotsman, Saturday 17 April 1948, reported 'Jews destroyed a mosque, village school, and 25 houses, killing three women in an attack on the Arab village of Saris early today (16th). There were about 500 attackers.' The New York Times carried the same report and gave the number of Arab dead as seven. A Haganah statement is quoted as saying that the battalion stayed in the village for about five hours, blowing up 25 buildings and burning others.

The settlement Shoresh was established 1 km south west of the remains of the village in 1948. Sho'eva was set up 0.5 km north east of the site in 1950. Both are on village land.

The Palestinian historian Walid Khalidi described the village land in 1992: "The site is covered with stone rubble; iron bars protrude from the collapsed roofs. There are many open wells and several caves with arched roofs. A large number of trees, including cypress, fig, and almond trees, grow on the site. An abandoned grove of almond trees is located on the eastern side. In the middle of the slope are the remains of an artificial pool. The village cemetery, surrounded by trees, is located southwest of the site. It contains several large tombs, one of which is surrounded by a small, roofless enclosure; an almond tree grows in the center. The Shoresh forest, named after the Israeli settlement, was established by the youth of the Jewish National Fund in Johannesburg, South Africa. Another forest in the area, dedicated to several notable Jews, have been planted under the auspices of the Center for European Jewry.

DHOTI

The Dhotî or Doti in Hindi, called Dhotiyu in Gujarati, Suriya in Assamese, Vaytti or Veshti(informal) in Tamil, Dhuti in Bangla, Dhoti or Kachche Panche in Kannada, Dhotar,Angostar,Aad-neschey or Pudve in Konkani, mundu in Malayalam, Dhotar in Marathi , Laacha in Punjabi and Pancha in Telugu is the traditional men's garment in India.

It is a rectangular piece of unstitched cloth, usually around 7 yards long, wrapped around the waist and the legs, and knotted at the waist.

In northern India, the garment is worn with a Kurta on top, the combination known simply as "dhoti kurta", or a *dhuti panjabi* in the East. In Tamil Nadu, it is worn with an *angavastram* (another unstitched cloth draped over the shoulders) or else with a *chokka* (shirt) in Andhra Pradesh or *jubba* (a local version of kurta). The *lungi* is a similar piece of cloth worn in similar manner, though only on informal occasions. The *lungi* is not as long and is basically a bigger version of a towel worn to fight the extremely hot weather in India. The sarong is another similar item of clothing.

Custom and Usage

The dhoti is considered formal wear all over the country. Apart from all government and traditional family functions, the dhoti is also considered acceptable at country clubs and at other establishments that enforce strict formal dress codes. The same is true across the Indian subcontinent, particularly in Bangladesh, Sri Lanka, and the Maldives. In many of these countries, the garment has become something of a mascot of cultural assertion, being greatly favoured by politicians and cultural figures. Thus, the *dhoti* for many has taken on a more cultural nuance while the 'suit-and-tie' or, in less formal occasions, the ubiquitous shirt and pants, are seen as standard formal and semi-formal wear.

In southern India, the garment is worn at all cultural occasions and traditional ceremonies. The bride-groom in a south Indian wedding and the host/main male participant of other rituals and ceremonies have necessarily to be dressed in the traditional pancha while performing the ceremonies.

Unspoken rules of etiquette govern the way the pancha is worn. In south India, men will occasionally fold the garment in half to resemble a short skirt when working, cycling, etc., and this reveals the legs from the knee downwards. However, it is considered disrespectful to speak to men or to one's social inferiors with the pancha folded up in this manner. When faced with such a social situation, the fold of the package is loosened with an imperceptible yank of the hand and allowed to cover the legs completely.

Pancha are worn by western adherents of the Hare Krishna sect, which is known for promoting a distinctive dress code amongst its practitioners, with followers wearing saffron or white coloured cloth, folded in the traditional style. Mahatma Gandhi invariably wore a pancha on public occasions, but he was well aware that it was considered "indecent" in other countries and was shocked when a friend wore one in London.

The genteel Bengali man is stereotyped in popular culture as wearing expensive perfumes, a light kurta and an elaborate *dhuti* with rich pleats ,the front corner of the cloth being stiffed like a Japanese fan and holding it in his hand; whilst feverishly discussing politics and literature. It is considered the most elegant costume and is worn at bengali weddings and cultural festivals.

Over the past century or more, western styles of clothing have been steadily gaining ground in the region, gradually rendering the pancha a garment for home-wear, not generally worn to work. It is less popular among the youth in major metropolises and is viewed as rustic, unfashionable and not 'hip' enough for the younger age-set. However, use of the pancha as a garment of daily use and homewear continues largely unabated.

Styles and Varieties

The garment is known as the *vaeshtti* in Tamil Nadu and Mundu in Kerala. It is called *pancha* in Andhra Pradesh and *panche* in Karnataka and dhuti in Bengal. The word is related to the Sanskrit *pancha* meaning *five;* this may be a reference to the fact that a 5-yard-long strip of cloth is used. It is also related to the sanskrit word 'dhuvati' .In one elaborate south Indian style of draping the garment, five knots are used to wrap the garment, and this also is sometimes held to have originated the word.

It is usually white or cream in colour, although colourful hues are used for specific religious occasions or sometimes to create more vivid ensembles. Off- white dhuti is generally worn by the groom in bengali weddings. White or turmeric-yellow is the prescribed hues to be worn by men at their weddings and upanayanams. Silk panchas, called *Magatam* or *Pattu Pancha* in Tamil Nadu and Andhra Pradesh respectively, are often used on these special occasions. Vermilion-red dhotis, called 'sowlay', is often used by priests at temples, especially in Maharashtra. Kings and poets used rich colors and elaborate gold-thread embroideries. Cotton dhotis suit the climatic conditions for daily usage. Silk panchas are suited for special occasions and are expensive.

There are several different ways of draping the panchas. The two most popular ones in south India are the plain wrap and the *Pancha katcham* or (five knots or five folds). The first style is mostly seen in south India as shown in picture. It is a simple wrap around the waist and resembles a long skirt. It will be folded in half up to knees while working. Second style is folding around the waist in the middle of the garment and tying the top ends in the front like a belt and tucking the falling left and right ends in the back.

The North Indian style, worn in the West by devotees of the International Society for Krishna Consciousness, consists of folding the cloth in half, taking the left side, pleating it vertically, passing it between the legs and tucking it in the waist at the back. The right side is pleated horizontally and tucked in the waist at the front

Along with dhoti, the angavastram or thundu (an extra piece of cloth) will be draped depending on the usage. Farmers carry it on one shoulder and treat it as sweat towel. Bride grooms use it as entire upper garment. It will be folded decoratively around the waist while dancing. South Indian Hindu priests wrap about the waist as the extra layer. North Indian priests (especially those of ISKCON) may drape it across the body with two corners tied at the shoulder (or they may wear a kurta instead).

It is also worn in East Africa, mainly by the Somalis and Afars, it is called a *ma'awees*.

Usage in Nepal

The word Dhoti is often used as an ethnic slur (derogatory term) against the Indians and sometimes to the Madhesi community of Nepal by the majority of the Nepali people. This may be because of the popularity of dhotis in the Terai region and the bordering Indian states.

KURTA

A kurta (also kurti for a shorter version worn by women) is a traditional item of clothing worn in Afghanistan, Bangladesh, India, Pakistan, and Sri Lanka. It is a loose shirt falling either just above or somewhere below the knees of the wearer, and is worn by both men and women. They were traditionally worn with loose-fitting paijama (*kurta-paijama*), loose-fitting salwars, tight-fitting churidars, or wrapped-around dhotis; but are now also worn with jeans. Kurtas are worn both as casual everyday wear and as formal dress. A kurta is also referred to as a panjabi, (usually spelled lower-case) in Bengal, Britain, and Canada.

Women often wear kurtis as blouses, usually over jeans. These kurtis are typically much shorter than the traditional garments and made with a lighter materials, like those used in sewing kameez.

Imported kurtas were fashionable in the 1960s and 1970s, as an element of hippie fashion, fell from favor briefly, and are now again fashionable.

Formal kurtas are usually custom-made by South Asian tailors, who work with the fabric their customers bring them. South Asians overseas, and Westerners, can buy them at South Asian clothing stores or order them from web retailers.

Styles

A traditional kurta is composed of rectangular fabric pieces with perhaps a few gusset inserts, and is cut so as to leave no wasted fabric. The cut is usually simple, although decorative treatments can be elaborate.

The sleeves of a traditional kurta fall straight to the wrist; they do not narrow, as do many Western-cut sleeves. Sleeves are not cuffed, just hemmed and decorated.

The front and back pieces of a simple kurta are also rectangular. The side seams are left open for 6-12 inches above the hem, which gives the wearer some ease of movement.

The kurta usually opens in the front; some styles, however, button at the shoulder seam. The front opening is often a hemmed slit in the fabric, tied or buttoned at the top; some kurtas, however, have plackets rather than slits. The opening may be centered on the chest, or positioned off center.

A traditional kurta does not have a collar. Modern variants may feature stand-up collars of the type known to tailors and seamstresses as "mandarin" collars. These are the same sort of collars seen on achkans, sherwanis, and Nehru jackets.

Material

Kurtas worn in the summer months are usually made of thin silk or cotton fabrics; winter season kurtas are made of thicker fabric such as wool (as in Kashmiri kurtas) or *Khadi silk,* a thick, coarse, handspun and handwoven silk that may be mixed with other fibers.

Kurtas are typically fastened with tasseled ties, cloth balls and loops, or buttons. Ready-made kurtas often avoid the use of horn buttons, in deference to Hindu sentiments; such buttons are frequently made from cow or buffalo hooves or horns. Buttons are often wood or plastic. Kurtas worn on formal occasions might feature decorative metal buttons, which are not sewn to the fabric, but, like cufflinks, are fastened into the cloth when needed. Such buttons can be decorated with jewels, enameling, and other traditional jewelers' techniques.

Decoration

South Asian tailors command a vast repertoire of methods, traditional and modern, for decorating fabric. It is likely that all of them have been used, at one time or another, to decorate kurtas. However, the most common decoration is embroidery. Many light summer kurtas feature Chikan embroidery, a speciality of Lucknow, around the hems and front opening. This embroidery is typically executed on light, semi-transparent fabric in a matching thread. The effect is ornate but subtle.

Etymology

The word "kurta" is a borrowing from Urdu and Hindi, and originally from Persian (literally, "a collarless shirt") and was first used in English in the 20th century.

BINDI (DECORATION)

A bindi (from Sanskrit *bindu,* meaning "a drop, small particle, dot") is a forehead decoration worn in South Asia (particularly India) and Southeast Asia, not to be confused with a tilaka. Traditionally it is a dot of red colour applied in the center of the forehead close to the eyebrows, but it can also consist of a sign or piece of jewelry worn at this location.

Modern Use

Nowadays, bindis are worn throughout South Asia (India, Bangladesh, Nepal, Sri Lanka and Pakistan) by women and girls, and no longer signify age, marital status, religious background or ethnic affiliation. The bindi has become a decorative item and is no longer restricted in colour or shape. Self-adhesive bindis (also known as sticker bindis) are available, usually made of felt or thin metal and adhesive on the other side. These are simple to apply, disposable substitutes for older tilak bindis. Sticker bindis come in many colors, designs, materials, and sizes. Fancier sticker bindis are decorated with sequins, glass beads, or rhinestones.

Outside South Asia, bindis are sometimes worn by women of Indian origin. Some Western women who have converted to Hinduism, such as in the Hare Krishnas, also wear bindis. Sometimes they are worn as a style statement. International celebrities such as Gwen Stefani, Shakira, Madonna, Nina Hagen, Nelly Furtado, and Shania Twain have been seen wearing bindis.

Alternative Names of Bindi

A bindi can be called:

- *Tikli* in Marathi
- *Pottu* in Tamil and Malayalam
- *Tilak* in Hindi
- *Chandlo* in Gujarati
- *Bottu* or *Tilakam* (in Telugu)
- *Bottu* or *Tilaka* (in Kannada)
- *Teep* (meaning "a pressing") (in Bengali)

- *Nande* is a term erroneously used to describe the bindi in Malaysia. It may contain pejorative connotations although not in most cases.

Religious Significance

The area between the eyebrows (where the bindi is placed) is said to be the sixth chakra, *ajna*, the seat of "concealed wisdom". According to followers of Hinduism, this chakra is the exit point for kundalini energy. The bindi is said to retain energy and strengthen concentration. It is also said to protect against demons or bad luck.

Related Customs

In addition to the bindi, in India, a vermilion mark in the parting of the hair just above the forehead is worn by married women as a symbol of their married status. During North Indian marriage ceremonies, the groom applies sindoor on the parting in the bride's hair. Ancient Chinese women wore similar marks (for purely decorative purposes) since the second century, which became popular during the Tang Dynasty.

INDO-WESTERN CLOTHING

Indo-Western clothing is the fusion of Western and South Asian fashion. With increasing exposure of India to the Western world, the merging of women's clothing styles was inevitable. Many Indian women residing in the West still prefer to wear traditional salwar kameez and sarees; however, some women, particularly those of the younger generation, choose Indo-Western clothing.

The clothing of the quintessential Indo-Western ensemble is the trouser suit, which is a short kurta with straight pants and a dupatta. Newer designs often feature sleeveless tops, short dupattas, and pants with slits. New fusion fashions are emerging rapidly, as designers compete to produce designs in tune with current trends.

Additional examples of the fusion that Indo-Western clothing represents include wearing jeans with a choli, salwar or kurta, adding a dupatta to a Western-style outfit, and wearing a lehnga (long skirt) with a tank top or halter top.

Distinctive Elements in Indo-Western Fashions

- **Sleeve length** - The traditional salwar has long or short sleeves. An Indo-Western design might forego sleeves altogether, or replace the sleeves with spaghetti straps, resembling the style of a tank top or halter. There are also poncho-styled tops and one-sleeve designs that follow contemporary Western trends.
- **Shirt length** - Indo-Western kurtas and salwars tend to be much shorter than those traditionally worn, so that they resemble Western-style blouses.
- **Necklines** - Some Indo-Western tops are available with plunging necklines, in contrast to the traditional styling of salwars and kurtas.

WESTERN CULTURE

Western culture (sometimes equated with Western civilization or European civilization) refers to cultures of European origin.

The term "Western culture" is used very broadly to refer to a heritage of social norms, ethical values, traditional customs, religious beliefs, political systems, and specific artifacts and technologies. Specifically, Western culture may imply:

- a Graeco-Roman Classical and Renaissance cultural influence, concerning artistic, philosophic, literary, and legal themes and traditions, the cultural social effects of migration period and the heritages of Celtic Germanic etc. ethnic groups, as well as a tradition of rationalism in various spheres of life, developed by

Hellenistic philosophy, Scholasticism, Humanisms, the Scientific Revolution and Enlightenment, and including, in political thought, widespread rational arguments in favour of freethought, human rights, equality and democratic values averse to despotism, irrationality and theocracy.

- a Biblical-Christian cultural influence in spiritual thinking, customs and either ethic or moral traditions, around Post-Classical Era.
- Western European cultural influences concerning artistic, musical, folkloric, ethic and oral traditions, whose themes have been further developed by Romanticism.

The concept of Western culture is generally linked to the classical definition of the Western world. In this definition, Western culture is the set of literary, scientific, political, artistic and philosophical principles which set it apart from other civilizations. Much of this set of traditions and knowledge is collected in the Western canon.

The term has come to apply to countries whose history is strongly marked by Western European immigration or settlement, such as the Americas, and Australasia, and is not restricted to Western Europe.

Some tendencies that define modern Western societies are the existence of political pluralism, prominent subcultures or countercultures (such as New Age movements), increasing cultural syncretism resulting from globalization and human migration.

Terminology

From its very beginnings in Mesopotamia and Ancient Greece the East-West distinction has been somewhat difficult to define with precision. The Greeks were not so different from their Eastern neighbors for example. In the Middle Ages, where Islam was contrasted to the West, it is notable that most of the Islamic Middle East, having - since the time of Alexander the Great - been Hellenized, ruled by Rome and Constantinople and part of the Orthodox communion, was as much under the influence of Byzantine and Biblical-Christian history as "Christendom".

In the later 20th to early 21st century, with the advent of increasing globalism, it has become more difficult to determine which individuals fit into which category, and the East–West contrast is sometimes criticized as relativistic and arbitrary.

Globalism has, especially since the end of the cold war, spread western ideas so widely that almost all modern countries or cultures are to some extent influenced by aspects of western culture which they have absorbed. Recent stereotyped Western views of "the West" have been labelled *Occidentalism*, paralleling Orientalism, the term for the 19th century stereotyped views of "the East".

Geographically, "The West" today would normally be said to include Europe as well as the overseas territories belonging to the Anglosphere, the Hispanidad, Lusosphere or Francophonie.

History

Western culture is neither homogeneous nor unchanging. As with all other cultures it has evolved and gradually changed over time. All generalities about it have their exceptions at some time and place. The organisation and tactics of the Greek Hoplites differed in many ways from the Roman legions. The polis of the Greeks is not the same as the American superpower of the 21st century. The gladiatorial games of the Roman Empire are not identical to present-day football. The art of Pompeii is not the art of Hollywood. Nevertheless, it is possible to follow the evolution and history of the West, and appreciate its similarities and differences, its borrowings from, and contributions to, other cultures of humanity.

The origins of the word "West" in terms of geopolitical boundaries started in the 1800s and 1900s. Prior to this, most people would have thoughts about different nations, languages, individuals, and geographical regions, but with no idea of "Western" nations and culture as some of us think today. Many world maps were so crude, inaccurate, and not well known before the 1800s that specific geographical and political differences would be harder to measure. Few would have access to good maps and even fewer had access to accurate descriptions of who lived in far away lands. Western thought as we think of it recently, is shaped by ideas of the 1800s and 1900s, originating mainly in Europe. What we think of as Western thought today is generally defined as Greco-Roman and Judeo-Christian culture, the Renaissance, the Enlightenment and colonialism. As a consequence the term "Western culture" is at times unhelpful and vague, since the definition involved a vast variety of distinct traditions, political groups, religious groups, and individual writers over thousands of years.

Furthermore, "Western culture" has taken many of its elements from neighboring areas in the Middle East and North Africa. Europe (whose borders are arbitrary) is an area geographically connected to Asia (forming Eurasia) and Africa, and important cultural exchanges such as trade and migration take place. Cities and complex political societies emerged first in places like Mesopotamia and Egypt, with civilizations far more advanced than anything in Europe at the time of their peak.

The Classical West

In Homeric literature, and right up until the time of Alexander the Great, for example in the accounts of the

Persian Wars of Greeks against Persians by Herodotus, we see the paradigm of a contrast between the West and East.

Nevertheless the Greeks felt they were civilized and saw themselves (in the formulation of Aristotle) as something between the wild barbarians of most of Europe and the soft, slavish Easterners. Inspired by Eastern example, and yet felt to be different, ancient Greek science, philosophy, democracy, architecture, literature, and art provided a foundation embraced and built upon by the Roman Empire as it swept up Europe, including the Hellenic World in its conquests in the 1st century BC. In the meantime however, Greece, under Alexander, had become a capital of the East, and part of an empire. The idea that the later Orthodox or Eastern Christian cultural descendants of the Greek-speaking Eastern Roman empire, are a happy mean between Eastern slavishness and Western barbarism is promoted to this day, for example in Russia, creating a zone which is both Eastern and Western depending upon the context of discussion.

For about five hundred years, the Roman Empire maintained the Greek East and consolidated a Latin West, but an East-West division remained, reflected in many cultural norms of the two areas, including language. Although Rome, like Greece, was no longer democratic, the idea of democracy remained a part of the education of citizens, as if the emperors were a temporary emergency measure.

Eventually the empire came to be increasingly officially split into a Western and Eastern part, reviving old ideas of a contrast between an advanced East, and a rugged West.

With the rise of Christianity in the midst of the Roman world, much of Rome's tradition and culture were absorbed by the new religion, and transformed into something new, which would serve as the basis for the development of Western civilization after the fall of Rome. Also, Roman culture mixed with the pre-existing Celtic, Germanic and Slavic cultures, which slowly became integrated into Western culture starting, mainly, with their acceptance of Christianity.

The Medieval West

The Medieval West was at its broadest the same as Christendom, including both the "Latin" or "Frankish" West, and the Orthodox Eastern part, where Greek remained the language of empire. More narrowly, it was Catholic (Latin) Europe. After the crowning of Charlemagne, this part of Europe was referred to by its neighbors in Byzantium and the Moslem world as "Frankish".

After the fall of Rome much of Greco-Roman art, literature, science and even technology were all but lost in the western part of the old empire, centered around Italy, and Gaul (France). However, this would become the centre of a new West. Europe fell into political anarchy, with many warring kingdoms and principalities. Under the Frankish kings, it eventually reunified and evolved into feudalism.

Much of the basis of the post-Roman cultural world had been set before the fall of the Empire, mainly through the integrating and reshaping of Roman ideas through Christian thought. The Greek and Roman paganism had been completely replaced by Christianity around the 4th and 5th centuries, since it became the official State religion following the baptism of emperor Constantine I. Roman Catholic Christianity and the Nicene Creed served as a unifying force in Western Europe, and in some respects replaced or competed with the secular authorities. Art and literature, law, education, and politics were preserved in the teachings of the Church, in an environment that, otherwise, would have probably seen their loss. The Church founded many cathedrals, universities, monasteries and seminaries, some of which continue to exist today. In the Medieval period, the route to power for many men was in the Church.

In a broader sense, the Middle Ages, with its tension between Greek reasoning and Levantine monotheism was not confined to the West but also stretched into the old East, in what was to become the Islamic world. Indeed the debate between these two streams of thought which is said to define the west was preserved best there for a while, with Greek literature, and even some Eastern theology, making their way back to Western Europe via Spain and Italy.

The rediscovery of the Justinian Code in the early 10th century rekindled a passion for the discipline of law, which crossed many of the re-forming boundaries between East and West. Eventually, it was only in the Catholic or Frankish west, that Roman law became the foundation on which all legal concepts and systems were based. Its influence can be traced to this day in all Western legal systems (although in different manners and to different extents in the common (Anglo-American) and the civil (continental European) legal traditions). The study of canon law, the legal system of the Catholic Church, fused with that of Roman law to form the basis of the refounding of Western legal scholarship. The ideas of civil rights, equality before the law, equality of women, procedural justice, and democracy as the ideal form of society, and were principles which formed the basis of modern Western culture.

The West actively encouraged the spreading of Christianity, which was inexorably linked to the spread of Western culture. Owing to the influence of Islamic culture and Islamic civilization — a culture that had preserved some of the knowledge of ancient Mesopotamia, Egypt, India, Persia, Greece, and Rome, and improved on them significantly — in Islamic Spain and southern Italy, and in the Levant during the Crusades, Western Europeans translated many Arabic texts into Latin during the Middle Ages. Later, with the fall of Constantinople and the Ottoman conquest of the Byzantine Empire, followed by a massive exodus of Greek Christian priests and scholars to Italian towns like Venice, bringing with them as many scripts from the Byzantine archives as they could, scholars' interest for the Greek language and classic works, topics and lost files was revived. Both the Greek and Arabic influences eventually led to the beginnings of the Renaissance. From the late 15th century to the 17th century, Western culture began to spread to other parts of the world by intrepid explorers and missionaries during the Age of Discovery, followed by imperialists from the 17th century to the early 20th century.

The Modern Era

Coming into the modern era, the historical understanding of the East-West contrast is the opposition of Christendom to its geographical neighbours began to weaken. As religion became less important, and Europeans came into increasing contact with far away peoples, the old concept of Western Culture began a slow evolution towards what it is today. The Early Modern "Age of Discovery" in the 15th, 16th and 17th centuries faded into the "Age of Enlightenment" continuing into the 18th, both characterized by the military advantages coming to Europeans from their development of firearms and other military technologies. The "Great Divergence" became more pronounced, making the West the bearer of science and the accompanying revolutions of technology and industrialisation. Western political thinking also eventually spread in many forms around the world. With the early 19th century "Age of Revolution" the West entered a period of World empires, massive economic and technological advance, and bloody international conflicts continuing into the 20th century.

Religion in the meantime has waned considerably in Western Europe, where many are agnostic or atheist. Nearly half of the populations of the United Kingdom (44-54%), Germany (41-49%), France (43-54%) and the Netherlands (39-

44%) are non-theist. However, religious belief in the United States is very strong, about 75-85% of the population, as also happens in most of Latin America.

As Europe discovered the wider world, old concepts adapted. The Islamic world which had formerly been considered "the Orient" ("the East") more specifically became the "Near East" as the interests of the European powers for the first time interferred with Qing China and Meiji Japan in the 19th century. Thus, the Sino-Japanese War in 1894–1895 occurred in the "Far East", while the troubles surrounding the decline of the Ottoman Empire simultaneously occurred in the "Near East". The "Middle East" in the mid 19th century included the territory east of the Ottoman empire but West of China, i.e. Greater Persia and Greater India, but is now used synonymously with "Near East".

The Cold War West

During the Cold War, the West–East contrast became synonymous with the competing governments of the United States and the Soviet Union and their allies.

Politics

Despite the Western empires in the past, concepts of democracy and an emphasis on freedom has been seen as distinguishing Western peoples from non-western neighbors.

In the Middle Ages and early modern times, the concept of a separation of Church and state developed, allowing for the development of more distinctive political norms, such as the doctrine of the separation of powers, which make modern Western democracy distinct from democracy in general.

In comparison to many other cultures in the world, western cultures tend to emphasize the individual. Much of this respect for difference and individual liberties remain, however, still theoretical, in many ways, among mainstream society, when the individual factor encounters a strong opposition from social customs and consensus, and thus resists to be accepted or understood. This situation, anyways, has tended to change among most progressive sectors of society, as a consequence of the many social and counter-cultural movements that the last decades have come to see.

Creativity and the expression of the individual is commonly encouraged in Western culture. New subcultures, art and technology constantly emerge. Furthermore, capitalism which is found in almost every western country, supports a highly individualistic ideology.

The forms of government usually adopted in western societies, as a part of a wider, nowadays ruling social-economical liberal capitalist structure, are multi-party parliamentary or presidential (also 'congressional') systems, frequently referred to as *figurative* democracy, which favors some sort of majority consensus when coming to adopt collective decisions.

Widespread Influence

Elements of Western culture have had a very influential role on other cultures worldwide. People of many cultures, both Western and non-Western, equate *modernization* (adoption of technological progress) with *westernization* (adoption of Western culture). Some members of the non-Western world have suggested that the link between technological progress and certain harmful Western values provides a reason why much of "modernity" should be rejected as being incompatible with their vision and the values of their societies. These types of argument referring to imperialism and stressing the importance of freedom from it and the relativist argument that different cultural norms should be treated equally, are also present in Western philosophy. Also Marxism, sometimes seen as an alternative to Western culture, comes from the West.

What is generally uncontested, is that much of the technology and social patterns which make up what is defined as "modernization" were developed in the Western world. Whether these technological and social patterns are intrinsically part of Western culture, is more difficult to answer. Many would argue that the question cannot be answered by a response from positivistic science and instead is a "value" question which must be answered from a value system (e.g. philosophy, religion, political doctrine). Nonetheless, much of anthropology today has shown the close links between the physical environment and daily activities and the formation of a culture (the findings of cultural ecology, among others).

Music, Art, Story-Telling and Architecture

Some cultural and artistic modalities are also characteristically Western in origin and form. While dance, music, story-telling, and architecture are human universals, they are expressed in the West in certain characteristic ways.

The symphony has its origins in Italy. Many important musical instruments used by cultures all over the world were also developed in the West; among them are the violin, piano, pipe organ, saxophone, trombone, clarinet, and the theremin. The solo piano, symphony orchestra and the string quartet are also important performing musical forms.

The ballet is a distinctively Western form of performance dance. The ballroom dance is an important Western variety of dance for the elite. The polka, the square dance, and the Irish step dance are very well-known Western forms of folk dance.

Historically, the main forms of western music are European folk, choral, classical, Country, rock and roll, hip-hop, and Electronica.

While epic literary works in verse such as the Mahabarata and Homer's Iliad are ancient and occurred worldwide, the novel as a distinct form of story telling only arose in the West (with the possible exception, though isolated, of the Japanese Tale of Genji, five greats epics of Tamil and Persian Shahnama) in the period 1200 to 1750. Photography and the motion picture as a technology and as the basis for entirely new art forms were also developed first in the West. The soap opera, a popular culture dramatic form originated in the United States first on radio in the 1930s, then a couple of decades later on television. The music video was also developed in the West in the middle of the twentieth century.

The arch, the dome, and the flying buttress as architectural motifs were first used by the Romans. Important western architectural motifs include the Doric, Corinthian, and Ionic columns, and the Romanesque, Gothic, Baroque, and Victorian styles are still widely recognised, and used even today, in the West. Much of Western architecture emphasises repetition of simple motifs, straight lines and expansive, undecorated planes. A modern ubiquitous architectural form that emphasizes this characteristic is the skyscraper, first developed in New York and Chicago.

Oil painting is said to have originated by Jan van Eyck, and perspective drawings and paintings had their earliest practitioners in Florence. In art, the Celtic knot is a very distinctive Western repeated motif. Depictions of the nude human male and female in photography, painting and sculpture are frequently considered to have special artistic merit. Realistic portraiture is especially valued. In Western dance, music, plays and other arts, the performers are only very infrequently masked. There are essentially no taboos against depicting God, or other religious figures, in a representational fashion.

Many forms of popular music have been derived from African-Americans' folklore and music during 20th and 19th centuries, initially by themselves, but later played and further developed together with White Americans, British people, and Westerners in general. These include Jazz, Blues and Rock music (that in wide sense include Rock and roll and Heavy metal branches), Rhythm and blues, Funk, Rap, Techno and also Ska or Reggae in an African-Caribbean, Jamaican background. Several other related or derived styles were developed and introduced by western pop culture such as Pop, Pop-Rock, Technopop, Dance, Rave, Nu metal, etc.

Scientific and Technological Inventions and Discoveries

A feature of Western culture is its focus on science and technology, and its ability to generate new processes, materials and material artifacts.

It was the West that first developed steam power and adapted its use into factories, and for the generation of electrical power. The Otto and the Diesel internal combustion engines are products whose genesis and early development were in the West. Nuclear power stations are derived from the first atomic pile in Chicago (1942). The electrical dynamo, transformer, and electric light, and indeed most of the familiar electrical appliances, were inventions of the West.

Communication devices and systems including the telegraph, the telephone, radio, television, communication and navigation satellites, mobile phone, and the Internet were all invented by Westerners. The pencil, ballpoint pen, CRT, LCD, LED, photograph, photocopier, laser printer, ink jet printer and plasma display screen were also invented in the West.

Furthermore, ubiquitous materials including concrete, aluminum, clear glass, synthetic rubber, synthetic diamond and the plastics polyethylene, polypropylene, PVC and polystyrene were invented in the West. Iron and steel ships, bridges and skyscrapers first appeared in the West. Nitrogen fixation and petrochemicals were invented by Westerners. Most of the elements,were discovered and named in the West, as well as the contemporary atomic theories to explain them.

The transistor, integrated circuit, memory chip, and computer were all first seen in the West. The ship's chronometer, the screw propeller, the locomotive, bicycle, automobile, and aeroplane were all invented in the West. Eyeglasses, the telescope, the microscope and electron microscope, all the varieties of chromatography, protein and DNA sequencing, computerised tomography, NMR, x-rays, and light, ultraviolet and infrared spectroscopy, were all first developed and applied in Western laboratories, hospitals and factories.

In medicine, vaccination, anesthesia, and all the pure antibiotics were created in the West. The method of preventing Rh disease, the treatment of diabetes, and the germ theory of disease were discovered by Westerners. The eradication of that ancient scourge, smallpox, was led by a Westerner, Donald Henderson. Radiography, Computed tomography, Positron emission tomography and Medical ultrasonography are important diagnostic tools developed in the West. So were the stethoscope, electrocardiograph, and the endoscope. Vitamins, hormonal contraception, hormones, insulin, Beta blockers and ACE inhibitors, along with a host of other medically proven drugs were first utilised to treat disease in the West. The double-blind study and evidence-based medicine are critical scientific techniques widely used in the West for medical purposes.

In mathematics, calculus, statistics, logic, vector, tensor and complex analysis, group theory and topology were developed by Westerners. In biology, evolution, chromosomes, DNA, genetics and the methods of molecular biology are creatures of the West. In physics, the science of mechanics and quantum mechanics, relativity, thermodynamics, and statistical mechanics were all developed by Westerners. The discoveries and inventions by Westerners in electromagnetism include Coulomb's law (1785), the first battery (1800), the unity of electricity and magnetism (1820), Biot–Savart law

(1820), the first electric motor (1821), Ohm's Law (1827), and the Maxwell's equations (1871). The atom, nucleus, electron, neutron and proton were all unveiled by Westerners.

In finance, double entry bookkeeping, the limited liability company, life insurance, and the charge card were all first used in the West.

Westerners are also known for their explorations and adventures of the globe and space. The first expedition to circumnavigate the Earth (1522) was by Westerners, as well as the first to set foot on the South Pole (1911), and the first human to land on the moon (1969). The landing of robots on Mars (2004) and on an asteroid (2001), and the Voyager explorations of the outer planets (Uranus in 1986 and Neptune in 1989) were all achievements of Westerners.

CHURIDAR

Churidars, or more properly churidar pyjamas, are tightly fitting trousers worn by both men and women in South Asia and Central Asia. They are a variant of the common salwar pants. Salwars are cut wide at the top and narrow at the ankle. Churidars narrow more quickly, so that contours of the leg are revealed. They are usually cut on the bias (at a 45 degree angle to the grain of the fabric) which makes them naturally stretchy. Stretch is important when pants are closefitting. They are also cut longer than the leg and finish with a tightly fitting buttoned cuff at the ankle. The excess length falls into folds and appears like a set of bangles resting on the ankle (hence 'churidar'; 'churi': bangle, 'dar': like). When the wearer is sitting, the extra material is the "ease" that makes it possible to bend the legs and sit comfortably. The word "churidar" is from Hindi and made its way into English only in the 20th century. Earlier, tight fitting churidar-like pants worn in in India were referred to by the British as *Moghul breeches, long-drawers,* or *mosquito drawers.*

The churidar is usually worn with a kameez (a form-fitted overshirt) by women or a kurta (a loose overshirt) by men, or they can form part of a bodice and skirt ensemble, as seen in the illustration of 19th century Indian women wearing churidar with a bodice and a transparent overskirt. Traditionally attired Kathak dancers, from northern India, still wear churidar with a wide skirt and a tight bodice; when the dancers twirl, the leg contours can be discerned — as can be seen in many Bollywood movies featuring Kathak dancing.

DUPATTA

Dupatta, alternative names include chadar (in Pakistan), orni, chunri, chunni, orna, and sometimes unni (mainly Gujarati)) is a long, multi-purpose scarf that is essential to many South Asian women's suits. Some "dupatta suits" include the shalwar kameez and the kurta. The dupatta is also worn over the South Asian outfits of choli or gharara. The dupatta has long been a symbol of modesty in South Asian dress.

History and Origin

The origin of the dupatta can be traced to the Mohenjo-daro civilization of the Indus Basin, where the use of textiles was highly prevelant. A sculpture of the Priest King of Harrapa, whose left shoulder is covered with some kind of a chaddar, suggests that the use of the dupatta dates back to the early Indus Valley Civilization. From here it spread across the Indian subcontinent, especially during the rule of the Muslim Mughal Empire.

Use

A dupatta is traditionally worn across both shoulders. However, the dupatta can also be worn like a cape around the entire torso. The material for the dupatta varies according to the suit: cotton, georgette, silk, chiffon, and more.

There are various modes of wearing an unsewn dupatta. When not draped over the head in the traditional style, it is usually worn with the middle portion of the dupatta resting on the chest like a garland with both ends thrown over each respective shoulder. When the dupatta is worn along with the salwar-kameez it is casually allowed to flow down the front and back.

The use of the dupatta has undergone a metamorphosis over time. In current fashions, the dupatta is frequently draped over one shoulder, and even over just the arms. Another recent trend is the short dupatta often seen with kurtas and Indo-Western clothing. Essentially, the dupatta is often treated as an accessory in current urban fashion.

GAMCHHA

A gamchha (alternate spellings *gamocha, gamchcha, gamcha, et al.*) is a thin, coarse, traditional cotton towel found in India and Bangladesh that is used to dry the body after bathing. The term "gamchha" derives from the *gâ mochha,* which means "wiping (the) body". Gamchha is the local term for indian towel.However its appearance varies from region to region. Gamchhas are most commonly found with check and striped patterns of red, orange or green. Plain white gamchhas with coloured (embroidered or printed) borders from Orissa and Assam are local handicrafts, and may be worn around the neck with traditional Indian attire. In western parts, gamchhas are primarily made in red colour and are plain like cloth. In southern india, gamchhas are more coarse and are available in various dyes. Even home made light weight fur towels are also popularly termed as gamchhas. Gamchhas remain popular in India because they are not as thick as Western-style towels and better suited to the country's tropical, humid climate.

Gamchhas are also worn as loin cloths by people of the poorer sections of society, especially menial labourers and farm workers.

MUNDUM NERIYATHUM

Mundum neriyathum *(set-mundu or mundu-set)* is the traditional clothing of women in Kerala, South India. It is the oldest remnant of the ancient form of the saree which covered only the lower part of the body. In the mundum neriyathum, the most basic traditional piece is the *mundu* or lower garment which is the ancient form of the saree denoted in malayalam as 'Thuni' (meaning cloth), while the *neriyathu* forms the upper garment added very recently to the mundu. The mundum neryathum consists of two pieces of cloth, and could be worn in either the traditional style with the *neriyathu* tucked inside the blouse, or in the modern style with the *neriyathu* worn over the left shoulder.

The mundum-neryathum is the extant form of the ancient saree referred to as "Sattika" in Buddhist and Jain literature. The mundu is the surviving form of lower garment of the ancient clothing referred to as antariya (lower garment). The neriyath is the modern adaptation of a thin scarf worn from the right shoulder to the left shoulder referred to in ancient Buddhist-Jain texts as the *uttariya*. It is one of the remains of the pre-Hindu Buddhist-Jain culture that once flourished in Kerala and other parts of South India. The narrow borders along the mundum neriyathum drape are probably an adaptation of the Graeco-Roman costume called "palmyrene". In the palmyrene costume, the piece of cloth known as "palla" was a long piece of unstitched cloth with a coloured border and was worn over a long garment, pinned at the left shoulder. The tradition of coloured borders along the present day mundum neryathum or pallu might have been influenced by the Graeco-Roman "Palla" or Palmyrene. It should be noted that the Malabar coast had flourishing overseas trade with the Mediterranean world since antiquity. However, the pallu in its modern form was not in common use until very recently. In fact, as late as the 1970s, some populations in Kerala still did not use the pallu as the upper garment.

Basic Drape

The mundum neryathum is traditionally white or cream in colour and consists of two pieces of cloth, which have a coloured strip at the border known as *kara*. The piece of cloth that drapes the lower garment is called the mundu. It is worn below the navel and around the hips, similar to the mundu worn by men in Kerala. The piece of cloth that is worn as the upper garment is called the neriyathu. One end of the neriyathu is tucked inside the pavadai or petticoat and the remaining long end is worn across the front torso. The neriyathu is worn over a blouse that reaches quite above the breast bone. It is worn diagonally from along the right hips to the left shoulder and across the midriff, partly baring it. The remaining loose end of the neriyathu is left hanging from the left shoulder, resembling the 'nivi saree'. Today the 'nivi drape', is the most common form of the saree. A mundum neriyathum is starched before being draped and is worn over a blouse that matches the colour of the border or kara.

Ornamental and Festive Use

The mundum neryathum is worn as everyday costume and also as distinct costume on festive occasions, in which case the Kara is ornamental in couture. During the Keralite festival of onam, women of all ages wear the mundum neryathum and take part in folk dance meant only for women called *kaikottikalli*. The mundum neryathum for festive occasion has golden coloured borders or a broad zari border known as *Kasavu*, lending the costume another name of "Kasavu Saree" . The colour for the blouse of the mundum neryathum for this occasion is determined by the age and marital status of the woman. Young unmarried girls wear green coloured blouse, while married middle aged mothers wear red blouses.

The kasavu or the golden border is either pure golden layer, copper coated or artificial. The fabric of mundu-sari is cotton and is always woven by hand. Kara or simple line designs adorn the bottom of these saris, while at times small peacock or temple designs embellish the pallu. The mundum neriyathum is also known as *Set mundu,* Kasavu mundu, Mundu-sari, set-sari, or set veshti. The veshti is another version of the saree which consists of a small upper clothing resembling a blouse-like garment worn without the pallu along with a mundu as lower garment.

Set-Saree

The set-sari is worn as a garment that closely resembles the mundum neriyathum though it is not considered as a true mundum neriyathum by classic definition. This is because the setu-sari consists of a single piece of cloth while a traditional mundum neriyathum consists of a two piece cloth. Otherwise, the set saree closely resembles the mundum neriyathum and is often worn by Malayali women as a quasi mundum neriyathum.

When *set-mundu* (mundum neriyathum) is worn, the *kasavu* border will be clearly visible on left side (the left thigh) of the person who wears it. This *kasavu* border is that of the *neriyathu* which is worn on the top of the mundu.

Cultural Symbolism

The mundum neriyathum is the cultural costume of women of the Malayalee community and often referred as *Kerala saree..* The grace and appeal of the golden borders contrasting with the otherwise plain white mundum neryathum of keralite women has come to symbolize malayalee women. Both the traditional and modern styles of the mundum neryathum are depicted in the paintings of the Indian painter Raja Ravi Verma. The mundum neriyathum was modified in several paintings depicting shakuntala from the mahabharatha to a style of draping now popularly known as the 'nivi saree' or 'national drape'. In one of his painting the Indian subcontinent was shown as a mother wearing a flowing nivi saree.

SHERWANI

Sherwani is a long coat-like garment worn in South Asia, very similar to an Achkan or doublet. It is worn over the Kurta and *Churidar, Khara pajama,* a shalwar. It can be distinguished from the achkan by the fact that it is often made from heavier suiting fabrics, and by the presence of a lining.

History

The Sherwani appeared during the period of British India in 18th century, as a fusion of the Shalwar Kameez with the British frock coat. It was gradually adopted by most of the Indian aristocracy, mostly Muslim, and later by the general population, as a more westernized form of traditional attire.

It is the national dress of Pakistan for men, as it is not specifically associated with any of the provinces. The Founder of Pakistan, Mohammad Ali Jinnah frequently wore the Sherwani. Most government officials in Pakistan such as the President and Prime Minister wear the formal black Sherwani over the shalwar qameez on state occasions and national holidays.

In India, it is generally worn for formal occasions in winter by those of North Indian descent, especially those from Rajasthan, Uttar Pradesh and Hyderabadi-muslims.The Sherwani is closely associated with the nation's first Prime Minister, Jawaharlal Nehru. This led to a modified version of Sherwani known as the Nehru Jacket, which is popular in India.

Many South Asian grooms wear them as wedding dress. Sherwanis are usually embroidered or detailed in some way.

Also, in Pakistan, Sherwanis for women are becoming popular.

Sherwanis have been designed by Rohit Bal for British Airways cabin crews who are on Southern Asian flights.

UTTARIYA

An uttariya is a piece of dress in ancient India. It is scarf-like, and descends from the back of the neck to curl around both arms, and can be used to drape the top half of the body. It was usually made of fine cotton, but almost never of silk.

It was usually used in combination with the antariya, an ancient version of the dothi, held with a sash or kayabandh. The uttariya could also be used as a turban, by both men and women.

Lay brothers of the Buddhist community would typically be dressed with the antariya, accompanied by an uttariya and a larger chadder, all colored in saffron.

●●

Index